D0439377

"It is rare for a deeply engaged reader of ancient scriptural texts to have also a deep insight into the human heart and the grittiness of everyday life. It is rarer still when such a reader is also a gifted writer who expresses insights in plain yet graceful prose. Alice Camille's brief meditations on appointed scriptures for the church year have these special qualities. Each commentary is grounded in the practical side of spiritual life, each illuminates scripture from a refreshingly down-to-earth viewpoint, and each is a jewel of concise wisdom."

W.M. Baillie
Bloomsburg University, PA

"Alice Camille's *God's Word Is Alive* should meet the needs of those who wish to make the Sunday and Feast Day Scriptures more meaningful in their lives. Ms. Camille has skillfully blended her commentaries with meditations and practical suggestions. She lives up to her book's title, blending erudition and personal experience."

Rev. Phillip J. Cunningham, C.S.P.
Author of *Exploring Scripture: How the Bible Came to Be;*
Mark: The Good News Preached to the Romans; and
A Believer's Search for the Jesus of History

"*God's Word Is Alive* is the product of a lifetime of reflection on the relevancy of Sacred Scripture to our daily lives. Alice Camille, as well as anyone we have read, has accomplished what the 1994 document of the Biblical Commission on the interpretation of the Bible has urged: 'actualization of the scriptural message, so that the Christian life of Faith may find nourishment.'

"This book is well named, for God's Word does come alive on its pages. It is directed primarily toward the laity in the pews; yet Bible study groups, lectors, and homilists will welcome these fresh insights into every reading of the three liturgical cycles."

Rev. Msgr. Francis P. Friedl
co-author of *Homilies Alive: Creating Homilies That Hit Home*

"The great, classic sources of Christian spirituality are the Scriptures and the liturgy, and it is above all in the liturgy that we most often hear the Scriptures. In these reflections on the lectionary readings for Sundays and feasts, Alice Camille combines a solid grounding in Scripture with extensive experience of different kinds (e.g., RCIA, bible study groups) to lead us into a deeper, spiritual, and personal appropriation of the Word of God. On many levels, I recommend this work highly."

Michael D. Guinan, OFM
Professor of Old Testament and Semitic Languages
Franciscan School of Theology
Berkeley, CA

"Alice Camille's work, *God's Word Is Alive*, does just what the title implies: it makes God's Word come alive for the reader. Freed from artificial complacencies, her insights are as fresh as the Pentecostal wind. Her intuitions are succinct but free from cliches. This is a challenging work for anyone who is interested in developing a passionate appreciation for and blazing love of God's Word."

Very Rev. T. Ronald Haney
Executive Editor, *The Catholic Witness*
Author of *Christ's Passion for Peace and Justice:
Meditations on the Stations of the Cross*

ALICE L. CAMILLE

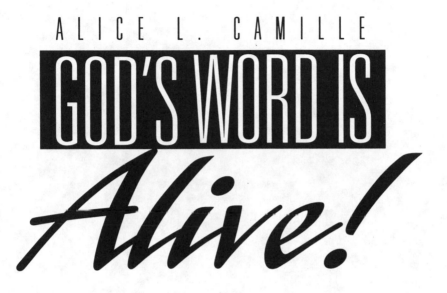

GOD'S WORD IS
Alive!

Entering the Sunday Readings

TWENTY-THIRD PUBLICATIONS

Mystic, CT 06355

Second printing 2000

Twenty-Third Publications/Bayard
185 Willow Street
P.O. Box 180
Mystic, CT 06355
(860) 536-2611
(800) 321-0411

ISBN 0-89622-926-2
Library of Congress Catalog Card Number 98-60276
Printed in the U.S.A.

Dedication

To Paul, for your companionship in faith
and holy example through the years.
You teach me what it means to say
the Word became flesh and dwells among us.

Acknowledgments

I work with a remarkable team of faith-filled people at Twenty-Third Publications who deserve my public gratitude. Thanks to Mary Carol Kendzia, the editor of *Exploring the Sunday Readings* and this book, who swam the extra miles to get this book on the shelf. She guided me through the murkier parts of the project with her usual humor and humanity. Thanks also to Dan Connors, my other editor, who originally auditioned me for *Exploring...* and continues to make publishing a friendly business. My friend Tom Artz, formerly at Twenty-Third, first insisted that I write for publication and I'm glad, at last, that he did.

I am also grateful to the Franciscan School of Theology in Berkeley for the pastoral education I received there, which shapes my theology and my heart. The Paulist Fathers at Old St. Mary's Church in San Francisco taught me what it means to be church, to lead, and to serve. The RCIA teams, catechists, and new Catholics in many cities shared their time and stories and witness over the years in ways that were inspiring and built my faith. My parents and sisters and brothers are my primary faith community, and everything I write reflects their love and belief at the center.

Table of Contents

Liturgical Calendar

Cycle A

Cycle B

Cycle C

Feast & Solemnities

Appendix A

God's Word Is Alive!

Liturgical Calendar: Year A

Liturgical Calendar: Year B

Liturgical Calendar: Year C

Introduction

God's word is alive; it strikes to the heart. It pierces more surely than a two-edged sword. (from Hebrews 4:12)

I came to Scripture in a roundabout way, through an early love of books. From the time that I can first remember, I couldn't put a book down. I read on my lap at the dinner table; I carted novels to school and read them during class. I read on the beach and in the bathroom, and any time I was forbidden to read, I disobeyed. My disobedience was pure. My primary allegiance has always been to the story.

I came to the Bible as an adult, though I knew many of its stories since childhood. A lifelong Catholic and graduate of parochial schools, I didn't think there would be much in the Bible that I hadn't already heard. I began reading the Bible systematically, with a plan to read a few chapters a day. Two years later, I emerged from the Book of Revelation, blinking in the light of a new world. This story of salvation history changed me more than anything I'd ever read, and I had to know more. And so I became a student of the great Story.

Stories wield a certain power over our lives. We have a fascination with people who are not us but who are like us. Stories teach and entertain, but they also comfort with the uncanny recognition of who we are and what we want. Our dreams and fears, our best and worst selves are demonstrated in stories, both biographical and fictional. We encounter ourselves in stories in a way that is almost confessional: this is who I am; this is who I could be.

Anyone who encounters the word of God as a person of faith is open to this same experience. In fifteen years of serving the Church and nine years of facilitating inquiry groups for the RCIA, I have listened to many people relate how contact with the stories of Scripture, however randomly met, transformed their hearts. In Bible studies, faith-sharing groups, seminaries, and parishes where the Liturgy of the Word is powerfully proclaimed and preached, more and more people are awakening to the deep call of God's story and feel summoned to radical response. God's Word reveals to us the beauty of the image in which we were made and meant to be. Having looked into that mirror, it is hard to accept the worldly image of what it means to be human any longer.

The Bible is a love story, sometimes funny, sometimes tragic, but always full of longing and presence and constancy. When we come to know ourselves as simply the most recent participants in this ongoing story, Scripture becomes alive for us as we pick up the trail of "those who have gone before us, marked with the sign of faith." Scripture is not the story of religious people who once knew God long ago. It is the ongoing testimony of sinners and saints (and some who are both) who tell us what they have learned and what we might learn if we take up the trail after them. Reading the Bible, then, is not for the sake of getting the history straight but for the purpose of finding our place in the story.

This collection of meditations on the Sunday lectionary emerged from the newsletter *Exploring the Sunday Readings*, with additions made for special feast days not covered in the original series. It is arranged in four sections: one for each of the three lectionary cycles, and a fourth for feasts and solemnities, some of which are celebrated irregularly.

The series is a conversation for ordinary Catholics and other followers of the three-year lectionary cycle of readings about the relationship between Scripture and personal experience. It includes brief reflections on each of the readings, as well as questions to help you make the connection between God's Word and everyday life. A suggested action concludes each Sunday's commentary, for those who want to know what, precisely, one might do in response to the Gospel.

I have been having the conversation that is this book with friends, catechumens, and parishioners for some time. Others may find it helpful for both private and group use. Lectors may consult these reflections for insights into the meaning of the passage they are preparing to proclaim. Homilists can use them as a starting point for their own preparations. Scripture study groups and those in the catechumenate process may like the faith-sharing questions for their open-endedness (yes-or-no answers are seldom possible). I have tried hard not to ask a question I can't answer myself or don't find relevant to my own life of faith. Of course, the supplied questions may spawn more meaningful questions from the group which should always take precedence.

In the end, a relationship with God's Word is a personal encounter. Though homilists and commentary writers and catechists do their best to mediate this word for others, each of us has to make room for the Word to be planted down deep in us. Once it sleeps in the soil, a seed can produce astonishing new life. I hope this astonishment and life comes to you.

Cycle A

Light and Darkness

FIRST READING: ISAIAH 2:1–5
Let us walk in the light of the Lord!

If God were to have the divine way with the world, what would it look like? We know how to respond if it is our way we are imagining: someplace beyond natural disasters, with no anxiety and lots of what we most need and want. Isaiah imagines a day of the Lord coming when God's people finally know the life that God intended for them. Nations actually seek wisdom and instruction, intending to walk in the way of truth. Justice is rendered, peace replaces violence.

It all begins, of course, with a recognition that God is in charge. Swords do not get beaten into plowshares until the mighty realize that a Mightier One has arrived. Peace has its roots in every act of humility.

SECOND READING: ROMANS 13:11–14
It is now the hour for you to wake.

Our waking habits are very individual. Some people spring up at dawn, grateful to be alive, breathing in the air with exuberance. Some of us open one eye miserably, snap it shut, and try to pretend it is still night for a few minutes more. Paul says time is short, do not play games, morning has broken!

If we honor God's ways, we honor one another and do not live half-hidden, with a private agenda submerged in our words, relationships, and choices. Do we dare to move out of the shadows, beyond cynicism and resentment, and live in the light without pretension? (The night is far spent: slow risers might want to begin right away!)

GOSPEL: MATTHEW 24:37–44
You must be prepared.

If Isaiah painted a picture of the day of the Lord as being glorious, a revelation of justice and truth, then Jesus counters that image: this day will also be mysterious, unexpected, and rather dangerous. Frankly, Isaiah's image is a bit more comforting. I am all for peace and justice arriving tomorrow. But a thief breaking into my house? This is not what I usually intend when I pray "thy kingdom come!"

Isaiah's understanding of that day necessarily includes the warning Jesus offers. When God is fully revealed, and justice is served, what will that justice look like? We pretend it is going to come down hard on the Bad Guys— we get the peace, they get the justice. But the fact is, we've all got a stake in the material world: the power, the glory, the sheer amount of stuff that weights us to this world like an albatross. When Jesus comes, all that is rooted in this world will disappear.

Questions for Reflection

• Isaiah envisions a world without conflict. What areas of your life would change in such a world? (Think of personal grievances, racial or ethnic tensions, institutions that you do battle with.)

• Paul's checklist for dishonorable living lists the vivid extremes like carousing, and the more hidden sins like jealousy. What would a list of honorable attributes for living contain?

• When Jesus breaks into your house like a thief in the night, what are you likely to lose?

Action Response

Review the areas of your life that would change if Isaiah's prophecy materializes. How many of those things do you have the power to change now? How much of the conflict in your life originates with you? Begin to move toward the kingdom now.

The Voice of the Herald

FIRST READING: ISAIAH 11:1–10

No harm or ruin on my holy mountain.

Good news! Incredible reversals are about to take effect. Society will no longer be run like a beauty contest, where the ones who look good and dress smart get all the praise and all the prizes. Justice will be for the poor and the plain ones, too. The vulnerable will be safe in the company of predators. Poison will not threaten the well-being of our children, not in its literal or more subtle forms. From now on, nobody hurts the innocent, and the wicked will be struck down with a word.

This is good news! Unless, of course, you stand to benefit from the world as it is. Are we sure we're on the side of the one upon whom God's spirit rests?

SECOND READING: ROMANS 15:4–9

Accept one another as Christ accepted you.

Acceptance is not much to ask for. Not to be rejected outright because of the way we look or talk, who are parents were, what we may have done in the past, or what we have or lack. But we all know it is not that simple. One group excludes another, historically, politically, and how can we as individuals withstand the pressure to conform to that? The norms of our culture teach us who's in and who's out, and if we attempt to change the rules, there's hell to pay.

Paul says: Jesus comes to change the rules. This world's hell is heaven in the world to come, so whatever the cost of doing justice, consider it a downpayment on a dream home. Acceptance of one another is the first step on the path of justice.

GOSPEL: MATTHEW 3:1–12

Reform your lives!

Bad news! Some baptizer is calling for reform. He dresses weirdly and eats bugs. Everybody's falling at his feet, getting dunked in the river. There's hysteria in the air, and the authorities are out of their minds about him.

He says awful things about our religious leaders, tells them their claims to God's favor mean nothing. God would just as soon have rocks for children! He says God's going to clear out all the deadwood in the forest. (I wonder if that includes me!) And he says if you think *he* is a reformer, wait till you see who is coming up. A dunk in the river will be nothing compared to a shower of Spirit and fire!

Real bad news. Unless this is the herald you've been praying for.

Questions for Reflection

• Who are the people who compose your immediate community (family, friends, neighbors, coworkers, parish)? How will Isaiah's reversals affect the people you know?

• What people or groups are outside of acceptance in your town? What or who keeps them out?

• Would John the Baptist be a threat to you? Your family? Your church? Your neighborhood and town? Why?

Action Response

Identify one concrete step you can take to further the acceptance of outsiders in your community. Welcome a stranger, forgive a fellow sinner; don't let fear or prejudice divide your heart.

THIRD SUNDAY OF ADVENT

Kingdom Coming

FIRST READING: ISAIAH 35:1-6, 10

Be strong, fear not.

What if the weak were suddenly made strong? We see it all the time in cartoons: Popeye eats his spinach and beats Brutus black-and-blue (and Brutus could use a beating, we think). We see it in the news as well. Countries long victimized by a powerful class undergo revolutions in which the former victims oppress their oppressors. Human justice wears a brutal face, as those who suffer unjustly take on the character of injustice themselves.

Divine recompense is different. Judgment is reserved to God, and the poor are restored to wholeness without becoming part of the cycle of evil. There is no need to turn and wreak vengeance on the strong ones. Those who are truly restored have room only for singing and joy in their hearts.

SECOND READING: JAMES 5:7-10

You too, must be patient.

"Patience is a virtue," my mother would intone, whenever algebra problems would wear down my eraser and good humor. This did nothing to increase the virtue in me. You cannot speak of patience to the impatient!

The patient know the fruits of waiting. They see the kingdom coming in the seeds they sow, words of kindness, deeds of compassion. They speak prophecy, knowing that what they say is already coming to pass. They know that God is in the seen and the unseen; and behind the scenes, God has already prepared a place for us. They believe that tenderness today means more love for tomorrow. And they are willing to make sacrifices now, trusting in God's promises. Patience is the premier virtue for Advent.

GOSPEL: MATTHEW 11:2-11

"What did you go out to see?"

Our expectations dramatically affect what we experience. Depressed people tend to gather evidence that life is not working. Angry people collect grievances. The self-righteous hunt for the sins of others. We're all looking for something, and we generally find it.

John in prison is reevaluating his claims about Jesus. He has prophetic expectations that he is unsure have been met. Jesus quotes him some Scripture as reassurance. But then Jesus directs the same concern to the crowds. What were you looking for in John? The message or the messenger? Because if you think it all ends with John, you will never guess that it begins with Me.

John announced the end of an age, the axe laid at the roots of some very old ways of being and thinking. Jesus announces the coming of a new age in which the humblest member would be greater than John. We have to believe that John in prison would be grinning to hear that. He was quite prepared to decrease for such an increase.

Questions for Reflection

• As the weak gain power and a voice in our culture, the strong tremble. Who are the weak in your circles? When they gain power, will they perpetuate injustice?

• How are you practicing patience during the holiday crush to get it all done?

• What do you expect to happen this Advent, and how does this expectation affect your experience of this season?

Action Response

The kingdom is coming! Everybody has a share in the harvest, but also a share in the sowing. What are you doing to make the kingdom a reality for others? Choose one seed to plant—gentleness, forgiveness, gladness—and tend it patiently in prayer and practice.

What Child Is This?

FIRST READING: ISAIAH 7:10–14
Ask for a sign from the Lord.

Ahaz has a point, not wanting to tempt God by asking for a show of magic. But it was God who first offered to help Israel with a sign of confirmation in this time of distress.

Evidently it is all right with God that we of partial understanding and faulty vision ask for the assistance we need for discernment. But we have to be open to the outrageous: virgin births, guiding stars, visiting kings, angels talking to shepherds. God's signs are not the paranormal raps on a Ouija board, containable if irrational. If we ask for a sign, we might have to live with the astonishing results.

SECOND READING: ROMANS 1:1–7
You have been called to belong to Jesus.

Paul has a clear sense of vocation that should be a model for every Christian. He knows himself as an apostle, one sent by God, called and set apart to proclaim the Gospel. He is not the least ambiguous about it: God has him on a mission and he aims to fulfill it.

Most of us are pretty vague about the call, the mission, and the goal. Does God have a plan for my life? Is there something I should be doing? Where is my life headed, if anywhere? Has God even noticed me yet?

For those who are unsure of the details, Paul spells it all out in the letter to the Romans. "Spread the Gospel" is the bottom line of the Christian mission, but the how of it has to do with the way of "holiness, grace, and peace" that we are called into. We cannot learn it in a day; but we must learn it in a lifetime.

GOSPEL: MATTHEW 1:18–24
This is how the birth of Jesus came about.

It's a story about an old-world engagement—a deal cut, father and intended husband shaking hands on an exchange of resources. And then the upset—a pregnant girl, a spoiled contract. But a good man does not hand over a child to a mob for stoning, so he opts for a discreet annulment of the deal. Joseph had no idea that he had made a contract with Heaven over the redemption of history itself.

An angel explains the details: the Holy Spirit, the son on the way, the end of sin as we know it. Joseph is not losing a wife, he's gaining a Savior! Grace happens. And Christmas happens too, in part because a good man chose not to stand in its way.

You and I have a part to play in the story of redemption. Our Eucharist is a contract with heaven, and all we have to do is get our agenda out of the way and let grace happen. Glory be to God for this gift!

Questions for Reflection

• What matters of discernment might you need to bring to God at this time? What prevents you?

• How would you describe your vocation as a Christian to someone who does not share your faith?

• Grace is happening in your life right now. Are you participating in it, or are you an obstacle in its path?

Action Response

Christmas is the best time of year to work on enlarging your heart. In exchanging gifts, do not forget those who cannot reciprocate your generosity. Remember the poor and the lonely in this season for families.

How Beautiful

FIRST READING: ISAIAH 52:7-10

How beautiful upon the mountains are the feet of those who bring good news!

Have you ever lost your home? Some of us have literally lost our homes in natural disasters, or the need to flee a native country and go into exile. Some have lost homes in economic disasters, or marital ones. It is actually easier to "lose home" than we might think. Sometimes our sense of home slips away as we fall into depression, loneliness, or overwork. Sometimes we divide ourselves from home and family through deliberate acts of sin.

How relieved we are in such isolating times as these, when we greet the messenger of good news. The exile is welcomed back! We can go home. We walk in wonder, in disbelief at such news. How beautiful the thought of home is to those who are isolated and in exile.

God went into exile once, far from divinity, far from home. God came into place and into time, abandoned unity for singularity, left omnipresence and took on limitation. God entered the strangeness of flesh and its isolation. God went into exile once, so that all of us could find our way home. We celebrate the feast of home today. Wherever you are, God is welcoming you and offering you the shelter of your truest home.

SECOND READING: HEBREWS 1:1–6

This Son is the reflection of the Father's glory.

History, seen through the eyes of faith, is like building a jigsaw puzzle. We pick up a straight edge here and know we have the border. We see a bit of blue and know it is the sky, or perhaps the water. As we continue to piece the fragments together, the image grows clearer, and we know as the end nears what we are looking at.

Salvation history teaches us through the fragments, stories of Abraham and Moses, Hannah and Ruth. We get the picture of who God is, what this relationship with God is all about. Sometimes we find an ambiguous piece—this story of Abraham and Isaac, is this sky or water?—and we pause to consider our options. But in the end, when Jesus appears, all the pieces fall into place. From his birth to his death, and yes, through his resurrection and his Spirit, Jesus continues to show us what the puzzle of existence is about and how to put the pieces of our daily choices together.

GOSPEL: JOHN 1:1-18
The light shines on in darkness, a darkness that did not overcome it.

The Gospel of John is a love story. It does not contain a story about Jesus born as a baby, the Christmas story we expect to hear. But it does give us poetry, the language of love and longing. It tells us about love taking on flesh and coming to live with us. It says we will all have a share in this love, for "love follows upon love."

We know about love stories. Some of them endure throughout our lives and become the strength which sustains us to do all the good we do. Some of us had the steadfast love of parents, siblings, teachers, mentors, and special friends. Some of us, too, have suffered the disappointments of love: the parent who deserted, the companion who could not or would not stay. The wounds of love go deep, just as the gifts of love transform and heal us.

The love that John announces in his love story is the love that is here for eternity. This love does not disappoint. This love is to be trusted and is for real. This love will heal us, sustain us, and lift us up. And this love will transform us so that we become heroic and generous lovers ourselves. As in any love story, if you want to be where love is, you have to follow the Beloved.

Questions for Reflection

• Reflect on times when you have lost your sense of home and how you were brought back.

• What are some of the ambiguous pieces of life's puzzle for you? How does Jesus shed light on them?

• What are the richest sources of love in your life? For whom are you a source of love?

Action Response

In this season of gift giving, remember to give love. Give love in warm presence, kind attention, sympathetic listening. Give love in patience and forgiveness. Give love so that you can become love.

The Holiness of Family

FIRST READING: SIRACH 3:2–6, 12–14
Kindness to a parent will not be forgotten.

In this day and age, when so much has been said about bad parenting and offspring who refer to themselves as survivors of their childhood, it is peculiar to talk about the honor due to parents from their children. Putting aside the nightmare scenarios we've all heard about, it is enough to say that every generation is indebted to the last one in ultimate ways, and youth should not ignore the needs of elders.

The human family is a real and vital relationship, a community of people who need one another and who must depend on one another for the survival of all of us. If I assist the older woman trying to make change on the bus, or share my lunch with the old man who's been sitting on the curb every day, I have honored my parents. Every person in need is an invitation from God to see myself as sister or son or mother in Christ.

SECOND READING: COLOSSIANS 3:12–21
Over all these virtues put on love.

Paul presents a smorgasbord of counsel in this passage. Dress yourself with virtues. Give each other a break. Exercise forgiveness. Do peace. Be grateful. Make a home in your heart for Scripture. Any one of these would make a fine new year's resolution.

But then comes the awkward passage about wives and husbands! Rather than ignore or apologize for Paul's culturally dated advice, I think preachers should take the opportunity to challenge the dynamics of human domination and submission. Paul says elsewhere and eloquently that the holiness of the body of Christ mandates that every part exists in communion with the others in mutual service of one life. There is only one head to this Body, and that is Christ. The rest of the members are to submit to Christ, and to one another in the way that love always submits to the beloved.

GOSPEL: MATTHEW 2:13–15, 19–23

Take the child and his mother and flee.

This is a strange story to use to celebrate the feast of the Holy Family, because this is a frightening story about a family in crisis. Fleeing your homeland for fear of death squads murdering children does not sound like a placid family portrait to me. (Sounds like Jesus has more in common with people who "survived" their childhood!) Out of chaos, and not stability, rose the life of Jesus.

But what makes this family holy is their attentiveness to God's word, in a visitation by an angel, in a dream, always willing to move in the direction that God prompts. They were not a model family living a perfect existence. They were a real family who faced real emergencies and tests to their lives. And from the start, they were ready to follow the will of their Lord.

Questions for Reflection

•How are you invited to be parent or child or sibling to the people in your life?

•Which phrase of Paul's counsel in this passage speaks loudest to you? How does it encourage you to grow?

•What makes a family holy? Whether you live in a nuclear family or not, what is your responsibility to contribute to the holiness of your family of the heart?

Action Response

It is new year's resolution time: have you made the usual list? Be sure to add a spiritual agenda to your hopes for the coming year. Review Paul's advice in Colossians 3. And let the word of God, rich as it is, dwell in you in the coming year.

Walking Together

FIRST READING: ISAIAH 60:1-6
Nations shall walk by your light.

Although independence is an icon for Americans, and isolationism the shadow side of that quality, to go it alone tears at the fabric of our creatureliness. Every dream of the prophets for peace included the hope of acceptance by other peoples, and even their admiration. When the glory of God is finally revealed, all nations would flock to Jerusalem to offer sacrifice and praise to the God of Israel.

The manifestation of God's glory that Israel hoped for is the literal definition of epiphany. The divine revelation is always accompanied by a rush toward unity, one God, one people, one peace. All that divides humanity would fall away in the wonder of that hour.

In the meantime, we who believe without seeking an epiphany must continue to harbor that hoped-for peace in our hearts.

SECOND READING: EPHESIANS 3:2-3, 5-6
Members of the same body and sharers of the promise.

The letter to Ephesus is Paul's great letter about the church, its universal mission, and its embrace of all peoples as sharers in the divine plan. Paul takes on a very touchy subject by tackling it head-on: the spiritual inheritance of the Jews is to be shared equally with the Gentiles.

To imagine the original impact of this claim, I think of what it would have sounded like to my parents before the Second Vatican Council to hear that God loved the Protestants just as much as the Catholics! And it may be as much of a surprise to some people today that God also loves Buddhists, Muslims, and Mormons with the same passion that we used to think was reserved only for Catholics.

It is no wonder that Paul got into trouble with the Jerusalem crowd, who saw the revelation of Jesus Christ to be a private, Jewish matter. The reconciliation of humanity to God through Christ has always been tough to swallow for anyone who lives with a divided heart.

GOSPEL: MATTHEW 2:1–12
"We observed his star at its rising."

The astronomers from the East made some brilliant calculations regarding the star, but they greatly miscalculated when they showed up at Herod's palace. If the wise men believed Herod when he said he wanted to worship the new king too, they must have been fatally innocent. Any child who hears this story knows that Herod is lying.

Still, these three do manage to find the child and recognize his greatness, despite the simplicity of his surroundings. And out of their coffers they surrender their wealth to the King of the poor.

The church has always seen these three as representatives of the universal nature of the good news of Christ. All nations will bow down in worship, as Isaiah foretold. God is the Lord of these three strangers from the Orient, who recognize the Savior even before his own people acknowledge him. And those who followed a star out of their lands are led back safely by a dream.

Questions for Reflection

• How is God's glory revealed in our world at this time? How does this revelation help you to hold peace in your heart?

• Cultural pressures dictate our prejudices and fears about those who are "other" than us. How do you mend the divisions that you may have been taught to uphold?

• Have you ever taken a journey in faith, as the wise men did? What mistakes did you make? How did God supply what you lacked?

Action Response

Pope Paul VI said, "If you want peace, work for justice." We manifest the glory of God in our world to the extent that we make justice and peace a reality. Brainstorm with your family or primary community one way that you can make a concrete commitment to justice this year.

"Give in for Now"

FIRST READING: ISAIAH 42:1–4, 6–7

I, the Lord, have called you for the victory of justice.

Folk ballads endure because they recall for us the personalities of heroic figures we want to keep alive in our hearts. The lover who does not forsake his love, though he loses his life preserving her safety. The soldier who wins the battle at the cost of his blood. The leader who is slain while carrying forward the cause. The servant songs of Isaiah are like ballads written about Jesus centuries before he was born. Like all ballads, they describe the noble figure and why he is to be revered. In the later verses, we will hear how he was slain for the sake of the truth, in fidelity to love, to liberate his people.

The fate of the servant of the Lord is unfair. But he brings real justice into an unjust world by his total surrender to God's purposes. He gave himself over to injustice for a time, so that God's justice might be known for all time. It is an odd bargain, but all of God's dealings are full of mystery from where we sit. Forgiveness of sin is hardly just, but who will turn it down?

SECOND READING: ACTS OF THE APOSTLES 10:34–38

"Anyone who fears God and acts uprightly is acceptable to God."

Peter didn't always get it, but when he got it, he got it good. His sudden breakthroughs caused him to shout that Jesus was the Messiah or to leap overboard and swim to shore at the sight of Jesus. Peter wasn't the most perceptive man in Galilee, but he wept at the knowledge of his own sin and admitted when he was wrong. That'll get you pretty far in the reign of God.

All along, Peter has had a hard time, like the rest of the disciples, seeing Gentiles as salvageable people. Prejudice runs deep, and the Hebrew prejudice against outsiders was bred to the bone—and for good reason. Outsiders never did the Jews a lick of good. Why should they care, or their God care, what happens to the Gentiles?

But in the time it takes for Peter to have one vision (see earlier in chapter 10), Peter sees his way through and repents his blindness. He brings the good news of Jesus to Cornelius and his household because of what he sees, and the light of the world shines further into the darkness.

"We must do this if we would fulfill all of God's demands."

Sometimes I like the job description of John the Baptist. He gets to stand in the river all day and dunk people, while preaching up a storm about everything he sees that God does not like. He does not have to practice diplomacy or be nice to his enemies; after all, they're God's enemies too. Being John the Baptist seems like a good job, if you don't count the beheading.

But even John has his off days. It is not always easy being the town baptist. When Jesus shows up, for example, he is confounded. Baptize "the one who is to come"? But all this baptizing is for the purpose of preparing for this very man! Jesus takes John aside. "Give in for now," Jesus urges gently. Do it God's way, and do not expect to understand everything.

Like John, we are susceptible to thinking we know what God wants and does not want. We think we have the corner on the market of God's plan for us, not to mention for everyone else. We have to be alert for the curve balls of faith, the events that twist us around and ask us to do what does not fit, what is not reasonable. Faith is not the same as reason. If it were, we would not have to believe; we would know.

Questions for Reflection

• Have you ever suffered an injustice for the sake of a greater justice, or have you observed someone who has?

• To whom do you bring God's good news, and from whom do you withhold it?

• When has a curve ball from God changed the way you see or understand your faith?

Action Response

Is there something in your life that you are resisting, the pursuit of a dream or allowing a wound to heal? Give in for now. Let God take you where the Spirit is prompting.

One Righteous Act

FIRST READING: GENESIS 2:7–9, 3:1–7

Then the eyes of both of them were opened.

The first consequence of knowledge is shame. What an unexpected development! We can imagine these seekers of divine wisdom tasting the fruit and expecting big returns. What would they learn? The secrets of creation? The power that controls the universe? How to fly like birds, or blaze like the sun?

What they learn is embarrassment. And as with all lessons, there is something to be gained in that. The acquisition of knowledge should always be accompanied by a certain humility, as science and theology have come to appreciate the hard way. Venturing onto holy ground, which the quest for understanding naturally entails, must be undertaken in a spirit of reverence, and never in a stealthy arrogance, hoping to cheat the deity. What we now call Original Sin could have been the First Great Cooperation, if humankind had chosen to grow with God rather than apart from the source of wisdom.

SECOND READING: ROMANS 5:12–19

A single righteous act brought acquittal and life.

Sin, death, condemnation, and acquittal. These are good themes for the beginning of the season of Lent, as Paul underscores for the community at Rome what the gift of Christ brings to our world. In a few paragraphs, he sums up what salvation history is all about. Sin—the deliberate movement away from God's will—comes into the world through human choice. Grace—the bridge that allows us access to God's way again—is offered to our world through Christ Jesus.

We who are wayfarers in this world can choose to heap sin upon sin, widening the separation between creation and Creator, or to choose righteous acts that widen the channel of grace as it seeks to penetrate every human heart.

GOSPEL: MATTHEW 4:1–11
God alone shall you adore.

The specter of Satan spouting Scripture at a fast-weakened Jesus in the desert is an eerie scene. Like the distorted image in a funhouse mirror, it is both familiar and grotesque in its resemblance to the temptation story in Genesis. In both stories, the tempter approaches its victim at a disadvantage: Eve's ignorance, Jesus' physical exhaustion. And the tempter uses the bargaining chip of divine power to supplant the limitation that his target currently faces.

Eve and then Adam fall for the lure; so human failure is ever illustrated. But Jesus withstands a trinity of assaults to become instead the supplanter of temptation itself, the personification of grace. Eve and Adam and all of us need never face the tempter alone again. There is no desert so barren that Christ will not stand with us against our demons.

Questions for Reflection

- Does growth in knowledge confirm or challenge your faith?
- As Lent begins, where do you stand in relationship to sin and grace?
- How does the power of your faith in Christ help you to withstand temptation?

Action Response

Make two lists as an examination of conscience for your lenten practice. First, list the areas of your life where sin still reigns, e.g., certain relationships, episodes of anger, lack of charity, self-involvement. Then, list places where grace is working: persons, activities, choices. Commit yourself to putting grace to work in countering the reign of sin.

Amazing Grace

FIRST READING: GENESIS 12:1–4

You will be a blessing.

At seventy-five, an age when most of us are well into retirement, Abraham is recruited for his great mission, to claim a land and to father a people. Now granted, biblical ages are not an exact science; yet the point is clear. There is no time in our lives when God is through making use of us.

We are schooled into thinking of vocation in a compartmentalized way: as a call to religious life that was best heeded in adolescence and left you alone entirely after a certain grateful age. But the root meaning of vocation is "summons," a call from an authority that can come at any time, to any purpose. So even if you are receiving your senior discount these days, you are not off the hook when God comes calling.

SECOND READING: 2 TIMOTHY 1:8–10

He has robbed death of its power.

It is very hard for us to understand that God does *not* save us or call us because we deserve it. God has a plan, and it does not depend on our merit. Years ago I tried to fathom God's pattern by scrutinizing the chosen ones, and this is what I came up with: Abraham was a liar, Isaac was not over-bright, Jacob was a con artist, Moses a murderer, Solomon a lady's man, David an adulterer…and the list goes on. It seems that God could have been a little more discerning in choosing the main players in salvation history. It is clear, at least, that the divine plan is not about us, but about something reason alone would find unreasonable.

When Paul writes to Timothy as one pastoral leader to another, he wants it to be clear that it is not by our own efforts that God makes grace available to us. What Timothy will need—and what we all require to do God's will—has been held out to us before the world began.

GOSPEL: MATTHEW 17:1–9
"Get up! Do not be afraid."

One minute, it is just their friend and teacher Jesus. The next minute, the light is so bright they can hardly see, and what they do see is astounding: Moses, the great lawgiver and Elijah, the great prophet! Peter, ever the man of action, tries to be helpful, but his speech is interrupted by a voice even greater than the three personalities before him. At this point, courage deserts the disciples, and they cower on the ground.

Can we blame them? We who do not see transfigurations are sometimes terrified by the touch of the divine in our lives. There have been days when what God is doing in my life makes me fearful to get out of bed. When the moment passes, the coast seems clear of epiphanies, and we dare to move on. But the trace of divine footprints makes it clear Who has been in our midst.

Questions for Reflection

- Do you know what God is summoning you to do? What can you do to discern this call more clearly?
- Name three reasons why God might find you "unsuitable" for service. Who in the Bible was similarly unsuitable?
- Under what circumstances has the face of God been most clearly revealed to you?

Action Response

Spend some time this Lent in active discernment of God's will for you. Consider a period of retreat, spiritual direction, or journal writing to enhance your ability to hear God's summons.

The Fountain Leaping Up

FIRST READING: EXODUS 17:3–7
"Is the Lord in our midst or not?"

It is easy for us to criticize the Israelites for their appalling vote of "no confidence" in Moses, not to mention Yahweh. After all, had not the Lord, through Moses, accomplished extraordinary rescues, time and again, for these people? But the fact is, you cannot argue with thirst. Dehydration is a dreadful condition, alarming in its immediacy, and like suffocation, imperils life in a way that doesn't admit much time for debate. The chosen people of God were at risk—didn't God see, or care?

This is a legitimate question, then and now, and no mere theology to anyone who is suffering. It is perhaps the most religious question one can ask. Moses accepts the urgency, and turns it over at once to the Lord. Which is, perhaps, the most religious response to the question of suffering.

SECOND READING: ROMANS 5:1–2, 5–8
The love of God has been poured out through the Spirit.

Who needs salvation? Sinners, essentially—the righteous need not apply. It should surprise no one, then, that Christ died for sinners, that the Holy Spirit is poured upon godless hearts like ours. Yet all of this is contrary to the human logic of just deserts. We tend to heap laurels on folks who do not need them, reward the wealthy with more wealth, the honored with more honor. If God were more logical, God would save the *good* people, and leave the nasty ones to their self-made hell. This is justice, we say.

Thank heaven, God is not as just as we are. God extends grace to us because of who God is, not because of who we are. God gives us what we need because we need it, not because we have earned it. And this is the source of our peace, which the world, in its ruthless version of justice, cannot give.

GOSPEL: JOHN 4:5–42
"Give me this water, sir."

The story of this first apostle to the Gentiles—a generation before Paul—is so rich and full, any brief reflection must be limited to a single image. Let's focus on the living water: what has living water got that other water does not? A connection to its source, biologists would say. Living water refers to oceans, streams, rivers—water that flows, pours, moves ceaselessly through its courses. Stagnant water, on the other hand, like the water in a cup, just sits there, and eventually becomes impure by its lack of a replenishing, renewing source.

The Samaritan woman has one advantage over Jesus: she has access to well water in a dry land. But the water that Jesus has, continually splashing up from the boundless generosity of God, is a far superior offering. Imagine having a fountain of water rising up within you, keeping your spirit ever refreshed and alive. Would you not, like this amazed woman, leave your old water jar behind?

Questions for Reflection

- How do you involve God when you are in a crisis situation?
- What does salvation through Jesus Christ offer you personally?
- In what ways do you settle for the stagnant water of the world? Where in your life is God's living water flowing?

Action Response

Dorothy Day once said: God does not give us the right to discriminate between the "deserving" and the "undeserving" poor. Since God's grace comes to us while we are still sinners, do a gracious act for someone "undeserving" this week.

A Showcase for God's Work

FIRST READING: 1 SAMUEL 16:1, 6–7, 10–13

People see appearances, but God looks into the heart.

The prophet Samuel is on the lookout for a king. If you were on a mission from God, in search of a would-be leader, what criteria would you use? Samuel's instructions are pretty clear, in some respects; he need look no further than Jesse's house, among a limited number of sons. But after that, the details get cloudy. Jesse, as it happens, has a generous supply of sons, and only one of them is the chosen one of God.

The Lord prompts Samuel—this is an open book exam!—not to be distracted by appearance, height, or other human considerations. This includes birthright, intelligence, and charisma. What criteria is left? The answer, for God watchers, is simple: surprise! Find the least likely fellow in the picture and that is the next king over Israel, for sure.

SECOND READING: EPHESIANS 5:8–14

Light produces every kind of goodness.

I ran into a table the other night, in my own apartment. Being reluctant to turn on the light, I stumbled in familiar territory. But when one is half-asleep, the very idea of light is threatening to that comfortable drowsy state.

Paul speaks to the sleeper in all of us: Christians, the light is available to us, so use it. People who do not know Christ might flail around helplessly, making wild life choices, having no criteria for discernment. But we, who believe, do. Still, we may choose to leave the light off, enjoying the sleepy environment of darkness and the luxury of not seeing clearly where our steps are taking us. This denial by no means lessens the consequences of our blindness, or the pain of the eventual impact.

GOSPEL: JOHN 9:1–41
"How were your eyes opened?"

The story of the man born blind is almost comedy. On the one hand, the disciples are clamoring at Jesus, "Whose fault is it that this man is blind?" On the other hand, the enemies of Jesus are asking, "Whose fault is it that this blind man now can see?" The passage is a series of questions, with nobody willing to accept the answers they are given. There is an anthill of activity, people running around excitedly, everybody in a panic over this dreadful miracle. If it were not Scripture, it would be slapstick.

The punchline, of course, is that we are all born blind, and like the man in the story, we are all offered sight through the power of Christ. But all of the "blind" in the passage—disciples, neighbors, Pharisees, Jewish authorities, and family members—reject the clear vision that Jesus presents in this fifth sign of John's gospel. Only the man who was once physically blind is able to perceive it, another twist in the irony. As Jesus says, this man was born blind to be a showcase for God's work. Depending on our choices, the same could be said of us.

Questions for Reflection

• If God were to choose a leader in your community, based on the criteria of surprise, who would the candidates be? How would you feel about such leadership?

• What light, available to you, do you fail to make use of?

• What is the greatest blindness you face? How does Jesus, the light of the world, alleviate this darkness?

Action Response

Take the Pharisees' question to prayer with you: "Since it was your eyes he opened, what do you have to say about him?" Ask it of yourself throughout the week, and listen for the continuing testimony from within.

Waking Lazarus

FIRST READING: EZEKIEL 37:12–14

I have promised, and I will do it.

Ezekiel's vision of the dry bones (found in chapter 37) is dazzling in its flamboyant imagery. First, a field of old dry bones. Next, skeletons knit together in the air! Finally, sinew and flesh creeping back over the forms so that human lives are restored to the world, planted firmly on the land that God ordained for them. The vision ends with these passionate words about resurrection, God's vow to bring life out of death for those who belong to the Maker of the Covenant.

These words are especially thrilling to us because we've all been there, in the valley of the dry bones, in illness, grief, emotional paralysis, shame, the endless ways in which people go dead in the midst of life. And our graves have been opened and will be opened again by the Promise-maker, who holds the key to every door.

SECOND READING: ROMANS 8:8–11

The spirit lives because of justice.

If Ezekiel prophesied that God would put flesh back on our bones, Paul seems determined to strip us back down to mere spirit. But this would be a faulty reading of Paul, who uses the Greek word for "flesh" in the larger sense of the material realm. Paul is not warning us against our bodies or the created world necessarily, but against placing our trust in things that are passing, otherwise known as materialism.

We who are of the Spirit cannot afford to bank on the flesh, because the only sure thing about the world is that it is heading toward extinction. The indwelling Spirit assures us that we are not born for corruption but for eternity. And eternity is a long way to drag your luggage.

GOSPEL: JOHN 11:1–45

"Lord, the one you love is sick."

There is no more powerful miracle story in the gospels than what happened that day in Bethany. The scene was taut with emotion: Martha's strength, Mary's grief, the mourners' wailing, Jesus himself moved to weeping at the pain and loss that death yields. And then Jesus lifts up his prayer, and a dead man wriggles awkwardly out of a hole, still bound by his shroud. What wonder, and terror!

Waking Lazarus from death is what finally condemns Jesus to his own death in John's gospel. He goes too far for the authorities, who are as spooked by the reports of this event as some of the witnesses themselves. To wake the dead is a testimony to power that is practically uncontainable. If not stopped, such power could change the established order for all time.

Questions for Reflection

• When has God called you back to life from a season of death? How did you hear the call to "rise"?

• In what ways do you still rely on "the flesh" and not the living Spirit of God?

• The story of Lazarus shows Jesus at his most human and divine moments. What is the most powerful lesson you learn at Lazarus' tomb?

Action Response

Someone you know is experiencing a season of death (grief, depression, failure). How can you help them to hear the call to "come forth" to life? Be a messenger of life this week.

Every Knee Must Bend

FIRST READING: ISAIAH 50:4–7
He opens my ear that I may hear.

The Servant Songs of Isaiah are profiles in courage. Articulate, obedient, long-suffering, resolute, the Servant of Yahweh is the image from Hebrew prophecy that Jesus draws upon in shaping his ministry. The cornerstone of the Servant's strength is the "morning after morning" of attentive listening to God's heart, which informs the rousing word he speaks and the road he walks.

Jesus continually turned aside to pray in his ministry, to rest, be filled, discern, and most of all to listen. In our attention-deficit culture, genuine listening rarely happens. Careful disciples will want to consider the "morning after morning" example of Isaiah's Servant.

SECOND READING: PHILIPPIANS 2:6–11
Jesus Christ is Lord!

One of my warmest memories of adolescence is of the charismatic priest who was our high school chaplain. No matter what curve ball life threw his way, he was always shouting "Praise the Lord!" At first I thought the man was unbalanced, having never seen an adult with such a passionate and overwhelmingly positive approach to life. But eventually his joy won me over to a new way of perceiving what God and faith are about.

Paul bursts forth with the same energetic enthusiasm in this Hymn to Christ. Jesus is humbled in this world to be exalted by the One who sent him. So too are we called to humbly bend a knee, to share in the exaltation of that proclamation that rings from here to eternity: Jesus Christ and none other is Lord.

GOSPEL: MATTHEW 26:14—27:66

Tonight your faith in me will be shaken.

All disciples come to this same dark night when our faith in the Lord is shaken. There may be earthquakes and explicit denials, troubling dreams and profitable betrayals. Or we may simply fall asleep when our presence is needful, or run away when called upon to risk a stand. We may join with the crowds and call for Barabbas over Jesus, even shout for the blood of the innocent. We may be the ones who jeer and mock, or simply the ones who say nothing in the face of injustice.

The night when our faith is shaken is the bleakest night our soul can know. But the disciples survive it to become the apostles, turning the shame of desertion into the courage of martyrdom. The only one who is not transformed is the one who condemned himself for his failure, fearing God's justice and forgetting God's mercy.

Questions for Reflection

• How do you make yourself available to God's word, morning by morning?

• How does your attitude compare to Christ's in the example of his humility?

• How do you behave in crises of faith? What shakes your faith?

Action Response

Practice putting on the attitude of Christ as Paul describes it. Let humility inform your choices this week.

Disciples At An Empty Tomb

FIRST READING: ACTS OF THE APOSTLES 10:34, 37–43

We are witnesses to all that he did.

I cannot help but thrill to Peter's words as he addresses the Gentile Cornelius and his family "I take it you know what is being reported about Jesus of Nazareth…." Yes, we know! We have heard of his generous love, of his life poured out for the likes of us, of wonders performed and gracious words that speak a new holiness into our world. Peter summarizes the great testimony of courageous love for an audience that he presumes is familiar with the details. In the telling, we can imagine Peter's radiance and joy (no longer the one who denies but the one who proclaims), and the family of Cornelius catching the awe of this good news.

There are two parts to this happy story, buried earlier in chapter 10. One is the conversion of Cornelius, drawn by a vision to seek the man of God and his message. The other is the conversion of Peter, who also comes to know through a vision that Gentiles are entitled to share this good news as surely as his own Jewish community. It is in the turning of our hearts that the word of God finds its home, and we our lasting peace.

SECOND READING: 1 CORINTHIANS 5:6–8

A little yeast has its effect all through the dough.

Making bread is hard work, from the measuring, testing, kneading, to the almost divine patience required to wait out the process and allow the "becoming" to happen. Much of the work is ours, to provide the right environment for bread to become. But at a certain time, there is nothing more we can do and we must "possess our souls in patience" and wait upon the bread.

Paul speaks proverbially about the tiny amount of yeast required to effect change throughout the flour. The proverb refers to the influence of evil and its progressively predatory effect. Paul says throw away the old yeast (whatever allegiances you have to old patterns of being), for the corruption of the whole is sure to follow, as fermentation follows the yeast. Bread without the leaven of the world will make a more wholesome food for a community called to wait upon the bread.

GOSPEL: JOHN 20:1–9
He saw and believed.

Define emptiness. You may find yourself using words like hollowness, a void, full of echoes. You may talk about meaninglessness, envision spider webs and nobody home. Whatever you may think of emptiness, when we talk about the empty tomb of Easter, we are talking about the most meaningful space ever discovered.

In John's account, Mary Magdalene is once again the first to find the empty tomb, but there are as yet no angels, no Gardener-Lord to explain the mystery. She flees, running at once to Peter and, presumably, John, with the troubling testimony of emptiness. Now it is Peter and John who are running, this time in the direction of emptiness, hoping that their eyes will tell them more than their hearts can presently understand.

They see a hollow space, hear the echo of their own footsteps, see wrappings that wrap nothing. There is truthfully nothing there to see except emptiness. Yet the emptiness contains truth itself, for those who believe. And they do, in the silence of that void, find faith.

It is easy enough to be faithful during epiphanies. But we are called to be disciples in the empty spaces of our lives as well, when only the sounds of our own footsteps accompany us. Can we look into the void and see divine purpose? Can we guess, in our Lord's apparent absence, the true Presence revealed in an empty tomb?

Questions for Reflection

• How do you turn your heart in preparation for the Gospel?

• What small amount of yeast in your life may be corrupting the whole of your journey in faith at this time?

• What are the lessons of emptiness that you have learned at the tomb?

Action Response

Jesus is risen! The promise of new life is spoken, but many of us have not yet heard it. Bring the message of life to someone who needs to know it through you: visit someone homebound, comfort a friend whose world is darkened by grief, forgive a trespass against you.

My Lord and My God!

FIRST READING: ACTS OF THE APOSTLES 2:42–47

A reverent fear overtook them.

Imagine the baptism of 3,000 people! That's how many in Jerusalem were mesmerized by Peter's impassioned speech in the street at Pentecost, and relinquished their lives to the Holy Spirit. It's hard to envision a homily with that kind of effect.

And how they lived after that, the Book of Acts tells us, was pretty incredible. A life in common, nobody holding an economic advantage over a neighbor, no one in need because everyone was generous. This is a community united in praise of God and obedient to the teachings of Jesus. Nothing has ever been as good as the early Christian experience—in fact, Scripture scholars tend to suggest that it was too good to be true even then, that Luke is idealizing more than a little bit what the original church was like.

But if we took it all seriously being the body of Christ—sharing God's life; the power of the Holy Spirit; the grace pumping through our world in every moment, available to us for the transformation of the world we know into the reign of God—would it be an exaggeration to say that reverent awe and exultant hearts would be the natural trademark of the Christian?

SECOND READING: 1 PETER 1:3–9

Rejoice with inexpressible joy touched with glory.

How strange it must have been for Peter to be writing to those who had never seen Jesus. His own experience was so rich with memories of fishing together, walking along dusty roads, looking for lodging, sharing meals. Or the more remarkable recollections: an extraordinary day of preaching at the Mount, miracles, the eerie brilliance of Jesus' face on the mountain, the dreadful night in the Garden, the impossible joy of his return.

Peter knows he is writing to folks who have heard of these things over time and distance, catching a glimmer of the reality of this good news through the accounts of eyewitnesses and the impact on their lives and hearts. This "birth unto hope" is for them as well—and for us—who believe without seeing and hunger to know this Jesus and his great mercy more personally.

GOSPEL: JOHN 20:19–31
Peace be with you, he said.

It was Sunday night. Three of them had already seen the vacant tomb, and Mary came back with stories of having seen the Rabboni himself. And then suddenly Jesus was there, past the locked doors and all their fear. He offered them peace and, with a breath, the Holy Spirit. He was hardly present before he was removed from their sight.

The disciples were convinced this was no corporate delusion. They had seen the Lord! Thomas, the brave one, the practical one, had gone past the locked doors and the paralyzing fear that gripped his friends. But he could not get past his skepticism at this report. Perhaps he had just been out to see for himself if the tomb really was empty, or if he could find two sets of footprints where Mary claimed to have seen Jesus.

It is so difficult for people like Thomas to act on faith. Which is why it is so important that Jesus came back, just for his sake. Some of us suggestible types can be easily dismissed as religious fanatics. We'll believe in anything: miracles, resurrections. But folks like Thomas do not profess faith unless brought to their knees by the reality of it. God is willing to accommodate us all according to our needs.

Questions for Reflection

• Would the description of the early church in Acts be good news or bad news for you if you had to live it?

• Peter says the goal of faith is salvation. What do you hope to be saved from?

• Is faith hard or easy for you? What would it take to get you to believe that someone you knew had "seen the Lord"?

Action Response

Write your own Creed. Start with "I believe..." and then write what you really believe about God, Jesus, the Holy Spirit, the church. How different is your creed from the profession of faith we make at Mass?

Burning Hearts

FIRST READING: ACTS OF THE APOSTLES 2:14, 22–28

My body will live on in hope.

A man starts to shout in the street. We look; it is hard to ignore his excitement. He is shouting about God. Oh no, we think, he must be crazy. We look away, intent on passing the crowd that gathers a respectful distance from his proclamations.

These street preachers! What are they trying to prove? Ranting about what God did, what we did or failed to do. This Peter claims that the man the state put to death a few weeks ago—a death our religious leaders had approved— was a man sent by God. And he says this Nazorean was not stopped by death, that the wonders he worked on God's behalf still continue.

If half of what these street preachers say is true, it would seriously disrupt the way we all do business.

SECOND READING: 1 PETER 1:17–21

Conduct yourselves reverently.

We are sojourners in a strange land, this first letter of Peter reminds us. Unlike those who choose their treasure from the offerings of this world— possessions, power, position—we find our hope and claim our citizenship in the City of the Lamb. Being sojourners, we travel lightly, knowing that we begin to belong to our belongings over time, if we bind our hearts to what the citizens of this world value. Pilgrims carry only what they can use for the journey, form relationships with those who are going along the same road, avoiding the contacts who tempt them to abandon the journey for the comforts of the byways.

Above all, pilgrims passing through alien lands are mindful of their destination at all times. It is this reverent focus that keeps them moving forward in joy or trial, companioned or friendless, when the way is clear or very uncertain. Our faith and hope, centered in God, make this sojourn we call church the only home a follower of Jesus can know.

GOSPEL: LUKE 24:13–35

"The Lord has been raised! It is true!"

In a play called *The Gospel According to the Angel Julius*, by Jack Pantaleo, Jesus greets his followers after the resurrection, then explains to them that he intends to take a little walk over to Emmaus. The disciples object: "Someone might recognize you!" Jesus answers wryly, "Believe me, I could walk from here to the twenty-first century, and very few people would recognize me."

I hope Jesus really has a sense of humor about our failure to know the Christ we serve. Certainly the Emmaus story is pretty typical for us religious types caught up in Jesus-talk; we all but let Jesus slip away unseen from our midst. It's an especially poignant story for Catholics, who in our commitment to Eucharist have a daily opportunity to open our eyes in the breaking of the Bread. The redemption of the Emmaus couple comes in that they *do* recognize Jesus in the end, that their hearts burn with that communion even before their eyes can see or their minds fully understand.

Can we trust the language of fire as it speaks within us?

Questions for Reflection

• How does the testimony of Peter affect the way you do business in the world?

• As a resident alien in this life, what essentials do you carry on the journey?

• Under what circumstances do you find truth burning in your heart?

Action Response

You have seen Jesus lately—on the news, in your neighborhood, in some event in your life which made your heart warm with holy compassion. Commit yourself to one concrete act of service to your Lord as you have seen him this week.

What Are We To Do, Friends?

FIRST READING: ACTS OF THE APOSTLES 2:14, 36–41

Save yourselves from this generation.

The response of the shaken crowd is heartfelt. "What are we to do?" If the one that we have put to death is both Lord and Savior, what can we possibly do to repair the loss? The dimension of the damage is cosmic in proportion. Our sin seems irredeemable. And it is the sin of every generation, not just an isolated people of twenty centuries ago.

Peter's reply is just as urgent and concise. Reform. Accept forgiveness. It is the same answer, repeated for every generation. I have to change my life, now, be washed clean of the barnacles that encrust my heart, and be forgiven for my many failures to love. I have to surrender the past, dedicate the present, and move decisively and fearlessly toward the future. Three thousand people heard Peter's message and were transformed by it that day. How many of us will feel the urgency in our time?

SECOND READING: 1 PETER 2:20–25

By his wounds you were healed.

This difficult passage is an exhortation to Christian slaves, who were caught in the tension between real economic bondage and the freedom they heard preached in the Gospel. Contemporary liberation theologies of the Third World challenge the institutions of oppression altogether, teaching that no form of subjugation is acceptable to God and should not be to us.

But the Epistles of the Christian Scriptures, reflecting an earlier worldview, do not address the systems of injustice as a whole. They speak instead to the poignant experience of the individual sufferer, finding consolation and strength in the parallel experience of Christ crucified.

It is possible to reject the first-century presupposition that slavery is an inevitable institution and still find instruction in these passages. Yes, injustice must be countered and unnecessary suffering alleviated—but when suffering does come, we look to the example of the One who used his own wounds to heal our brokenness.

GOSPEL: JOHN 10:1–10
I am the Gate.

A friend of mine once joked "I am going to change my name to Exit. That way, I'll see my name in neon lights wherever I go." Being an Exit would certainly guarantee that folks will be rushing in your direction on a regular basis. But what about being an Entrance? And which is it, exactly, that Jesus intends to be in his teaching?

Gates swing both ways, keeping some safely within and allowing others passage out. Jesus proposes to do both: to be the one who leads us safely out and guides us with his familiar voice on the way to a more abundant life. And to be the place of refuge, the pasture we seek to sustain us.

Jesus is clear there are others who come and go, marauders who usurp the authority and property of the shepherd. But there is only one way to pass through, one gate to fullness of life. All other claims on our allegiance are illegitimate.

Questions for Reflection

• Imagine Peter speaking his call to reform to you. What is he asking you to change?

• Think of examples when suffering for righteousness' sake has helped our world, or your life in particular.

• How do you distinguish the voice of Jesus from that of a marauder?

Action Response

Be an Entrance this week. Welcome someone who is seeking refuge. Be an Exit this week. Assist someone in the struggle to be free.

Which Way?

FIRST READING: ACTS OF THE APOSTLES 6:1–7

The word of God continued to spread.

Prejudice is a familiar byroad. We all take it now and again, preferring one kind of people over another, discriminating into camps of insiders and outsiders. It fractures our society and leads to tension, suffering, and violence.

The early church was no stranger to the impulse to travel that route. The disciples around Jesus disparaged people by categories: you are not going to talk to that woman! You are not going to help that Roman! Paul's letters are full of chastisements for the tendency of communities to close their hearts to one group or another. Here in the Book of Acts, we see the distinctions being made even in works of charity, in the cheating of the Greek widows.

A whole new ministry is formed, the diaconate, to counter the impulse to surrender to prejudice. We could use these kinds of deacons in the church again, whose job is to be sure that no one is unwelcome or excluded.

SECOND READING: 1 PETER 2:4–9

You too are living stones.

A famous old church in San Francisco burned down this year. I live in a city prone to disasters, and it is not unknown to us for buildings to come down. But the destruction of churches has a special poignancy for communities of faith. We all feel the loss that our neighbor Lutherans have suffered this year in losing their house of worship.

Yet we all know that the church does not reside within brick and mortar, and that you cannot kill a church by tumbling its walls. Christ our cornerstone calls us to be built into "an edifice of spirit," temples where God's holy Spirit lives and moves and has its being. The only church that matters ultimately is the church we *are*, the church that people encounter when they witness the testimony of our lives.

Which is why the Lutherans up the street, homeless for now, have nothing to fear. They have always had a remarkable ministry to the poor of our community, and their public testimony ensures that their church is alive and well as living stones.

GOSPEL: JOHN 14:1–12
I am the Way and the Truth and the Life.

The scene is in the upper room, at the last supper Jesus will share with his friends. He knows what lies in store for him, and he knows this is his last opportunity to teach those who are his own. After washing their feet, he begins to prepare them for his leave-taking. In this opening discourse, he tells his followers that he is going on ahead to prepare a place for them, and that the God whom Jesus knows as Father awaits them in this place.

Thomas and Philip both register confusion. How do we get to this "place" where Jesus is going, this house with many rooms? How can we know this "Father," whom Jesus knows well but whom we cannot see? The answer to both questions is the same. Jesus is the Way, and we only need to come to Jesus to see the God who sent him and the life God desires for us.

This is important for Christians to understand. We do not need to waste time and theology wondering about the nature of heaven or the demeanor of God. All we need to know can be known by choosing Jesus as our path. The truth of his Gospel is the heaven we seek. And the life of Christ we share as one Body is the divine life that leads us to the heart of God.

Questions for Reflection

• What kinds of prejudice operate in your community? Who are the deacons that minister to overcome these attitudes?

• What is the foundation of your church community? What particular charisms or gifts does your parish have to offer as "an edifice of spirit"?

• Jesus is the Way: which way does he point you? Jesus is the Truth: what truths does he teach you? Jesus is the Life: how does his life change yours?

Action Response

Consider yourself appointed deacon for a week, "filled with faith and the Holy Spirit," to serve your community with integrity and fairness. Be present to the needs of others, regardless of social distinctions. Combat prejudice in speech and action.

Truth on Wings

FIRST READING: ACTS OF THE APOSTLES 8:5-8, 14-17

Samaria had accepted the word of God.

Samaria. This was the home of those people the first-century Jews loved to hate, the Samaritans. These were the people who often starred as the heroes of Jesus' parables; it was the place where Jesus encountered a woman at the well who became a joyful apostle of good news to her town. With the coming of Philip, Samaritans at last hear of the resurrection of Jesus, and are baptized in his name.

How quickly in that first generation has the understanding of the people of God changed. Who would have ever thought that Samaritans would become disciples? When Jesus had his famous meeting with the woman at the well, his disciples had argued with him about the unseemliness of such contact. But now those same men—Philip, then Peter and John—embrace the Samaritans as kin in Christ, and pray for their full reception of God's Spirit.

Which makes you wonder: of those people we perceive as the enemies of God today, how many are closer to salvation than we can imagine?

SECOND READING: 1 PETER 3:15-18

Venerate the Lord in your hearts.

These two good messages need to be said loudly and often: not all suffering is Christian suffering; and not all testimony is Christian testimony. It is very tempting for religious people to baptize all pain and distress as salvific in nature (remember the line: offer it up for the conversion of Russia?), when some suffering is purely neurotic or flat-out earned by our own choices. Christian suffering is characterized as the suffering of the just for the sake of the unjust. I am afraid a lot of pain simply does not fall in that category.

As to the second message about testimony, this is one of the reasons that religion has such a bad name in the world and is viewed as a real drag by the non-religious. Peter's letter says we should offer the reasons for our hope "gently and respectfully." Most so-called Christian testimony comes down harshly and accusingly, not as an invitation but rather a condemnation. Few folks have ever been shamed into discipleship. Love and forgiveness are better bait.

GOSPEL: JOHN 14:15–21
I will not leave you orphaned.

Everybody always says they want the truth: in politics, in advertising, from the people they love. We style ourselves like the ancient figure of Diogenes with his lantern, ever in search of an honest person. The fact remains we generally do not appreciate hearing the truth when it makes us uncomfortable, as it often does. The truth comes with a price tag, and it is usually higher than we had thought to pay.

In the Last Supper discourse, Jesus promises to send the Paraclete (advocate), who is the very Spirit of truth. There are qualifications to receiving this Spirit, however; we must love Christ and be obedient (assume an attitude of listening) to him. Otherwise, we will be like those of the world, who cannot accept, see, or recognize the truth even if it dwells right within their own hearts.

Let's face it: God's Spirit is revealed in our world at every moment, unfolding the truth before our very eyes, the full flower of the kingdom available and at hand. The problem has never been a shortage of truth, only of acceptance and response.

Questions for Reflection

• Who are the contemporary Samaritans? Is the Gospel being proclaimed to them?

• Consider the Christian testimonies you hear about in the media. Are any of them gentle and respectful?

• Where do you seek the truth? What do you do with it when it finds you?

Action Response

Commit yourself to telling the truth, the Christian way. Make it kindly and reverent, an invitation to the hearer. Pray for the courage to witness to your faith this week.

Always

FIRST READING: ACTS OF THE APOSTLES 1:1–11
"Why do you stand here looking up at the skies?"

Trust the disciples to always look up the wrong end of a miracle. Jesus is risen from the dead! and all they can think to ask is, "Lord, are you going to restore the rule to Israel now?"

And then, as he is lifted up before their eyes, up into the heavens, their best response is to continue cloud-gazing for awhile. What are they waiting for? Do they think he might come right back?

Jesus' last instructions were plain: be my witnesses to the ends of the earth. But looking up at the sky is far easier. Sometimes religion degenerates into this kind of pious practice, sky gazing for signs of God, while the suffering world waits for our witness. Spiritual revelations are important and very powerful. I say, get as many as you can and hold on to them. But we cannot stop there. We have our orders. And we do not need to fear missing Jesus' return. When Jesus comes, the whole world will know it.

SECOND READING: EPHESIANS 1:17–23
The church is the fullness of Christ who fills the universe in all its parts.

What does ascension really mean? Is it about Jesus being carried away on a cloud? Is it about being physically lifted up, the Christian version of "Beam me up, Scotty?"

Paul writes about Jesus being exalted and glorified. This is a lifting up of a different order. Christ once emptied himself of the privileges of divinity in order to become the word made flesh and to live with us. Christ subjected himself to a humiliating death and was brought low by sin. And for this obedient subjection to God's will, Christ is raised not only from death but also from humiliation to glory. The one who hung naked and abandoned on the cross is now higher than every power on earth and every spirit in heaven.

This is not meant to be simply theologically interesting. Paul tells us this because we are going in the same direction. The last shall be first. The meek shall inherit. The dead shall be raised. So we believe.

GOSPEL: MATTHEW 28:16–20

"Know that I am with you always, until the end of the world!"

Jesus is not going to go away. After twenty centuries, all those who thought the Christian phenomenon was a fad have been disproved. Those who thought that crucifying Jesus would put an end to the matter were mistaken. Those who believed killing the eyewitnesses would stop the story from spreading miscalculated. Jesus is not going away.

The reason Jesus is still here is because of the church. Oh, I don't mean to say the church has always done an excellent job of presenting the Gospel to the world. We have made some huge miscalculations of our own. But Jesus commissioned those first disciples to baptize, teach, and unleash his Spirit wherever they went. And that Spirit has kept the church alive, though humans and their institutions have done everything possible at times to unhinge it.

Jesus is not going away, because you and I are here. We accept the Gospel as true for our lives and for the world. We embrace our baptism and learn all we can about our faith. We teach these truths to the next generation in our words and in our witness. And sometimes we let the Holy Spirit blow through our lives and into our world. Jesus said he would be with us always, and he meant it.

Questions for Reflection

- How do you respond to the spiritual revelations and miracles in your life?
- When it is your turn to ascend, what part of you will be lifted up, and what part brought low?
- Where and how does the church keep Jesus in the world "always"?

Action Response

Lift someone up who has fallen down. Lift the spirits of a friend who is sad. Lift up your heart in praise and gratitude for the gifts you have been given.

The Power of Unity

FIRST READING: ACTS OF THE APOSTLES 1:12–14

They devoted themselves to constant prayer.

These were the folks who had seen it all. They had been there for the ministry of Jesus, as well as the crucifixion, resurrection, and most recently, the ascension. Nearly immobilized with wonder, it took the prompting of angels to get them to stop staring stupidly at the sky and to get on with it. And what they had to get on with was simple and direct: they went home to pray. Constantly.

I have spent few seasons of my life in constant prayer, I must confess. And it takes something about as enormous as the motivation the disciples had to get me to surrender to it. But as I consider what great movements occur in my heart even when I give myself over to a season of mediocre prayer, I can imagine the thrilling results of such fervent and sustained communion. Jesus promised to be where two or more are gathered. Why not take advantage of this remarkable offer?

SECOND READING: 1 PETER 4:13–16

Do not be ashamed to suffer for being a Christian.

What does it mean to suffer for being a Christian today? In the realm of Christendom (that is, living in an ostensibly Christian society), no one is likely to put us to death for the faith. No one will deny us our rights, our jobs, a place to live, or in any way hamper our freedom. It is acceptable to be a Christian in the United States, we might think. It's almost too easy.

But that is only superficially true. The suffering comes, not in bearing the name of Christ, or in wearing the sign of the Cross, which has been reduced to a fashion statement by a culture that delights in disarming the disruptive witness. The suffering comes when we have to reconsider the call to right livelihood. The suffering comes when we have to end relationships or change patterns of behavior in conformity to the Gospel. The cost is felt when we have to give up pleasures and freedoms for the sake of justice, or when we are ridiculed for speaking the truth.

Christian suffering is not passé. There are still plenty of opportunities to share in "the glory that comes to rest" on those who suffer in the name of Christ.

GOSPEL: JOHN 17:1–11
They have believed it was you who sent me.

Jesus prays for unity on the eve of his death. What a wonderful prayer it is! He acknowledges his oneness with God, bearing the life of God as a Son bears within himself the life of the Father. Jesus also speaks of his bond with his followers and how, being given to him, they are also given to God.

This prayer that Jesus prays is not just about his friends at the Last Supper; he is praying for you and me as well. Just think: on the night before he died, Jesus prayed for you. He prayed that you would be one with God, just as he is. He asked that God would protect you and guide you as you sojourn in the world. As he contemplated the hour of his death, you were on his mind. After all, it was for our sake that he gave himself up that night in the garden.

Questions for Reflection

• Does your prayer life have a personal and communal expression? What opportunities for prayer might you be missing?

• Think of people you know who have suffered for being Christian; in the news, or in your community. How are you being called to take up the cross?

• How does the church continue the unity prayer of Jesus?

Action Response

If you belong to a regular prayer group, rededicate yourself to fervent prayer. If you do not, consider trying out a local prayer meeting, or pray together with your family or a friend this week.

The Seven Holy Gifts

FIRST READING: ACTS OF THE APOSTLES 2:1–11

All were filled with the Holy Spirit.

When we last looked in on the disciples, they had dedicated themselves to constant prayer. Liturgically speaking, they've been at it for ten days—who knows in real time how many days or weeks they poured themselves out in ceaseless communion with God.

What we do know is that this phase of their development as a community was met with an incredible response from God: Pentecost. The breath of God came down like wind, like fire. The Spirit of holiness filled them with language, Spirit becoming Word, Word becoming flesh.

What happened to those men and women in the upper room was an astonishment to the people in the streets, as they stepped outside and let the Spirit speak its passion through them. If the Spirit has not manifested itself in our midst like this recently, perhaps it is because we have not put ourselves at God's disposal with as much abandon.

SECOND READING: 1 CORINTHIANS 12:3–7, 12–13

There are different gifts but the same Spirit.

Never mind that the world does not attend to Paul's plea for unity-in-diversity. I wish at least our parishes would! But the usual scenario is more like this: the liturgy committee feels under-appreciated, the justice committee is smugly superior, the finance committee thinks it is the only one holding the whole thing together, the pastor is an island of alienation, and the rest of the folks in the pews don't think it matters whether they show up on Sunday or not.

Come on, people! We are many parts, we are all one Body. The Body is diminished if any one of us does not contribute our part. Let's listen together to the words of the special Sequence that is read (or sung) on this day, an exhortation for God's Spirit to bless us with seven holy gifts, each vital to the life of the church. Whatever part you have to play, whatever gift you are given to share, please come and be church.

GOSPEL: JOHN 20:19–23
Receive the Holy Spirit.

With a small breath, Jesus anticipates the wind of God that descends on Pentecost, bringing with it the power of the Holy Spirit. In this resurrection narrative, we can recall the story of Elijah, waiting on God's voice through a storm and an earthquake, hearing it at last in a small, still way (1 Kings 19). This gentle breath has the full force of the storm in its wake. In fact, as the Pentecost story belongs to the tradition of Luke, for the purposes of John's Gospel this *is* Pentecost.

We who hope for the action of the Spirit in our lives are poised between two traditions: which will it be? Should we look for the Spirit in tongues of fire, inspired speech, and charisma? Or should we expect it with no fanfare, in the softness of a breath, in the tender moment of forgiveness?

Certainly it is easier to spot the action of God in heroic hours, in the midst of wind and flame. But we would be wise not to miss the small, still way that God's Spirit is available to us, breathing new possibilities into our lives.

Questions for Reflection

• Pentecost is often called the birthday of the church. How do you experience the call to be church through the celebration of this feast?

• What are the gifts that are given to you as a member of the church? How do you put them at the service of the Gospel?

• Have you experienced the Spirit as wind or as breath? Where is the Spirit speaking in your life now?

Action Response

Remember the seven gifts you received at Confirmation: wisdom, understanding, knowledge, counsel, courage, holiness, and reverence? Pray for the grace to use these gifts, and to put yourself wholly at God's disposal.

The Mystery of Our God

FIRST READING: EXODUS 34:4-6, 8-9

"Do come along in our company."

Moses was a rare mortal who actually stood in the presence of God and saw the glory of the Divine—and lived. Whatever it was that Moses was privileged to see, it altered his appearance, shone from him so that the people had to cover his face with a veil. He glimpsed the mystery. Therefore his story was critical to the self-understanding of the Hebrews, and of no small value to us.

When the Lord announces the divine passage, the language is strong and clear (evidently too clear for lectionary editors, who cut verse 7). God's love is steadfast for thousands of generations, the sacrificed verse declares. And God's judgment is heavily felt for three or four generations. The God of Moses is a God whose judgment has a long and lasting effect, yet who is far and away a God of immense and everlasting tenderness for the people called to the Covenant.

Moses wants the company of such a Lord for his people. How much more do we seek God's company, we who have come to know the Divine through the New Covenant of forgiveness.

SECOND READING: 2 CORINTHIANS 13:11-13

The God of love and peace will be with you.

In Paul's emotional and personal letter to the Corinthians, he ends with the phrase now familiar to all Massgoers: the grace of the Lord Jesus Christ, and the love of God, and the fellowship of the Holy Spirit be with you all! Grace, love, and fellowship are a trinity of ways in which God has been revealed to us. The love of the Creator who bore us, the grace of the One who saves us, and the constancy of the One who will never leave us are three faces of one God, like facets of a diamond, unique yet equally brilliant.

The church asks us one day a year to sit with the mystery of the God who is Three-in-One, or unity-in-community, as theologians say. Having just celebrated the community of church last week, we now rejoice in the God who teaches us the indivisibility of union through the image we bear, the fullness of one, the love which is never alone.

GOSPEL: JOHN 3:16–18
Whoever believes in him may not die.

To hear many people talk, religion is all about condemnation and judgment. It's one of the reasons most often cited by people who leave the church (any church): it is all so negative and smug. It's also one of the main reasons some people, particularly fundamentalists, flock to churches. It gives them a high moral ground on which to stand and look down on others.

Jesus sounds exasperated in his exchange with Nicodemus, who is a teacher in his own right. Jesus wants him to understand that God's desire is not to consign sinners to hell, but to save the life once so generously brought into being. The coming of the Son cannot be separated from the original act of creation and generation. Both are for life, and not death. The God who loves the world and the Son who comes to save it are One.

Questions for Reflection

• Moses pleads for the Lord's company. How do you invite the companionship of God?

• The doctrine of the Trinity has been called the central tenet of Christianity. How does it affect your understanding of faith?

• Do you participate more in the saving of the world, or in its condemnation?

Action Response

Spend some time this week contemplating the three-ness of God. Find a way to honor God as Creator: enjoy the beauty of nature. Honor God as Redeemer: help a sister or brother in need. Honor the Holy Spirit of God: seek wisdom in prayer.

The Bread of Life

FIRST READING: DEUTERONOMY 8:2–3, 14–16

The Lord fed you in the desert with manna.

After forty years of struggle and miracle in the desert, Moses addresses the whole people of Israel as they stand on the verge of entrance into the promised land. He tells them the story of their long journey, and reminds them of the hardships and great protections. God tested you many times, Moses asserts. (And you failed each time—he does not say, but they know it is true.) Yet God still sent the manna, and water from the rock.

Wonder bread indeed, formed miraculously in the night, gathered easily at dawn. It was not the bread that sustained you, Moses declares, but the Lord's desire that you might live. Moses wants the people to be clear on this point: there is no magic in the bread, but rather wonder in the loving God who sends this food.

SECOND READING: 1 CORINTHIANS 10:16–17

Is not the cup of blessing...a sharing in the blood of Christ?

The word incorporate means, literally, to take into the body and become as one flesh. We incorporate the Body and Blood of Christ in our Eucharist, make it part of our own bodies, let it become one with our life. At the same time, we are incorporated into the body of Christ in mystical communion, and become one with the life of Christ. The dual realities of taking and being taken, feeding and becoming food, are the mysteries we celebrate. It is the matter of our thanksgiving, which is what Eucharist implies.

Sacraments are powerful acts, gestures of assent that Paul, at least, took very seriously and with great deliberation. I often wonder, when I take the cup of salvation in my hands, if I am really willing to drink of the cup from which Jesus drank.

GOSPEL: JOHN 6:51–58

My flesh is real food and my blood real drink.

Chapter 6 is known as the crisis in John's Gospel. Many of those who have followed Jesus up to now desert him after this teaching. It is at this time too that the decision is made to seek an opportunity to put him to death. This teaching about the Bread of Life was the most costly in all of the Gospels.

The Body of Christ has suffered much through the centuries for the sake of this understanding. The church has been rent into two camps, Protestant and Catholic, divided in our belief about the significance of this meal. These words of Jesus are startling and visceral, and to one without faith, they sound grotesque. Jesus, the Word made Flesh, has come to be our food. The life of God is offered to us as bread and wine. Take and eat, the priest recites at every Mass, for this is my Body, which is given up for you. We do this in holy memory, as Jesus bid us. In fear and trembling, in wonder and gratitude, daring and desiring, we take this food.

Questions for Reflection

• Imagine yourself on the threshold of the promised land, the new Jerusalem of our hope. Tell the story, as Moses did, of your journey, and the ways God has tested and sustained you.

• How does the church act as one bread, one body, in the world?

• How has your understanding of holy communion changed over the years? How has it remained the same?

Action Response

Having consumed the Body and the Blood, we become bread and wine for others. Seek a way to celebrate your vocation to be food: serve a meal in a soup kitchen, share lunch with a lonely person, bring the bread of your presence to someone who is in need.

John's Testimony... and Ours

FIRST READING: ISAIAH 49:3, 5–6
God is now my strength.

This passage from one of Isaiah's Servant Songs reminds us that God does not share our parochial view of the world. God's designs are vast, limited only by the size of our hearts. The Servant of the Lord is one made glorious in God's strength, raised up to witness to more than a tribe or race or nation.

Jesus read Isaiah like a job description, as the Gospels make clear. He understood the role of the anointed one in terms of Isaiah's Servant Songs. And he often made the folks at home bitterly angry with parables that made heroes of Samaritans, or by curing the children of Gentiles.

It is hard to get beyond the ideology, politics and biases of "our kind," whoever our kind happen to be. But it is a struggle we have to engage in, because God's kind are found just on the other side of every prejudice.

SECOND READING: 1 CORINTHIANS 1:1–3
Called to be a holy people....

We are not a society of letter writers, so we don't really have much of a formula for how it is to be done. "Dear Mom," and "Love, Diane" is about as far as our formula goes. But to the ancient world, deprived of phone, FAX, and e-mail (not to mention paper and pen!), letters were rare opportunities for communicating beyond the town. The proper form identified the sender, as well as his or her authority, and also recognized the receiver, and the terms of their relationship.

Imagine the surprise of your friends (and the disbelief of society at large) if you began identifying yourself in your communications as a Christian and acknowledging the God who dwells within your listeners. It might seem strange if you did it as Paul does, but in one way or another, that reality should be implicit in our dealings with those around us.

"Look there! The Lamb of God!"

John, before he was a baptizer, was the cousin of Jesus. And though the two of them grew up in separate towns, they must have had some knowledge of each other: family news, yearly reunions at the Temple in Jerusalem, gossip, if nothing else. Yet John is emphatic in this Gospel that he did not know who Jesus really was until the day of his baptism at the river.

Now John, we can suppose, was a pretty spiritually savvy guy. As a prophet, his job was to be attentive to the One who sent him, and he was very good at what he did. Although baptisms were not unknown practices in the first century, only John is known as "the Baptist."

But all of this did not make Jesus' identity clear to him until the day the Spirit descended before his eyes. Once he knew, he did not keep it to himself. The mere sight of Jesus had him leaping and shouting: "Look there! The Lamb of God!" It does not matter how long it takes us to know who Jesus is. What matters is that, once we know, we've got to testify.

Questions for Reflection

• Make a list of the biases of your group or community. How does the word of God challenge you to overcome them?

• Do people know you are a Christian? Do they know by your treatment of them that you see Christ in them?

• How did you come to recognize who Jesus is? How does that knowledge shape your life?

Action Response

"Testimony" is a word that belongs to courts—and to fundamentalist Christians—but the idea of Christian witness is vital to growth in faith. When you do good works, or make tough decisions, be clear with people how your faith motivates you. And when blessings come your way, don't call it luck. Give the glory to God.

Pledging Allegiances

FIRST READING: ISAIAH 8:23—9:3

Dispelled is darkness.

This prophecy is part of a longer passage subtitled "Prince of Peace" in some Bibles, and goes on to include the well-known verses, "for unto us a child is born." The land reference makes it obscure. It helps to know that Zebulun and Naphtali were two of the twelve tribes of Israel, and tracts of land settled by those tribes included land west of the Sea of Galilee. The degradation of this land occurred during the occupation by Assyria, at the time of Isaiah's writings. The glory of Galilee would come when Jesus chose it as the place to begin his public ministry.

Maybe the geography and history of a faraway place do not seem to tell us much about God's action in our world. God redeemed Galilee—does that mean there's hope for the coal region of Appalachia and the ghettoes in Los Angeles, too? Does the great light that brought joy and freedom to a small slice of territory in the Middle East have anything to offer our modern world aching under its own yoke and anguish?

The people who walk in darkness *will* see a great light if we will carry it there. We are the light of the world. We have this on the highest authority.

SECOND READING: 1 CORINTHIANS 1:10–13, 17

Has Christ been divided into parts?

Our Creed begins: we believe in one God. But our allegiance is often directed in many ways: to the former pastor that we liked better than the present one; to the traditions that got changed by the Second Vatican Council; to our old way of thinking about God or the church that kept us comfortable for many years. It is easy to find ourselves attracted to a charismatic individual or a familiar situation, and to forget that our loyalty is not to a person or a practice but to Christ.

The Christian community has been scandalously fragmented over the centuries because of this very thing that Paul warned the early community at Corinth about: pledging allegiance to the messenger and missing the message. Paul chose not to preach with an elegant show of sophistry (a particular brand of rhetoric much in favor in his day) because it would have won people to his discipleship and not to Christ. How to preach the Gospel without promoting yourself has been the dilemma of every preacher since Paul. Both preacher and hearer share the responsibility not to miss the good news by clinging to its outward sign.

GOSPEL: MATTHEW 4:12–23
The kingdom of heaven is at hand.

When Jesus winds up on the shore of the Sea of Galilee, he encounters several people who are plying their trades, business as usual. He is already known as a preacher, taking up the cry of John the Baptist, "Reform your lives! The reign of God is at hand." But when he sees the fishermen, he does not promise the kingdom or ask them to change their hearts. He just asks them to come away from what they are doing, and to follow. And mesmerized by the person of Jesus—and perhaps a little bored with fishing—they walk away as coolly and cleanly as if it were less than their lives they were leaving behind.

Chances are they did not understand the whole of it. We seldom do whenever we answer God's call. The willingness to cast one's lot with Jesus when he passes by is the grace that only disciples can know. The ones Jesus called who had excuses that day are probably still fishing.

Questions for Reflection

• What light do you have to carry to the community in which you work and live?

• Draw a circle, and divide it into slices that compose your personal allegiances. Do these help you to serve the Gospel or keep you from it?

• Imagine Jesus showing up in your area today, calling you by name and asking you to follow. What would you have to leave behind?

Action Response

There are people close to you who live in darkness, struggling with illness, loneliness, financial trouble, moral confusion. Choose one way you can help someone see the great light of Christ.

FOURTH SUNDAY IN ORDINARY TIME

The Day of Humility

FIRST READING: ZEPHANIAH 2:3, 3:12–13
Seek justice, seek humility.

Prophecies come in two kinds: the ones you can take standing up, and the ones you can only handle sitting down. Zephaniah, writing before the exile to Babylon in a peculiarly degraded period of Israel's relationship to Yahweh, has a little of both kinds of prophecy in his brief work. His first chapter contains a passage upon which the *Dies Irae* (a prayer of the church used in the Mass of the Dead) is based. But the *Dies Irae*—the day of wrath—is only one prediction that Zephaniah makes. The other is what we might call the day of humility.

I try to envision what a day of humility might be like: a time when the proud, the strong, the rich, the beautiful are not in charge. It is almost impossible to imagine a world like this, because our actual world is so different. But the day of humility is certainly closer to what God has in mind for the kingdom than our contemporary day of the powerful. If the thought of a day of humility makes us uncomfortable, we'd better get practicing.

SECOND READING: 1 CORINTHIANS 1:26–31
If you would boast, boast in the Lord.

Paul's passion for his message makes him less than tactful at times. Can you see him getting up in front of a Mass crowd at your parish, saying, "Not many of you are wise or influential, and surely not well-born!" Yet it is true that the Gospel is most attractive to the weak of this world. It is the sign of a healthy parish, if the lowly and the despised show up and are welcomed at your functions.

For what good would there be, Paul argues, if God made use only of the gifted and the strong? The world has room for those people, who succeed and are admired wherever they go. But when God makes use of the lowly ones, then the world must gasp. Clearly such folk would "count for nothing" if the power of God did not move in them.

How blest are the poor in spirit.

Jesus says some pretty doubtful-sounding things in the Sermon on the Mount, but the Beatitudes take the cake. How blest are the poor in spirit? Not very! And the sorrowing, the hungry, and the persecuted are not doing so well either. In fact, the merciful are mocked as soft, the peacemakers as "doves," and the single-hearted dismissed as lacking imagination.

What Jesus promises is a reward in heaven—of course he would not presume too much for the charity of this world. But the Beatitudes were delivered to two audiences with two purposes in mind: to the lowly, to increase their hope, and to the powerful, as a warning. It is no accident that, in Luke's version, the "blessed be" verses are followed by the "woe to you" section, to spell it out for the hard of hearing.

Good news for the weak is always bad news to the strong. That's why, if we stand in any position of power or have any resources at hand, we are warned to put our advantage at the service of the lowly. God will side in the end with the poor. I repeat: God will side in the end with the poor.

Questions for Reflection

• Consider Zephaniah's description of the day of humility. Whom do you know who best exemplifies the spirit of that day?

• How have your weaknesses been turned to strengths through the power of God?

• In what ways do the Beatitudes sound like good news to you? Are they also bad news in some ways?

Action Response

Choose one Beatitude—the one that strikes you most keenly—and find a way this week to make someone feel blessed in their lowliness. Make your presence/action/generosity a beatitude for others.

Called to Be Light

FIRST READING: ISAIAH 58:7–10

Your wound shall quickly be healed.

Israel is all but broken by the trauma of exile, and seeks to repent by ritual fasting. But Isaiah is clear: fasting without almsgiving is a ritual with no meaning. Why take on the "feel" of the poor with no attempt to alleviate their plight? Outward signs of repentance do not impress the Lord: a change of heart and behavior is what is needed.

This is classic biblical medicine for every age. We cannot be religious people without being people of justice. We do not heal from that sin that wounds our hearts until we turn to bind the wounds of others. Everybody who has ever reached out to the afflicted reports the same experience: "I thought I was doing it for them. Turns out I was doing it for me." Light will rise for us in the darkness when we lift the gloom of our sisters and brothers.

SECOND READING: 1 CORINTHIANS 2:1–5

Your faith rests on the power of God.

It was a huge temptation, but Paul didn't fall for it. Most wandering philosophers of his day were making a nice living for themselves—not to mention winning lots of esteem—by treating the crowds to a show of wisdom. People are impressed by brilliance, even if they cannot understand half of what is said.

Paul wanted his message to be understood, however, and he did not see his mission to draw attention to his "school of thought." So he abandoned the rhetoric of the academic circles he had known in his rabbinical education, and stuck to "Jesus Christ and him crucified." He subordinated wisdom talk to the power of the Spirit, relying on God's Spirit to gather and form the community of faith. Thanks to Paul's humility, the Corinthians fell in love with Paul's message and not his mystique. Would-be evangelists: take good notes.

GOSPEL: MATTHEW 5:13–16
Your light must shine before all.

The second-century historian Pliny declared that nothing is more useful than salt or sunshine. Yet salt that cannot be tasted and light that cannot be seen are absurdities, devoid of the properties that make them valuable. Jesus warns us that we who call ourselves disciples had better do what Christians do if we are not to be rendered ridiculous.

Is there anything more foolish than the preacher who speaks of God's love and treats people with contempt? Or people who pray to the God of mercy while presiding with intolerance and judgment over others? It is equally ludicrous to hear the good news that Jesus proclaims and to quietly deposit it in your purse or back pocket as a possession of your own. Sometimes we behave as though baptism saves our souls and communion sanctifies our hearts, with no responsibility implied. It is not enough to be salt and light! We have to be salt "of the earth," and light "for the world."

Questions for Reflection

- How have corporal works of mercy brought healing to you as a worker of mercy? As a beneficiary of mercy?
- Does your faith rest on human eloquence or the power of God's Spirit? Are you easily swayed by religious rhetoric?
- Who sees your light? For whom are you "salt of the earth"?

Action Response

Someone near you needs your light—maybe in charity or maybe in testimony. Find one concrete way to lift the gloom for a friend or stranger this week.

Choosing Your Path

FIRST READING: SIRACH 15:15–20

There are set before you fire and water.

There are few stronger statements in Scripture on the nature of free will. Human history is not a random flow of genes, nor is it a predetermined game that God is playing with us. Each of us makes choices, toward life or death, and each choice has consequences, some we can foresee, others quite unpredictable.

As we stretch forth a hand, toward fire or water, Sirach admonishes us to consider that we make a world of difference with our choices. Another beer? Another night in front of the TV? Another fight with a spouse? In every moment is also the seed of another opportunity to choose life, to choose God's way.

SECOND READING: 1 CORINTHIANS 2:6–10

Eye has not seen what God has prepared.

Paul of Tarsus has seldom been accused of comedy, but he does have a wry humor even in moments of deadly earnest (an attribute for which he is better known.) After trouncing wisdom teachers for their self-interest, he playfully asserts that the "spiritually mature" do possess a certain wisdom. But it is God's wisdom, not that of philosophy which depends on the virtuosity and eloquence of mortals. God's wisdom is shrouded in mystery, hidden beyond sight and sound. To know it is not the same as coming to any kind of human knowledge.

God's wisdom will not ultimately depend on years of scholarly study or mental gymnastics of the rational mind. God's wisdom comes to us through the Spirit, which is the only way we can apprehend "the deep things of God." Those who would be spiritually mature have to give up being athletes of the intellect—how hard this is in our rational age!—and make ourselves regularly available to the prompting of God's Spirit.

GOSPEL: MATTHEW 5:17–37

Whoever fulfills these commands shall be great in the kingdom.

Messiah watchers were trying to size up the ministry of Jesus. Perhaps they had heard that he broke the Sabbath rest upon occasion and wondered if he might have come to abolish the Law and to make life easier. This law of love certainly sounded like a relaxed approach to religion. The Beatitudes constituted a kinder, gentler spirituality than the Decalogue, to be sure.

Jesus makes short work of that theory in this sterner passage from the Sermon on the Mount. His standards were much higher than the law of Moses required. The law of love wasn't about mere obedience to statutes, but about taking their spirit to heart. If we are forbidden to kill, should we not also refrain from oppressing, hating, shunning, and excluding? If we cannot do harm, should we not also respect and seek to honor?

Those who followed Jesus would discover, to their horror, to what end the law of love might lead. The road to the cross was paved with acts of love.

Questions for Reflection

• Fire and water are before you today. What are they in your life, and which will you choose?

• How do you provide the Spirit an opportunity to teach you "the deep things of God"?

• What is the hardest part of Jesus' Sermon on the Mount for you?

Action Response

There's a sore spot for everyone in the Sermon on the Mount. Choose life this week by finding one way to avoid the near occasion of your most common offense against the law of love.

The Perfect, Holy Fool

FIRST READING: LEVITICUS 19:1–2, 17–18

Be holy, for I am holy.

God asks us to be holy. What can it mean for us to be a holy people? I have met folks in and out of parishes who think being holy means praying a lot, retiring to a monastery somewhere, being otherworldly. But the Lord says to Moses quite plainly that being holy is behaving like the Lord your God.

What's it like to be holy like God? A being called Love has no room for hatred, vengeance, bitterness. If we kept our hearts free from the choking effect of these conditions, we might have an experience of holiness that would bring us closer to the nature of God than we had ever imagined. Holiness is born, not in pious acts, but in unfettered love.

SECOND READING: 1 CORINTHIANS 3:16–23

You are God's temple.

Paul asks us to be foolish. What a request, as we scurry about in great concern over our dignity, prestige, and the opinion of others! No one wants to face the mockery of others: to choose downward mobility in an upwardly mobile culture, to champion love over reason, to take risks for justice rather than prudently permit the oppression of the weak. Paul instructs us to go against the flow. It is an amazing proposition.

But if we love the world's esteem, we are assured that we lose nothing of importance. In ultimate ways, the present and the future are ours, for we are Christ's, and Christ is God's. No temple has ever been built on firmer ground.

GOSPEL: MATTHEW 5:38–48

You will rightly be called children of the Most High.

Jesus asks us to be perfect. (And you thought "holy" and "foolish" were hard to swallow!) He asks that we measure ourselves, not against each other or a bald commandment, but against the ideal of love. Anyone who hears this must yearn for the days when all a person had to do was obey the law! The standard of love is an everlasting stretch, growth without end, a journey with an elastic horizon.

The way of love is also efficacious. Jesus didn't see turning the other cheek and praying for persecutors as a limp response to opposition. The crucifixion was not surrender! The stark courage of not returning evil for evil invites the conversion of the enemy. Eye-for-an-eye justice does not challenge the method of the wrongdoer, nor does it cause a heart to soften. But unmerited compassion and forgiveness can turn a stone heart to flesh. The shadow of the cross has been doing exactly that for twenty centuries.

Questions for Reflection

- How do you love yourself? Do you love your neighbor that way?
- Is your life wise or foolish by worldly standards?
- Have you ever loved an enemy? What did it do to them? To you?

Action Response

Consider the threefold call to be holy, foolish, and perfect. Have you known anyone who lived these teachings closely? What did their lives look like? Choose one occasion this week in which to be a perfectly holy fool.

Keepers of the Mysteries

FIRST READING: ISAIAH 49:14–15

Can a mother be without tenderness for the child of her womb?

Have you ever believed that love has forsaken you? I have been there. The accusations, the self-reproach, the mourning for what was and the ache of what is. The loss of love in our lives seems worse than not having known love at all.

Isaiah speaks to the people who believe they have been deserted by God. Did God forget the Covenant? Has God tired of the people once dearly possessed? The prophet assures them that mothers do not forget their children. But even if a mother should abandon her child, God's love would still stand firm.

We live in a world where parents *do* abandon their children, where fifty percent of marriages end in divorce, where the pledge between an employer and employee can be pink-slipped into history tomorrow. Nothing stays, and few relationships, it seems, can be counted on for the long haul. As the poet William Stafford wrote, "Oh friends, where can one find a partner/for the long dance over the fields?" Only in God can we find such a partner. Let the dance begin.

SECOND READING: 1 CORINTHIANS 4:1–5

Think of us in this way, as servants of Christ and stewards of the mysteries of God.

Paul has a way of blowing you away with a phrase. Imagine yourself a steward of God's mysteries. Your job is to preserve, protect, and allow others access to what belongs to God. How in the world do you do that?

Paul says the first job of the steward is to be trustworthy. You cannot be a cheat, lazy, or unreliable. God's the one who is the judge of how well you do, so don't worry about how others judge your performance. But you do have to concern yourself with God's judgment, because it is not only coming but also final. The steward is given a privileged place because he or she has proven responsible in smaller matters. We have already received the commission to stewardship in our baptism, so now it is time to do the job.

If we are obedient (good listeners), faithful, and creative with our commission, the world will come to know God's mysteries in the way we live.

"Is not life more than food?"

"You cannot give yourself to God and money" should be posted in every seminary, every chancery, and every lay institute. Those of us who do church-work for a living know personally that you will get opportunities to go either way, but you cannot do both. And anyone raising a family, taking care of their elderly, or any other holy way of living knows the same thing. You have to make a choice: whom or what do you serve, at the bottom line?

It's hard to remember that life *is* more than food, more than car payments, the second mortgage, braces, the college fund, the annual vacation, the debts from last Christmas, and keeping Mom comfortable at the nursing home. All of this is real and sometimes overwhelming. Life is full of things to be anxious about, and most of them are connected to money. Jesus does not mean to belittle our concerns. He is not saying these things are not important or worth our attention. But he does say that we have to know, resolutely, where our allegiance lies. Because if it is with stuff, we will be disappointed when the stuff passes away.

Questions for Reflection

- How well do you keep your promises to the people in your life?
- How do you reveal God to others in the way you love? In the way you make decisions? In your life-style?
- How much of your time, energy, and creativity goes into the pursuit of money? How much goes into the pursuit of a life of holiness?

Action Response

Contemplate the saying, "You cannot give yourself to God and money." Post it on the refrigerator, at the office, in the bathroom, or anywhere that it will be frequently before your eyes. Live with it for awhile, and let it take root in your heart.

House Under Construction

FIRST READING: DEUTERONOMY 11:18, 26–28
"Take these words of mine into your heart and soul."

What words have you taken into your heart and soul? Something your mother said to you in a moment of pride, or what your father once said in anger? What lurks in your heart: the demons of self-doubt planted long ago, or the you-can-do-it praise of a teacher or mentor? Our hearts echo with the words of others which gradually take on a life of their own. In time, these angels and devils can transform our inner world and master our relationships.

Moses speaks to the people of blessings and curses. Following God's words will lead to blessings for one and for all. Denying God's will has an equally disastrous effect on the individual and the community. You can think of it in terms of rewards and punishments if you want, but it is equally true that a world created by goodness for goodness is going to balk at the choice for evil. Though the world was originally made for goodness, our free will gives us the right to remake it or unmake it if we choose. Like the world around us, we are a house under construction.

SECOND READING: ROMANS 3:21–25, 28
God made Christ the means of expiation for all who believe.

Paul does great theology, but he would have been a lousy homilist. He hardly ever tells stories; he prefers to write in the abstract. So it is easy, especially when you are listening to his letters read aloud, to lose his train of thought entirely.

Paul would have preached more successfully about justification if he had done it this way: once upon a time there was a fellow who lived in a society governed by law. He broke the law, fearfully, knowing that the sentence was death. But a new governor came into town during his trial and judged that the man should go free. Not, mind you, because the man was an honest citizen, since he had clearly failed to keep the law. His reprieve said nothing about the man, and everything about the new governor. The lawbreaker, in gratitude, put his faith in the new governor, and knew that the law had no more power over him.

But what if the man had not put his faith in the governor? What if he had clung to his old familiar world of law and judgment? He could have refused the pardon, and gone to his death. Or he could have accepted the reprieve and gone on to break another law, and gone to his death anyway. People do that all the time. Choosing the amnesty of Christ is mind-boggling, and some of us cannot make that leap.

GOSPEL: MATTHEW 7:21–27

"The wise one's house did not collapse; it had been solidly set on rock."

A lot goes into building a house: mounds of paperwork, choosing a site, laying the foundation, walls, wires, and pipes, hooking up to existing resources, choosing colors to paint the rooms. People put a lot of money and energy into creating a home. It is where life is going to take place for them.

What a tragedy, then, if the house is lost! Earthquakes, fires, floods, and inability to make payments are some of the many ways that homes are lost. Sometimes the marriage comes down even as the house goes up. Many homes, for many reasons, are impossible to live in. Jesus says: build your homes carefully. Start with the foundation. If the foundation is not in me, then forget the accents in the children's rooms, forget the wires and the pipes. No matter what you do, this house will not stand. But if you build on me, then the mightiest earthquake will not take it down.

Questions for Reflection

• Make a list of statements that are foundational in your life. Where do they come from? How do they shape you?

• How much of your faith lies in doing things right, and how much is in Christ?

• Upon what is your life truly built? If you had to name the four pillars and the cornerstone, what would they be?

Action Response

Find a stone and paint a word on it. It can be any word you choose, so long as it helps you to remember what the cornerstone of your life is supposed to be. Plant it in your garden, set it on the windowsill, use it as a paperweight on your desk. Whenever you see it, pray.

Adding, Not Subtracting

FIRST READING: HOSEA 6:3–6

For it is love that I desire, not sacrifice.

How much easier it is to subtract than to add! It is much easier for us to spend money than to make it. It is much easier to give up cookies during Lent than to do justice. It is simpler to cut someone out of our lives than to say we are sorry, or to offer forgiveness. We would much rather subtract than add.

This is an ancient truth. Early people had religious sacrifices down to a science. Ritual burnings and bloodlettings kept the seasons and the gods in order. The Israelites had a system of atoning for the sin of the world that kept God from getting too mad, they imagined. It was much simpler to sacrifice a sheaf of wheat, or a lamb, than to stop sinning.

God raises the divine fists in frustration through the prophet Hosea: "What can I do with you people?" Love is the answer, not destruction. For the one who loves much will be forgiven much. It is a lesson we learn, from one testament to the next.

SECOND READING: ROMANS 4:18–25

Abraham believed, hoping against hope.

You have to love folks like Abraham and Sarah. They are old people without a plot of ground or a single child to call their own, yet they believe God when they are promised that a country and a nation will come out of them. And it is not like God's promise is served up overnight, or even in nine months. They wait years, long years, to see anything come of the wonderful words. Yet they do not forget or lose heart.

That kind of faith gets rewarded, and Paul reminds us that the same can be said of us. Faith in Christ makes up for all of our inadequacies and errors. Faith makes up for the way we sometimes laugh behind the tent at God's outrageous propositions for our life, like Sarah. Or the way we tell white lies to save ourselves, like Abraham. Faith will take us all the way to the land of promises, if we can hold fast to it above all.

GOSPEL: MATTHEW 9:9–13
"I have come to call not the self-righteous, but sinners."

Who do you suppose fell into the category of "those known to be sinners" in Jesus' day? Collaborators with the Romans, like the tax collectors, certainly. Prostitutes, adulterers, and women who kept company with men outside of marriage, for sure. People who didn't go up to the Temple at the prescribed times and pay their tithes. People who gave up trying to keep the law and just ate, drank, and made merry.

Go into any bar in America, or talk with the unchurched, or have lunch with a friend who's on his or her third marriage, and you get the picture. "Those known to be sinners" are members of your family, friends of yours, and maybe even you. The reality is, we are all sinners, but not all of us are known that way.

Jesus chose notorious people for his intimate circle of friends. He had dinner in their homes and laughed at their jokes. We like to think of Jesus as above that sort of thing but it is true. The religious people of his day had as much trouble with the idea as we do when we look at our plaster statues and try to imagine Jesus spending the afternoon in a bar. Yet Jesus knew that the place to win souls was a barroom, not a church. Those people are just waiting to be added to something or someone.

Questions for Reflection

• How has love atoned for sin in your life?

• When has your faith been strongly tested? What made you endure?

• How much of your time do you spend with people just like you? How much time would you be willing to spend with people who are very different, and may need you?

Action Response

In our busy lives, it is hard to think of adding on anything. So add something simple: pray while you drive, bless children as you pass a schoolyard, make the time you already spend with others more loving and inviting. Love is the answer.

Gathering the Harvest

FIRST READING: EXODUS 19:2–6

I bore you up on eagle wings.

It is common for religious people to talk about salvation. But what does it mean, really, to be saved? The people of Israel knew. When they said, "Our God is a God who saves," they were referring specifically to the Exodus event, the deliverance of a people from slavery to freedom. God destroyed their enemy's army in the Red Sea, brought them to the desert of Sinai, and fed them bread from heaven, sweetening bitter waters to quench their thirst.

They knew themselves to be chosen by God, a special possession, dear, holy and dedicated. Gathered from the lowest place, they were called to be "a kingdom of priests." But that seems to be God's way, to consecrate the humble to holy purposes.

SECOND READING: ROMANS 5:6–11

While we were still sinners, Christ died for us.

Once when I was attending a Baptist church, I heard the most unusual communion call. The minister said, "This table is set for sinners. The righteous can all go home now; and will the sinners come forward to share this food!"

What a surprise to Catholic ears, used to the notion that you should be in a "state of grace" to be worthy of communion. The fact is, the idea that we are ever "worthy" of the Eucharist is probably blasphemy. We can never merit the gift of God's life given to us as food. We are, as human beings, sinners in need of God's mercy at all times. Paul points out that it is precisely as God's enemies that Jesus came to reconcile us. What need was there of the death of the Son, if we were the friends of God all along?

It is humbling to be called to the table of the Lord as sinners. But truly, those who are righteous have no need of this food.

GOSPEL: MATTHEW 9:36—10:8

The gift you have received, give as a gift.

The sick, the unclean, the possessed, the poor: no wonder Jesus looked out at the crowds with great pity. There was no one in those crowds but sinners and the desperate, as far as the eye could see. Who ever said ministry would be a glamorous job?

This came home to me when I supervised a seminarian during his field education placement at our church. After several months of working together, the seminarian threw up his hands in disgust. "Everybody in this parish is so...dysfunctional!" he complained.

"Of course," I smiled, "who did you think you would be serving?" The reign of God is to be announced to the sheep without a shepherd, to the least and lowliest, to the people of the highways and the byways who are invited to the feast because the great of the land are too busy being great to attend. Think charitably of the poor seminarian. Little does he suspect that God looks at all of us with the same genuine pity. He will learn.

Questions for Reflection

• In what circumstances of your life have you known yourself to be saved?

• Make a list of "the godless," as Paul calls them. How do you feel about the idea that Christ died for them? Is your name on that list?

• Jesus asks us to freely give of what we are freely given. What have you been given, and how do you give it away?

Action Response

Each of us is called to join the twelve disciples as laborers for the harvest. Consider how your choices will reap the kingdom this week.

Holy Courage, Proper Fear

FIRST READING: JEREMIAH 20:10–13

The Lord is with me, like a mighty champion.

As a prophet, Jeremiah is a heartbreaker. Called while still young, he confronts kings with God's anger against them, and suffers the taunts, threats, and imprisonments that one might expect would be the lot of someone who challenges the seats of power so openly. Despite his bold prophecies, he is tormented by doubt, and at times his book reads as plaintively as a diary, chronicling his bouts with despair.

It is the remarkable humanity of Jeremiah in the midst of his inspired courage that has prompted scholars to view him as a prototype of Jesus. Suffering God's will and the disapproval it reaps, he does not cease to proclaim his message, trusting in God whether he stands in the palace of the king or at the bottom of a muddy cistern. Meeting a martyr's end, his moving testimony continues to prophesy to a world sorely in need of such a faithful, persevering witness.

SECOND READING: ROMANS 5:12–15

The gift is not like the offense.

Imagine being sorely, grievously offended by someone, wounded to the heart, a cruelty without merit. And further imagine forgiving the offender, and not only forgiving, but showering her or him with kindness, compassion and a lasting, all-embracing love. Sound like a fantasy, or a fool thing to do? It's also the story of salvation, and the holy fool is God.

Paul was quick to understand the irony. The original sin brought death into the world, and as all flesh is given to sin, each un-original sin repeats the death sentence. Yet, though every one of us chooses death, it is the death of the sinless One that restores all of us to life. It is not sensible, nor is it just, by any human standard. For which we should be grateful that God's ways are not like ours.

GOSPEL: MATTHEW 10:26–33

Every hair of your head has been counted.

I like to tease my aging male friends: "Don't worry, every hair that has fallen from your head has been counted." (As are the rapidly graying hairs on my own head.) It is nice to know that God is in charge of this process, every detail lovingly orchestrated and observed.

Jesus makes it clear that the God who is well aware of my waning youth and every tiny sparrow is certainly not hidden from the more critical and vital concerns of my life, the real dangers I might face. What can harm my bodily life—the loss of possessions, health, friendship, security—though painful, is not to be feared. Only that which could challenge my life in Christ is an enemy to me.

Questions for Reflection

• Jeremiah knows the terror of oppression, yet can still sing to the Lord. How does his lament speak to your experience?

• Have you ever been forgiven for an offense with an outpouring of unmerited love? What does this teach you about the forgiveness of God?

• What sparrows have fallen in your life this week? Are you conscious of God's presence and concern in even these small matters?

Action Response

What are your greatest fears at this time in your life? What should you be afraid of? Commit yourself to the "perfect love which casts out fear" and live beyond your courage this week, trusting that God will supply what you lack.

A Welcome for the Prophet

FIRST READING: 2 KINGS 4:8–11, 14–16

"I know that he is a holy man of God."

It is not always apparent who the holy ones are. Sometimes the world is deceived by a show of piety or religious talk. But even the devil, we know, can quote the Scriptures with great familiarity, as in the story of Christ's temptation. It takes some discernment to know who the holy ones are, and the Shunemite woman had enough to recognize Elisha as the real McCoy. She also had enough initiative to persuade her husband to establish a permanent guest room for a sojourning prophet. With no expectation of a reward, she receives miraculous recompense.

To establish a permanent dwelling place for holiness in our lives can never be without fruitfulness.

SECOND READING: ROMANS 6:3–4, 8–11

You must consider yourselves dead to sin but alive for God.

Everybody knows that baptism means new life; "born again" is how some Christians put it. But it is also true that baptism means death, the plunging into the water as much a drowning as it is a cleansing. Water, like most powerful things, carries the dual possibilities of death and life in its wake.

We die to ourselves in the sacrament, die to our old ways of being, are lost forever to the power of sin to harm us irretrievably. As Paul explains these things, he points out that the life into which we are raised up is now life for God. This is one for the refrigerator magnets. We Christians should prominently display the words where we can meditate on them often—*my life is life for God, in Christ Jesus.*

GOSPEL: MATTHEW 10:37–42

The one who seeks only the self brings that self to ruin.

In a wonderful old movie, a young child catches his first glimpse of his own face in a pond. Saddened to understand that he is not of the same race as his guardian, he runs to him with the poignant words, "But I don't want to look like me! I want to look like you!"

A child might be selfless enough to identify with another face so completely. But as adults, we have learned to seek our own reflection in all things, enthroning the ego as lord of our lives. Enslavement to the self makes the real welcome of another nearly impossible. Even when we extend our concern to include our families, we are still protecting our own property and denying access to the stranger, who is Christ.

Jesus promises that if we empty ourselves of narcissism, we will discover who we are. What joy to be able to say to the Lord, "But I don't want to look like me! I want to look like you!"

Questions for Reflection

• How have you established a place in your life for holiness to bear fruit?

• Where in your life is sin struggling to claim a victory over you? How can you die to this sin and be free to live for God?

• Consider the sins of the ego: pride, self-righteousness, judgmentalism, selfishness, self-pity. Are you denying welcome to prophecy, holiness, or charity by loving your own reflection too dearly?

Action Response

A prophetic word is always knocking on the door of our hearts. Spend some time in contemplation, emptying your own agenda and preparing a space for this word to speak to you.

Majesty and Meekness

FIRST READING: ZECHARIAH 9:9–10

Shout for joy, O daughter Zion!

What would a Prince of Peace be like? Our generation has seen few leaders who answer to that description. Wars and rumors of wars are the mainstay of the news. As much as we dread it, we wearily expect that the violence will continue.

In this prophetic oracle, Zechariah dreams of the day when the warrior's bow is banished, the last gunshot fired, its echo dying away with sober finality. The king who comes is not riding on a chariot, or even seated on a horse, the preferred vehicles of the warrior. He comes in peace, on an animal of peacetime. He comes in humility, yet his rule extends to all the earth. His arrival is greeted with shouts of joy and great relief.

If we dare to dream of such a day, we invite this kingdom to come.

SECOND READING: ROMANS 8:9, 11–13

We are debtors, then, my friends, but not to the flesh.

It's a question of citizenship. We have a certain loyalty to the country that is ours. We obey its laws, and share in its privileges. We make a home and reside squarely in the land whose name we bear, in whose identity we find our own.

Paul's letter to the Roman Christians is unsettling to the notion of citizenship. Are they choosing ultimate allegiance to life in the world ("the flesh"), with all of its advantages and opportunities and obligations? Do they intend to make a home in the flesh, and find their identity in a mortality that, for all its glory and glamour, will end?

Or will they, in choosing the name of Christ, claim their citizenship in the world of the Spirit, and live by its values? The citizens of every empire must choose their loyalties wisely.

GOSPEL: MATTHEW 11:25–30
What is hidden from the learned has been revealed to the children.

In chapter 11, Jesus proclaims the Gospel through many cities, only to find the people curiously unrepentant. Even deeds of power leave them only momentarily entertained. After delivering a series of chastisements, he offers this prayer in praise of children, and all who are young enough in the life of the Spirit to understand.

The good news of Jesus is for those who have known only the bad news of the earth, the weary and the burdened. Our gentle, humble Lord, in meekness and majesty, comes to offer rest from the world's cares. In return, we are asked to shoulder a new burden, that of truth and love.

After being crushed under the weight of the other, we will find this burden surprisingly easy on our hearts. Doesn't the yoke of love, weighty as it is, always make you feel light enough to dance?

Questions for Reflection

• How do you participate in bringing about a reign of peace?

• In what ways are you a citizen of the world? Of the Spirit? Where do these loyalties collide for you?

• The truths of God are revealed to children. What do we gain by being like children? What do we lose?

Action Response

Practice ushering in the reign of peace. Hold your tongue when prompted to words of violence, gossip, uncharity. Be a reconciler. Think gentleness and humility.

Sowing the Good Word

FIRST READING: ISAIAH 55:10–11
My word shall not return to me void.

God has a plan. Our faith confesses that this is true, and furthermore declares that it is a plan for salvation and not condemnation. The God who created a world and called it good will not leave it to corruption and destruction. As the rain falls, as the seed is sown, so does the creative and life-giving word of God come to us, achieving its end in due season.

In the creation story of Genesis, we are told that God "spoke" the world into being for six days and then retired. But Isaiah presents a God who still speaks, who continues to will life and purpose into the events of history, the matter of creation. If we press our ear to the heart of the world, perhaps we can catch the rhythm of those words: let there be...let there be...let there be.

SECOND READING: ROMANS 8:18–23
All creation groans and is in agony.

Theologians love to talk about "realized eschatology," the already/not yet nature of God's reign. Eschatology means whatever-it-is that happens when we run out of "world" and "time"; realized, in this sense, means we are as good as there now.

This makes no sense to us, of course, creatures consigned to time, where either a thing has happened already, or has not happened yet, but cannot be both at once. Naturally, God—who stands outside of time—experiences the past, present, and future as a holy and eternal "now." But that is not a perspective we can share, being subject to the limitations of personal history.

Paul catches a glimpse of the Holy Now when he is able to see his present sufferings in relationship to the future realm of glory. All of creation, subject to time and decay, suffers the anguish of the passage of years and the loss of vigor. But we who know ourselves to be children of God appreciate that behind the waning of this life stands the life to come, a realized life that makes this one a mere shadow by comparison.

GOSPEL: MATTHEW 13:1–23
Blest are your ears because they hear.

Years ago, I admit, I tore the cover off a missalette I found in church. I still have it in my apartment. It shows four vertical strips of illustrations: birds pecking hungrily at seeds on the ground, small plants struggling feebly through rocks, green shoots hopelessly surrounded by evil curling thorns, and slender golden grain blowing lightly in the wind. It depicts the parable of the sower.

At the time I vandalized the missalette, I wanted to be like that picture of the grain more than anything I could think of. I still daydream in front of it, admiring the richness and the freedom of those long stalks. But in those days, I felt more like victim seed, swallowed by birds, crushed by rocks, pierced by thorns. When God's word came to me, I watched it fall to the ground, sterile and lifeless, at a distance from my heart.

Yet God continued to send sowers out to sow in the field, scattering words of life all along my path. And the day finally came, after the hard work of clearing out my field, that a seed came to sprout up from the heart of me. Once received, it can never be denied. Praise God.

Questions for Reflection

• Isaiah compares the word of God to the processes of the natural world around him. In contemplating the world around you, what can you learn about how God works?

• Consider your life from the perspective of the Holy Now: your past, the present, what may lie ahead in your future. What does God have to say about what you see?

• What parts of your life can be compared to the four soils of the parable of the sower?

Action Response

Sow the Good Word this week in unlikely places. Use kindness where none is given. Speak hope into someone's darkness. Witness your faith to a non-believer. You never know when a seed will take root.

A Window on Heaven

FIRST READING: WISDOM 12:13, 16–19
Those who are just must be kind.

I heard a canon lawyer give a talk on morality. "In a world where we *can* do almost anything, how do we decide what we *should* do? And in a world where we *can* do almost anything, how do we decide what we should *never* do?" These are wonderful questions for people who live in a free society like ours. The more power we have to choose, the more just we need to be. And the more just we seek to be, the more we need to exercise mercy.

The Book of Wisdom teaches us this. God is the ultimate power, unchallenged by any other force in the universe. And the One who knows perfect power is also the very source of justice, and that justice is clement. We who know the unrestrained power of the worldly know that power does not have to be just, or kind; and often is not. This makes the mercy of God a marvel, and good ground for our hope.

SECOND READING: ROMANS 8:26–27
The Spirit intercedes for the saints.

Some things cannot be put into words. The desire between two people is often exchanged as a long, lingering gaze. Need can be eloquently spoken with an outstretched hand, or love known more clearly for what it does than what is said.

When we pray, we bring all these experiences and more to the moment. We desire to surrender ourselves to the God we cannot see, and our speech is lame in relation to what we hold in our hearts. The Spirit is available as a messenger of our great longing, a new language which is given to us, eyes and hands and hearts to carry the fire within us.

GOSPEL: MATTHEW 13:24–43
I will announce what has lain hidden.

The kingdom. The reign of God. Heaven. If you ask a roomful of average Christians to describe it, you may get as many answers as there are people. Even Jesus has more than one image to offer, and he's the only one among us who's not guessing.

Jesus calls the reign of God a season of harvest and ruin, a time of final judgment. He also sees it in terms of an unpromising seed that blooms into grandness beyond all expectation. Then he adds the familiar image of a woman making bread. Now, doesn't that make it all clearer for you? Not for me either. Nor for the disciples, evidently, who asked him, "Explain to us the part about the weeds in the field." They never even asked about the other two images, maybe too fearful after the first explanation to hear any more.

Jesus ended this passage with a caveat: let each person heed what they hear. Perhaps it is human nature that we will hear different things, and so Jesus uses a multiplication of images so that one of them will take root in us, the one we best can understand. When talking about a room as wide as heaven, it is best to open many windows.

Questions for Reflection

• What power do you wield in your life? Is it just? Is it kind? What measure can you use to make it so?

• Are you aware of the presence of the Spirit when you pray? How do you invite the Spirit into your prayer?

• Describe your image of the reign of God. Does it resemble any of the parables that Jesus tells?

Action Response

The wheat is left to grow among the weeds, so Jesus tells us. Consider the nature of the weeds in your life that are destined for destruction. How much more time do you want to give over to the dead-end proposition they represent?

Getting It Right

FIRST READING: 1 KINGS 3:5, 7–12

Give your servant an understanding heart.

There is an indication that Solomon was already on the road to wisdom when he asked for it. As God points out, he could have requested a long life, a fortune, the sweetest of revenges. Instead he asks for what he really needs, the ability to lead an uncountable people, he a young man of little experience. This is not only wisdom, but a sense of vocation.

If we clearly perceive what we are called to do, it helps to shape our prayer for the spiritual gifts that are available to us. Often prayer becomes a conversation with no real subject, a meandering stream of words that is frustrated at the source, or a hysterical rant at God because things are not going well. When we have these conversations with one another, they seldom are resolved with any satisfaction. It is no wonder that the person who approaches God with discernment, like the conversation that knows its object, will be much more likely to receive an answer.

SECOND READING: ROMANS 8:28–30

God makes all things work toward the good.

This passage has been used by fundamentalists to prove a doctrine of predestination, the Calvinistic idea that some are pre-selected for salvation and others for perdition—which is just a Christian way of saying it is all in the cards. Rather than implying that we've each been dealt an immutable hand (where's the possibility of conversion in that?), Paul suggests that we are involved in a gradual process of being claimed by God. Each of us, anticipated before the world began, has been dedicated to the likeness of Christ—which is how we can see Christ in even the most despicable of characters. The call is issued to come forward to claim our heritage.

In parochial school, I used to worry myself sick about the people going to hell. I asked the Sister, "Is there no way to get them out? Isn't there something God can do?" Sister told me that God was bigger than everything I could understand about justice, big enough to redeem a world and everybody in it. "Maybe, in the end, no one goes to hell," she said. Maybe she's right.

GOSPEL: MATTHEW 13:44–52

The reign of God is like a buried treasure.

Jesus speaks of the kingdom more than fifty times in Matthew's Gospel, warning people to repent in the face of it, promising its joy to the poor, assigning seats in it, barring some from entering it, praying for it to come, announcing it as good news, offering up images and stories about it, confiding the secrets of it, handing over the keys to it.... It is one of the central themes in Matthew, and it is instructive to read all twenty-eight chapters alert for the references.

After you've read everything that Matthew has to say about the reign of God, try painting a picture of it, if only in your mind. Buried treasure. A fabulous pearl. A dragnet tangled with garbage and gifts from the sea. A place where the poor are blessed and happy. A place with no lawyers and Pharisees (apologies, my lawyer friends!) and lots of prostitutes and the IRS (you can't have everything.) Wheat fields and weeds, yeast and seeds, angels and devils, fire and fruit, weddings and feasts, sheep and goats!

It's a wild-sounding place, and one thing is for sure: some of us are going to love it there, and a lot of us are going to hate it. And it is coming. And we'd better repent.

Questions for Reflection

• Consider the circumstances to which you are called in life: relationships, career, responsibilities. In light of these, what might you ask God for?

• We are all called to the likeness of Christ. Which parts of your life "look" like Christ? Which do not?

• What is your favorite image of the reign of God from the parables of Jesus? What does this image teach you about the Coming we await?

Action Response

Jesus says the kingdom is not simply a place where we're headed, but that it is already at hand. There are many ways to realize the kingdom for others: speaking truth, doing justice, bringing good news to the poor, living peace. Spend this week conscious of your citizenship in the kingdom.

Enough to Go Around

FIRST READING: ISAIAH 55:1–3

Listen, that you may have life.

These are passionate words in a desert culture: all you who are thirsty, come to the water! Obtaining water was a daily concern, an hourly need, in a land as dry and primitive as the one Isaiah knew. To prophesy that there would be water enough, and food enough, for all of Israel was a daring message. And it would all be free.

Isaiah used these powerful images to convey to his people what the renewal of the Covenant would bring to Israel. After idolatry, decadence, and the scourge of exile, God was willing to try again, if they were. We can imagine the corporate relief of the nation at the prophet's words: You mean we get another chance?

Water, grain, wine, milk, and another chance. Out of God's abundance comes our literal salvation.

SECOND READING: ROMANS 8:35, 37–39

Neither death nor life, neither angels nor principalities....

The apostle Paul and I are old sparring partners. I force-fed myself the Epistles for years, a spoonful of verses at a time, feeling the reluctance of digesting so many abstractions, such technically complex theology. Yet even in our most uncomfortable moments, these lines from Romans shone like jewels to me, and let me know that Paul was a friend.

With utter heroism and sheer devotion, Paul wonders what it would take to separate us from God, the Beloved from the Lover. He calls upon all the dreadful possibilities of torment and need—are any of these dire enough to conquer us? Then he concludes with words as powerful as cannonballs: "For I am certain neither death nor life, neither angels nor principalities...." Nothing, *nothing* we can touch or imagine has the power to tear us away from the love of God.

For years, I have hung these words in my living room as a continual meditation. I do not ever want to forget that God's love holds me fast.

GOSPEL: MATTHEW 14:13–21
His heart was moved with pity.

He could have been irritated or even angry. After all, Jesus had just learned of the death of John the Baptist, and he had gone aside to a lonely place to mourn his kinsman and to pray. But the crowds pursued him, offering their sick. Despite his own suffering, Jesus responds to them with compassion.

Night approaches, and this same crowd is hungry. Who asked them to follow him out to this lonely place to begin with? The disciples are all for dismissing the lot of them to forage for themselves. But Jesus says no, *you* feed them.

Feed them with what, exactly? The disciples point to their relative poverty of supplies: a bit of bread, some fish. Jesus could have said something like: "And what resources do you suppose I had to draw on, when the crowds set upon me this afternoon?" Jesus does not exploit the comparison, however. He just looks to heaven as usual, and soon thousands are fed. The leftovers exceed the original supply.

It's easy to produce excuses: I am tired of giving. I have done my share. This need is beyond my resources. Yet no need is beyond the resources of heaven. All we have to do is begin somewhere, with compassion.

Questions for Reflection

• Have you ever been given another chance in a relationship? What did you do with it?

• What conditions make you feel separated from God? How do Paul's words offer you hope?

• Jesus shows us we must begin to feed the hungry, and God will do the rest. When have you experienced this partnership between your action and God's?

Action Response

If we don't contribute something to the hungry this week, there is no defense for us. Consider what you have—time, money, or food—and start with compassion to do what you can, inviting God to do more.

God's Whereabouts

FIRST READING: 1 KINGS 19:9, 11–13
The Lord will be passing by.

Here is a very peculiar story about a theophany. (A theophany is the way God behaves when the Divine would like to be noticed.) The usual acts of God—storms, earthquakes, fire—are disavowed here as genuine theophanies and are seen only as precursors to the event itself.

And what is the event itself? A tiny whispering sound. One translation calls it "a sound of fine silence." Elijah recognizes the silence as a word from God, and responds with proper humility.

We are always looking for the tracing of God's hand in the tumultuous events of our lives. God's fingerprint is just as discernible on the quietest hour, the simplest circumstance, for those with a prophet's appreciation of the sound of silence.

SECOND READING: ROMANS 9:1–5
There is great grief and constant pain in my heart.

Paul laments the stubbornness of his own people in refusing the good news. His litany of their advantage is tinged with disbelief: Israel got "the glory, the covenants, the law, the worship," not to mention the Messiah. They got it *all*, Paul says, but they don't *get* it. He would gladly accept damnation if by doing so his people would receive salvation.

Paul is not writing to the Jews, of course, but to the Romans. So we can imagine that his purpose in offering this lament is for the benefit of the Gentiles and not the Jews. The implication here is this: listen, Romans, maybe you didn't have the patriarchs and a grand history of prophecy to guide you to Jesus. But you do have me and Peter and Apollos instead. So do not blow your advantage—do not be too sure of yourselves, like the Israelites.

We who sit in the pews, equipped with our salvation accessories, are hereby warned. We may have it all, and still not get it.

GOSPEL: MATTHEW 14:22–33
"It is a ghost!" they said.

I have a soft spot in my heart for Peter. He always seems to be in the way of Jesus' backhand. Here he is, in the midst of this black night, this terrible storm, confronted with what seems to be the ghost of Jesus. Like the rest of the disciples, he's scared witless. But unlike them, he has the courage to address the Lord, and the absolute guts to scramble out of the boat and walk on water.

Okay, so he falters. But he still has the horse sense to scream, "Lord, save me!" knowing full well from whence comes his help. To him, and only to him, does Jesus say, "How little faith you have!"

I want to start a campaign to protest Peter abuse. He's the only one in the bunch who ever acts, and he always gets zinged for it. The main reason I am defensive of Peter is because so often I find myself in the same boat (so to speak). I take comfort in the fact that it is to this faithful one, so often rebuked, that Jesus delivers the keys to the kingdom. I guess Jesus could see past Peter's impetuous miscalculations to his eager, ready heart.

Questions for Reflection

• Name three recent theophanies in your life. What did God have to say to you?

• Is it possible to receive the sacraments and keep the laws of the church and not be saved? Why or why not?

• Jesus on the lake is shown in a full-scale, old-fashioned theophany. Would Jesus be less impressive to you if he had simply taught?

Action Response

Locating God's whereabouts in our days is one of the ways we can discern God's call. Consider spiritual direction, keeping a faith journal, or developing a prayer partnership with someone who can help you sight the theophanies that come your way.

About Those Gentiles

FIRST READING: ISAIAH 56:1, 6–7
My justice is about to be revealed.

I was raised in a small town where there were two kinds of people: Catholics and non-Catholics. Having been an insider in a group that defined outsiders in such a black-and-white way, it is hard for me to identify now with the term Gentile. Yet to the orthodox Jewish mind, there are also two kinds of people. According to that system, most people reading this are probably Gentiles.

We therefore have a stake in what prophecy has to say about the fate of Gentiles. The later chapters of Isaiah are quite bold about it: God can choose the non-chosen people, the foreigner, the Gentile. When God's salvation comes, and divine justice is revealed, the Gentiles will stand in the holy place along with the Jews.

This was not good news to Isaiah's audience! Nor is it good news to many Christians to imagine that non-Christians may one day stand in the holy place with them, equally justified by God's desire to have "a house of prayer for all peoples." Every religious group in history has tried to define a careful wall between the saved and the damned. But God can—and will—topple that distinction with a breath.

SECOND READING: ROMANS 11:13–15, 29–32
God's gifts and call are irrevocable.

Paul has grieved over Israel's rejection of the Gospel. Now he turns to the Gentile Romans to make it clear that God is not done with Israel yet. In the omitted verses, Paul uses the image of cutting and grafting branches onto an olive tree. In God's desire to bring all people to the Gospel, Israel had to be cut to make room for the Gentiles. Once the Gentiles were grafted on, the Jews who rejected Jesus would eventually rejoin the tree.

I get theologically nervous around a too literal approach to Paul's olive tree. Maybe the lectionary planners felt the same uneasiness, and so they pruned those verses right out. Paul's bottom line to the Romans is this: God is heading in the direction of universal salvation. No group is categorically in or out. So prejudice has no place in the kingdom.

GOSPEL: MATTHEW 15:21–28
"Woman, you have great faith!"

In this unusual story, the miracle takes a back seat to the conversation—and it takes some conversation to upstage a healing. In this corner is the woman with a demon-filled daughter. Parents of troubled children can probably relate. She is desperate for a cure, willing to appeal outside of the confines of her own people for help. She shows no interest in becoming part of the Jewish story. Her meeting with Jesus is a kind of accident—he is crossing her territory on the way to somewhere else.

In the other corner are the disciples, hoping Jesus will "get rid of her." By all appearances, Jesus tries to. First, he ignores her. Then, he draws a fence around his ministry. Finally, he tells her frankly that it would be unjust to help her when his own people need him. And she does not go away. Her comeback plea is so humble and yet so firm that even the Son of God cannot resist.

Her daughter gets better, yes. We are told that almost as an aside. But the real miracle in the story is that a woman changes Jesus' perspective on his mission.

Questions for Reflection

- Which groups of people do you have the hardest time imagining will be saved?
- What will have to happen before Jews and Gentiles can live in peace, grafted onto the same tree?
- What troubles you about the story of the Canaanite woman? What excites you?

Action Response

Consider the group of people you feel are least likely to fit in God's plan of universal salvation. What can you do to reach out to them? Make a concrete step in the direction of reconciliation.

Who Gets the Keys?

FIRST READING: ISAIAH 22:15, 19–23

I will fix him like a peg in a sure spot.

It's a story of two men, one brought low from a high place, one raised up to a level of new authority. We hear the echo of this motif everywhere in the Scriptures. The first shall be last; the last, first. We know the moral of this story by heart. Power, prestige, position will not protect us. The one whom God chooses gets the keys, the power of opening and shutting, binding and loosing.

I think about the power of binding and loosing. On the surface, it does not sound like much. But when I was a kid, I was locked inside a church for several hours. It grew dark; my voice was weak from shouting. I threw dozens of hymnals out into the street, hoping to attract attention. When I was finally rescued, I took in the fresh air of freedom in large, grateful gulps, between tears. The power to withhold freedom or to set people free is an awesome thing.

SECOND READING: ROMANS 11:33–36

Who has known the mind of the Lord?

It's a mystery, Catholics like to say. That's another way of saying, "God knows: I don't." Lots of things are beyond our understanding: why the innocent suffer, what happens after death, whether angels dance on pins or dance at all. We all have our private lists of what we want to know some-day: why did my brother die so young? Why was my aunt's life nothing but sorrow? We have our questions. God has the answers. For now, mystery is our best description of the impasse.

I used to wonder if reliance on mystery was a Catholic copout. The more I have come to understand the other formulas for meaning—science, philosophy, politics, psychology—the fonder I am of the sacred character of mystery. It exacts from me a hybrid of heroism and humility that seems very whole and true. The surrender to mystery is a surrender to faith in the wisdom and ultimate goodness of God. Until the veil is lifted, I think I can rest on that.

GOSPEL: MATTHEW 16:13–20
"Who do you say that I am?"

A rare moment in the Gospels—Peter has the right answer! He must have been as surprised as anybody to hear Jesus praise him and call him blest. The scene is not unlike the instant in a casino when you hit the jackpot. Not only is Peter commended for his reply, but he gets a new name, position, and authority.

The words must have rushed passed his dazed mind like a waterfall: rock, church, death, keys, heaven, bound, loosed. Maybe there was a moment of anxiety: what was he getting himself into? Maybe Peter the Rock was going to be a harder position to maintain than Peter the Blockhead.

Happily, Peter was a man of slight imagination. If he could have envisioned Vatican City and the Chair of Peter to come, he might have passed out cold. For now, he would be the possessor of the keys, and contemplate the sturdy nature of a rock. God tends to give us only the authority we are ready for.

Questions for Reflection

• What would you like your life to be bound to? What would you like to be loosed from?

• Our relationship to mystery is often a reflection of our need for control. How do you stand in relationship to these two ends of the spectrum?

• "Who do you say that I am?" None of us can escape this question Jesus poses. How would you reply?

Action Response

Make a list of the kinds of authority you wield, as parent, boss, group leader, breadwinner, caretaker, confidante. How do you use the power of the keys? Pray that justice and mercy will companion your responsibilities.

Fire in the Heart

FIRST READING: JEREMIAH 20:7–9

It becomes like fire burning in my heart.

I copied these verses on the back of my notebook when I was a teenager. Jeremiah was not much more than a teenager when he wrote them, and they have the raw emotional force of youth behind them. Humiliation, rage, shame—it is all there, the dark side of adolescence.

I do not mean to suggest that we've outgrown Jeremiah's lament. I still feel framed by God's will at times; I feel the flush of mockery, the unpopularity of a prophet's role. But there is also the alternative: the ache of words not spoken, a witness not dared, a truth not championed. As Jeremiah testifies, it is harder to live with the cowardice of repressing God's word.

SECOND READING: ROMANS 12:1–2

Do not conform yourselves to this age.

Prophets have railed against "this age" in every age, as if theirs were the shallowest, meanest, most decadent era ever. Every era is wanting in significant ways, so conforming yourself to any generation and its values is a big mistake. At the root of every generation is the desire to get ahead—a mysterious phrase—as if there were a quantifiable destination to which all of this is heading. Which is funny, in a morbid way, since both science and religion agree that "all of this" is heading straight to total annihilation.

What else can we do? Upward mobility is a waste of time itself, but downward mobility sounds grim. Paul begs us to consider conforming ourselves to the God of Ages, who outlasts everything we see or know or can obtain. It's a gamble, of course, from our perspective. But we *know* the other way is a losing proposition. To learn what is truly "good, pleasing, and perfect," as Paul writes, sounds like what our hearts are yearning for.

GOSPEL: MATTHEW 16:21–27
"You are not judging by God's standards."

Peter is back in the doghouse. He just spoke what was in his heart: he does not want Jesus to be hurt. A moment ago, Jesus had told him he was inspired by God to speak as he did. Now Jesus tells him he must have a devil in him, to say such things. Poor Peter. He should have stayed in bed.

Peter is not alone in his inability to grasp the necessity of the crucifixion. For the first four centuries, many church heresies dispelled the death of Jesus as a divine mirage. It is incongruous to think of Jesus in his heroic self-giving being repaid with the infamy and agony of the cross. It must have been an illusion, the heretics insisted. No God would stand for such treatment, having the power to prevent it.

Yet within our experience, we know something that makes sense of this horror. We know that love is willing to suffer for the sake of the beloved. Love does not choose to suffer or prefer to suffer But love is willing to suffer. If our love can rise to such an act of courage, surely the God of Love was equal to the crucifixion.

Questions for Reflection

• When have you felt duped by God? How did your reaction compare to Jeremiah's?

• In what ways does your life conform to this age? Conform to God's will? Is there territory claimed by both sides?

• When was the last time you tried to talk God out of the divine plan, like Peter did with Jesus? What were the results?

Action Response

Is there a fire burning in your heart: words of forgiveness not spoken, a lie not confessed, an encouragement not offered? Find a way to express it this week.

How to Speak the Truth

FIRST READING: EZEKIEL 33:7–9
"I will hold you responsible."

I heard these words a lot, growing up in a household of many children: you are the one who is responsible. Being older, I was responsible for a lot of things: I was the one who knew better. It did not matter that the younger ones did it—I was there!

Ezekiel hears the same message from God. As a prophet, he knows better than most people what is on God's mind. He has a charge to be God's messenger. If people suffer the consequences of their poor choices despite his words, that is all right. But if they suffer because he failed to speak—woe to the prophet.

This kind of zeal drives groups like the Jehovah's Witnesses to stand on the corner, rain or shine. If they fail to witness, they are lost. It is regretful that most churchgoing folks do not feel compelled in any way to speak from the richness of their spiritual treasure. Nonetheless, we are responsible for what we know.

SECOND READING: ROMANS 13:8–10
Love never does any wrong to the neighbor.

There will always be legalists, I suppose, literal-minded people who do exactly what they are told and no more. These people find law comforting, because it gives them both instruction and boundaries. Law requires no imagination and little understanding, only obedience.

It is easy to adhere to all of the laws Paul mentions and miss the point entirely. You can be exemplary in the "thou shalt nots" and never get to the "why thou shoulds." So Paul says, as Jesus said before him: aim for love. If you love, all these rules will be honored besides. But the reverse is not true. You can honor all the rules, and have no love.

Paul wrote the best poem in the world above love (see 1 Corinthians 13) so he should know.

GOSPEL: MATTHEW 18:15–20

If your brother should commit some wrong against you....

Have you ever been to a conflict-resolution seminar? Arbitration is hairy stuff. They advise you to say your piece without blame and without giving offense. My preferred method of dealing with conflict is primal screaming. But that seldom leads to resolution, I am afraid.

Jesus explains precisely how Christians should go about resolving their differences. First, say that there is a problem, and say it to the right person. Most conflict terminates right here, in the morass of things unsaid, or in grumbling and gossip to everyone but the offender. Second step (when necessary): get support for the next confrontation. Third step: get the church involved. Jesus does not mean run to the priest but get the whole assembly united behind you.

The antithesis of this strategy is: my lawyer will talk to your lawyer. It's the American way, of course. But few, if any, ever have a conversion experience in a courtroom.

Questions for Reflection

• What truths do you hold in your spiritual storehouse? How do you witness to them?

• Measure yourself against the Ten Commandments. How well do you perform? Measure yourself against the law of love. Is there a greater shortfall?

• How do you deal with confrontation? As the confronter? As the confronted? What can you learn from Jesus' advice?

Action Response

Practice speaking the truth (not just telling the truth.) Spend a week consciously saying what you know to be true, even if you risk the esteem of others. Do not hold grudges, but rather confront your sister or brother in a loving and timely manner.

TWENTY-FOURTH SUNDAY IN ORDINARY TIME

Mercy for Mercy

FIRST READING: SIRACH 27:30—28:7
Remember your last days, set enmity aside.

The Book of Sirach (also known as Ecclesiasticus) is one of the disputed books of the canon of Scripture. Inspired or not, it contains a highly pragmatic piety, written by Ben Sira as advice for his son.

Ben Sira does not appeal to the highest motivations in his admonitions to do right. He seldom says, "Do right because you love God, because love calls you to charity and justice." He is more prone to say, as he says here, "You had better forgive others if you want God to forgive you." Somehow this is not quite in the same spirit as "Forgive us our trespasses...."

Do not sin—Ben Sira writes—remember death and decay! He sees good works as an investment opportunity for the afterlife. He must have been a businessman, whose approach to morality is very much like banking.

There's a little Ben Sira in all of us, we must admit. We're all still hoping to earn our piece of the sky.

SECOND READING: ROMANS 14:7-9
When we die, we die as the Lord's servants.

We are not our own masters. This particular Scripture passage goes against the grain of every message our culture sends us. We are supposed to be rugged individualists, self-made, self-possessed, bending the knee to no monarch, no ruling class. To tell us that we are mastered is an American blasphemy.

Paul of Tarsus, a citizen of two worlds, Jewish and Roman, was not American. In his Jewish world, he was a member of an oppressed race, a dominated country. As a Roman citizen, he knew the freedom of the elite and well-born. Paul certainly knew the difference between mastery and subjection. He chose his words carefully, we can be sure.

When Paul described our role as servants (sometimes, as slaves) of the Lord, he was aware he was using strong language. He wanted the relationship to be clear. He knew firsthand the damage we do when we go off on our own way, blinded by self-righteousness.

GOSPEL: MATTHEW 18:21–35
"How often must I forgive?"

Peter has just attended Jesus' conflict-resolution seminar. He offers a heart-felt question: how much forgiveness is required of me? He may well ask. As a career bungler, he himself could use a seven-forgiveness cushion on which to rely. Peter is adding. Jesus, as usual, multiplies. To get his disciples into the right spirit, Jesus tells the story of a man who forgives, and one who does not. It ends on a grisly note, and seems to confirm Ben Sira's point (see the first reading): forgive your offenders, or else.

Or does it? There is an element to this story that is missing in Sirach. The king originally forgave the official his debt because of the king's own com-passion, not because of the official's worthiness. Forgiveness is not a matter for barter. Our lack of mercy may find us wanting mercy in the end, but God's mercy is not driven in exchange for ours. We can forfeit it, but we do not earn it.

Jesus exhorts us to forgive one another "from the heart." It is by the quality of our hearts that we are judged.

Questions for Reflection

• How much of your morality follows a pragmatic piety like Ben Sira's?

• We belong to Christ in death only if we belong to Christ in life. How do you deal with the temptation to be your own master?

• What was the hardest thing you ever had to forgive? What did unfor-giveness cost you? Were you able to forgive "from the heart?"

Action Response

Spend the week clinging to no offense, forgiving every unkindness or injury from the heart and letting it go.

The Problem with God

FIRST READING: ISAIAH 55:6–9

So high are my ways above your ways.

Isaiah's proclamation sounds very straightforward: seek the Lord while the Lord may be found. But when exactly is that? When is God near? The prophet does not say.

Human need leads us to cry out to God in time of trouble. We also turn our thoughts to God on the Sabbath, before meals, when we retire at night. Are these the best times? When should we seek God? Is a sunny day a good day to find God? Or should we wait till it rains? Is work a good place? Or the laundromat? Is it possible to find God in an enemy? Or only in the face of a friend? Will God draw near in the forest, or in the heart of the city?

God's ways and thoughts are peculiar to the Holy One, we are told. Chances are, God is in the least likely place we can imagine. Best to keep our eyes open at all times.

SECOND READING: PHILIPPIANS 1:20–24, 27

For me, to live is Christ.

Paul's letter to the Philippians has been called "the letter of joy." Even though Paul writes from prison, his affection for the community at Philippi shines larger than his concern for his own danger. He writes to them candidly about his fate. Death will mean a reunion with his Lord. Life will mean ongoing service to Christ. Either way, he is content to face the future.

Now that is a relaxed posture. We modern-day control freaks would prefer a little more input, more leverage. We take life-and-death decisions with a bit more gravity. (To be honest—we even take wallpapering decisions with more gravity.) To have our priorities straight like Paul is to have no priorities beyond Christ. "Whether I live or die, Christ will be exalted," he says. Is that true of us?

GOSPEL: MATTHEW 20:1–16
"Are you envious because I am generous?"

The story of the workers in the vineyard follows the encounter of Jesus with the rich young man. This context is interesting, because Jesus has just told the young man to give up all he has and become a disciple. As we know, the man turns away sadly.

Then Peter pipes up, observing that the Twelve have done exactly what Jesus asked—given up everything to follow him. "What will we get for that?" Peter asks. Jesus assures him the reward of disciples is great. Then he tells this story of the vineyard workers.

The jaws of the disciples must have dropped. You mean—we can hear them saying to themselves—you mean we who have been with you from the start will get the same wages as those who cast their lot with you in the end? Forget sitting at Jesus' right or left—they would end up in the bleachers with everyone else!

This is the problem with God. Divine justice sounds terribly unfair by our standards. Our thoughts are not God's thoughts, and our scales weigh things out quite differently. For most of us, needless to say, this is our only hope.

Questions for Reflection

• Where and when do you usually seek God? Where would you be least likely to look for Divine Presence?

• How is Christ exalted through your life?

• Consider the various shifts of workers in the vineyard. Upon which shift were you engaged? How does this affect your relationship to the others?

Action Response

Try finding God in new places. Pray in the supermarket, during the commute; vary the time and method of your prayer. Perhaps God will have something new to say.

A Different Sense of Fairness

FIRST READING: EZEKIEL 18:25–28
Is it my way that is unfair?

This prophecy of Ezekiel extends through all of chapter 18 and is worth reading in its entirety. What the Lord has to say to Israel is wonderfully new. The prophecy revolves around the proverb: the parents have eaten sour grapes, and the children's teeth are set on edge. It's another way of saying the sins of the parents are visited upon their children, or God punishes to the seventh generation the wrongdoing of the present.

Ezekiel proclaims a new word from the Lord: a resounding "no" to this senseless perpetuation of evil. The Lord says we only have to answer for the wrongdoing that is ours. The Lord also says it is God's desire that all should live and no one should die.

In this prophecy, God rejects bad theology that makes the Divine a vengeful despot, one who delights in the destruction of the wicked. The Puritanical vision of "sinners in the hands of an angry God" is *our* idea of justice, not God's. God hopes to save us all.

SECOND READING: PHILIPPIANS 2:1–11
Jesus Christ is Lord!

Paul pleads tenderly with the Philippians for unity, humility, and a Christ-like attitude among them. Then he recalls this beautiful hymn, hoping to clarify what he means by an attitude like Christ's.

Imagine the wealthiest and most powerful person in the land surrendering all advantage and going to live among the truly poor. Not just slumming it for a season, to see what it is like, but going to live the life of poverty and die the death of ignomiy. At any time, with one phone call, he could stop the process, go back to his estate, and live a long and pleasant life. But he never does. How are we to interpret such an act of solidarity, a terrifyingly complete surrender to love and justice?

With Jesus, the self-emptying is greater than our imagination, and the solidarity leads to salvation from our poverty. It is for this reason he receives the name above every other name, and can be the only true Lord of Love.

Tax collectors and prostitutes are entering the kingdom....

The chief priests and the elders come after Jesus on the matter of authority. By whose authority was he teaching, healing, editing the Law? He was, after all, not a priest or a scribe, not an elder or even an educated man. Without the official succession or a school of thought to point to, he was just a dubious fellow from Galilee.

Jesus takes the dialogue to another level. Rather than addressing authority, he casts the matter into a question of obedience. Authority resides—he says in effect—not with official channels but with the faithful servant. Only the one who does God's will can be called God's messenger. We carry our credentials in our deeds.

That's why tax collectors and prostitutes may enter the kingdom, while priests and elders may have to seek other accommodations.

Questions for Reflection

• How does God's sense of justice differ from yours?

• What verse in the Hymn to Christ speaks to you most powerfully?

• When have you behaved like the first son in the parable? The second son?

Action Response

Consider your deeds this week as your credentials in calling yourself a Christian. Concentrate on building a resume that is worthy of hire.

Grapes at Vintage Time

FIRST READING: ISAIAH 5:1–7

Judge between me and my vineyard.

To whom much has been given, much will be required. This parable from Isaiah bears out the Gospel injunction in detail. After lavish care is bestowed on the vineyard, bitter grapes are harvested. Woe to the vineyard, due to lose its protection and cultivation. Even the rain will not fall on this disappointing vine.

Strange how we see it all another way. As Franciscan Father Richard Rohr has said, "The more we have, the more we have to protect." We see our wealth and advantage as a call to more security, more stocks and bonds, more armies and bombs, higher and stronger borders, stiffer laws against immigrants. The more there is, the more there is for me.

If our advantage does not reap the harvest for which it was given, it will be treasure stored in a place where moth and rust and thieves will soon break in. The more we hoard, the more we stand to lose.

SECOND READING: PHILIPPIANS 4:6–9

Whatever is true, whatever is honorable, think about these things.

Paul's relationship to the folks at Philippi is warm and encouraging. They obviously caught the spirit of what he felt community in Christ should be. Yet he warns them that the reverse spirit is out there, and to guard against it. Whatever is just, pure, pleasing, and worthy of praise should be uppermost in their minds.

We have, as Paul had, an acquaintance of the reverse spirit, what we call today "toxic communities." These are closed systems that do not admit any breathable air. They have a pronounced dysfunction and tend to dwell on bad news, cynicism, negative energy, and bitterness. Whatever fails, whatever is displeasing, whatever is unjust, the toxic community trumpets and sees as vindication for its window on misery.

In this way, a family, a work environment, a parish, or even a nation can go toxic. I have worked and worshiped in places where the corporate mentality was, "This place is treacherous so watch your back." Sometimes the answer is to remove yourself from that community and go elsewhere. But often, all it takes is for a few people to put on another mind, as Paul recommends, and let the peace which passes understanding begin to dwell there.

GOSPEL: MATTHEW 21:33–43
"What do you suppose the owner will do?"

The chief priests and elders are in the Temple. They have just questioned Jesus' authority to teach and act as he does. He replies with a series of parables aimed at questioning their authority to do as *they* do. It's a fairly defining and ugly war of words, yet told as benignly as a series of children's stories. Jesus is so smooth!

Obviously, the religious leaders of the community are insulted to be identified with the ruthless murdering tenants in the parable. Jesus rubs it in when he says, "Did you never read in the Scriptures?" about the stone rejected by the builders. (Of course they have. They may be ruthless, but they are professional scholars.) For this affront, they want to arrest him on the spot.

I have felt threatened like that, when the truth has been spoken in my life. Since I cannot alter the truth, I want to silence the messenger. And soon enough, this messenger will be silenced by the cross. But the truth will go on being true, and the cross will become its most eloquent messenger.

Questions for Reflection

• Which areas of your life are bearing fruit now: prayer, worship, community, witness, justice, charity, service? Which are in need of tending?

• Examine your primary communities: home, work, parish, or neighborhood. Are they directed toward "all that is true and virtuous," or do they have toxic elements? How do you contribute to the atmosphere?

• How or where is truth spoken in your life? Do you encourage it or try to arrest it?

Action Response

Resolve to be a model "Philippian." Spend a week concentrating on "living according to what you have learned and accepted." Be a bringer of peace and accord in all the communities in which you move.

Rich Food, Choice Wines

FIRST READING: ISAIAH 25:6–10
The hand of the Lord will rest on this mountain.

Religion has the reputation of being a pious drag. Christians are not acclaimed as the people who know how to have a party. But that is to some degree our fault. We often forget to invite others to the feast, and concentrate our public persona in condemnations.

Perhaps you have a more hopeful witness in your local community. My parish has Mary Anne and Norman. They are the couple who celebrate everyone's victories and seek to right injustices by immediately turning their living room into the center of the feast. They serve rich juicy foods and pure choice wines, just like in Isaiah. They take up collections and mourn with those who mourn; they provide warmth and hope to friends and strangers alike. They are everyone's family, and their living room is everyone's church. The hand of the Lord rests on the mountain that is their open, ready love. They remind us all that church is a banquet, and God is Lord of the feast.

SECOND READING: PHILIPPIANS 4:12–14, 19–20
God in turn will supply your needs fully.

This is one of those times when it pays to check out the verses eliminated from the lectionary. Paul is very personally grateful to the Philippians for sending material support; they've been backing him for a while, even as other communities have forgotten him. I have been rich and I have been poor, Paul seems to be saying, but it is better for your sake that you help me out, since you store up wealth in heaven. This is the old jewels-in-your-crown argument many of us heard in parochial school. Be charitable now, and you will earn jewels in your crown in the afterlife. As theology goes, this is not particularly edifying—it is more like the delayed gratification of virtue.

Wouldn't it be nice if the Philippians took up a collection for Paul out of simple love for him and conviction about his mission? Wouldn't it be great if we gave because giving is good and "blesses him that gives and him that takes," and not because we hope God is taking notes?

GOSPEL: MATTHEW 22:1-14
"See, I have my dinner prepared!"

If the chief priests and elders did not like being compared to the evil tenants in the last parable, they are less happy about the choice presented in the parable of the wedding banquet. Either they see themselves as the arrogant guests who refused the invitation altogether, or they may liken themselves to the guest who came without the proper garment for the feast. How would you rather end up, burned with your city or wailing and gnashing your teeth in the darkness?

This parable left a strong impression on me as a child. I remember drawing a comic strip of it. I drew the legitimate guests who refused to come in triangular robes of Crayola goldenrod, the brightest color in the box. The folks from the byways arrived in similar robes of subdued purples and greens. But the fellow who gets in trouble was a penciled-in stick figure, alone in a blackened final frame, screaming, pinned hand and foot as the parable indicates.

Obviously I missed the point in second grade: it was his readiness for the feast that was being measured, not his appearance. But how *do* we make ready for the never-ending invitation to share in the feast? The priests and elders did not get it. Their response was to begin plotting for Jesus' destruction.

Questions for Reflection

•Is your parish an active witness of celebration in its liturgy, community and call to justice? If not, where else is the feast being celebrated?

•Is your generosity free or is it all "tax-deductible"? Where do you give with no rewards?

•How do you make ready for the never-ending invitation to share in God's feast?

Action Response

Consider having a party or gathering which is of no advantage to you (or your parish) financially, politically, or personally. Invite people who cannot return the favor. See how this transforms the nature of the feast.

Giving Caesar His Due

FIRST READING: ISAIAH 45:1, 4–6
It is I who arm you though you know me not.

A surprising prophecy comes from the Lord: Cyrus the Babylonian conqueror is acknowledged as the anointed of God. To an oppressed people in exile, this must have seemed a ghastly idea. Their God at work behind the ascendancy of the Babylonian emperor! Why, Cyrus does not even know their God!

Isaiah's prophecy admits that, and more. It is an oracle that admits the idea of God operating beyond the expected, respectable channels. God's will can be achieved through an evil czar as much as through the pope, if God so chooses. Even Pharaoh and his hard heart had their uses. It does not matter that Cyrus is not aware that God has appointed and led him to this moment in his career. There is no power besides the Lord: all that happens, happens as an incorporated piece of God's plan.

This may be good news just before election day, particularly if your candidate is not elected. If God can liberate Israel by means of Cyrus, then God can do some good work through our elected officials, whoever they may turn out to be.

SECOND READING: 1 THESSALONIANS 1:1–5
We know too, beloved of God, how you were chosen.

Paul admits that the power of the Holy Spirit and not mere human skill at preaching led the Thessalonians to conversion. Think of how much good the church could do if we, the church, were convinced of this. Instead, we worry about our lack of talent or lack of funds and say, alas, we are not prepared to witness. We forget we are mere vessels that God can fill with light.

Public speakers of every profession know this: you can be prepared and talented and equipped till the cows come home and still bomb. Or you can be unschooled and of modest verbal skills and bring life to thousands with your sincerity and love.

Once I saw author Henri Nouwen upstaged by a mentally retarded adult he invited to the podium to speak. Nouwen's eloquence as a speaker and writer are unchallenged, and he has my full admiration, more so as a result of this invitation. He was able to perceive and elevate this man's Spirit-infused experience so that all of us could share it.

If we surrendered ourselves to "the Holy Spirit and complete conviction," what grace might enter the world through us?

Give to God what is God's.

"Teacher, we know you are a truthful man," the Pharisees' disciples purr at Jesus. They flatter him with false and empty words. But Jesus is no fool and he throws the matter back to them with clever wordplay.

And it is more than wordplay, if we read between the lines. They ask about the emperor's tax, a concern of law-abiding Jews. And Jesus asks them to produce a coin, which they immediately do. Mistake number one: what are law-abiding citizens of Jerusalem doing walking around with Roman coins in their pockets? They have just betrayed themselves as being on the payroll of the Romans in one fashion or another. So Jesus answers them curtly: let them who deal with Caesar, pay Caesar his due. What is of God should be given to God. They are stunned by his keen perception, and they leave him directly.

We cannot be too quick to judge the Pharisees. Most of us carry the coins of many realms through our days. It is not always clear where our allegiance lies.

Questions for Reflection

• When have you known God to work through a surprising or "enemy" source?

• How has God used your weakness to Divine advantage?

• As a citizen of the reign of God, what other realms do you serve? When or where do you find your allegiances in conflict?

Action Response

Someone you know could use some good news. Let the Holy Spirit and complete conviction drive the encounter. Give to God what is God's: your willing heart.

Holding Our Neighbors' Cloaks

FIRST READING: EXODUS 22:20–26
I will hear the poor one, for I am compassionate.

The Native American prayer to the Great Spirit speaks a simple wisdom: grant that I may not criticize my neighbor until I have walked a mile in his moccasins. As the Law of Moses points out, the Israelites *have* walked for many generations in the shoes of the neediest and most vulnerable people of any culture. As they know precisely what destitution, helplessness, and friendlessness can mean, they have a special mandate to remember and to deal compassionately with others.

The citation about the poor neighbor's cloak is particularly touching. Should you take a cloak from a poor person as a pledge, it must be returned by nightfall, for what else does a poor person have to sleep in? Our assistance to each other, if it is genuine, cannot be offered with a new set of burdens all its own. Yet how often do we help our neighbors while holding on to their cloaks with both hands?

SECOND READING: 1 THESSALONIANS 1:5–10
Thus you became a model for all believers.

The community at Thessalonica became an overnight sensation in the burgeoning Christian world. They turned to God from idols so quickly and completely that the word spread for miles around and was an inspiration to many communities weaker and less certain in their conversion. If Christian witness were a source of fame today, we'd all be wearing Thessalonian T-shirts.

The sad truth is, there are few contemporary communities I can point to where "the word of the Lord echoes forth resoundingly." For many years I belonged to a parish that was the envy of the diocese. With a small membership and a microbudget, we offered more leadership, witness, liturgy and religious education per square feet than anyone else. We were the Thessalonians of our region.

But as a priest friend of mine often reminds me, "It doesn't take much to be a star in this show." The competition is meager, the fellow witnesses that should join hands with ours are scarce. Even a thousand points of light, if spread too far apart, get lost in the darkness.

GOSPEL: MATTHEW 22:34-40
"You shall love the Lord your God."

The Pharisees and Sadducees each have had a turn at Jesus, and the score is predictable: Jesus, two; Pharisees and Sadducees, zero. So the Pharisees are up at bat again, wielding another lawyerly question: which commandment of the Law is greatest? It is a question whose answer has got to offend someone; which is to say, it is a political setup. They do not want an answer; they want Jesus to stumble.

Compare this reading of the encounter with the benign versions in Mark 12 and Luke 10. Mark presents the scribe who asks the question as a wise and good man who receives the highest commendation Jesus gives anyone in that Gospel for his understanding. In Luke's Gospel, Jesus elicits the correct answer from the lawyer himself and simply approves it. Only in Matthew does the story assume an ugly color.

And Jesus' response is not a stumble, by any means. He takes the First Commandment of the Decalogue and combines it with a well-known law (Leviticus 19:18) from Jewish liturgy, and says, rightly, these two forms of love contain all law and prophecy.

And now, if you read on in this passage, it is Jesus' turn to ask the Pharisees some questions. Who do you suppose will win this inning?

Questions for Reflection

• In what ways can our assistance be self-serving or burdensome to those whom we assist? How can we let go of our neighbor's cloaks when we serve them?

• Is there a community whose example provides inspiration to you?

• Consider your words and actions this day in light of Jesus' twofold law of love. What would you have to change to conform to this law?

Action Response

Plan a good deed that will not benefit you at all or lay a burden on anyone who receives it. Give without counting the cost, and do not tell anyone about it.

Heavy Loads, Hard to Carry

FIRST READING: MALACHI 1:14–2:2, 8–10
Has not the one God created us?

Most of today's prophecy is actually cut from a larger diatribe aimed specifically at corrupt priests of the Lord. So if you are not one of those, you can breathe easier. Writing after the return from Babylon, Malachi is particularly incensed because the people, by now, should know better than to mess with the Lord. They have already experienced the despair of exile brought upon them by their miserable response to the covenant. God loved them and delivered them nonetheless. And now, once liberated, they are as depraved as ever.

The last verse of this passage is directed at the people of God as a whole, who are no better than their priests. This is where we might not breathe as easily as before. When the day of the Lord does come, it will either be a "great" or a "terrible" day, depending on how well we have kept our covenants.

SECOND READING: 1 THESSALONIANS 2:7–9, 13
We were as gentle as any nursing mother.

Here is a tribute to the worker-priest spirit: Paul does some of his best work in Thessalonica, employed full-time to earn his keep all the while, presumably as a tentmaker, which is his trade. He did not want the mission to be seen as parasitic, leeching off the community while presenting the Gospel.

The argument is not about whether ministers should have secular jobs or not. The issue is really the attitude of entitlement: should ministers presume they are owed their keep, because of what they offer? Obviously many traveling philosophers and teachers did make their living in this way in the first century, or Paul would not be at such pains to separate himself from them.

At the same time, he admits elsewhere his gratitude when communities like the Philippians send money to support his work. Paul appreciates financial support, but does not deem it his due. How easy it is for us to make the leap from gratitude at blessings received to imperious expectations of what we deserve.

Their words are bold but their deeds are few.

I do not know a priest who can get up without some embarrassment on the Sundays this reading is presented. Here you are, in the front seat of the assembly, wearing robes, being called father.... it is an awkward moment. Most good homilists meet the challenge head-on by admitting the description is a little close for comfort.

If you read on in chapter 23, this is Jesus' full counterattack on the Pharisees and Sadducees who have been on his back all day in the Temple with their testing and tricking. It is a condemnation of hypocrisy, not priesthood per se. Religious posturing may look good in front of the crowds, but God is not impressed by the outer side of the cup, as Jesus says further on.

We are all tempted by a variety of tassels and titles that people bestow on us as marks of respect. As a lay minister of fifteen years, I am just as tempted to surrender to some of the wonderful opinions people have pronounced about me—or similarly, to some of the invectives that have been applied to me as well. What is perceived about us is, in fact, of no consequence. What we carry in our hearts and bear out in service is the measure of who we are.

Questions for Reflection

• Make a list of the covenants you are obliged to keep, according to who you are. Grade your efforts. Which covenants need more attention right now?

• Where do you see yourself in mission to the church: full-time minister, part-time worker, willing volunteer, or pew-sitter? What are you given to make this situation viable?

• What is your attitude about professional ministers: positive, negative, or somewhere in between? (Even ministers can answer this!) What shapes your reaction?

Action Response

Consider the covenant you singled out above as in need of most attention at this time. Take steps to be more faithful to your commitments.

The Beginning of the End

FIRST READING: WISDOM 6:12–16
Wisdom makes her own rounds.

Wisdom is a surprisingly rare find in an educated society like ours. That's because wisdom is not the same thing as knowledge; anybody who had to memorize the seven gifts of the Holy Spirit for confirmation knows this. So does anyone who has met a particularly dense individual with a degree after his or her name. In this technological age, we have to know tons of information to survive. But everything we know and everything we have memorized does not make us necessarily wise.

A geek, properly defined, is a person who has absorbed tons of information but does not know how to find clothes in the right size. From the perspective of Wisdom, most of us are geeks, full of catechism and religious trivia but without the wherewithal to clothe ourselves with what is prudent, let alone resplendent. Yet Wisdom waits for us at the gates, making her rounds, seeking lodging with those who have prepared for her coming.

SECOND READING: 1 THESSALONIANS 4:13–18
Console one another with this message.

This passage sure sounds like Rapture to me. You've heard of the Rapture: the fundamentalist belief in the snatching up of the faithful at the end of time to meet the Lord in the air before the destruction of all things. Paul didn't make this stuff up: Jewish apocalyptic tradition has similar themes. And there are parallel images in Luke 17 and Matthew 24.

So what are Catholics to make of the Rapture? Catholic scholarship is vague and impersonal in its treatment of the concept. Many other descriptions of the last things appear in Scripture and all can be seen as metaphorical in nature. Where scholarship does come alive is on the subject of the resurrection of the dead and our ultimate union with God.

That is clearly the emphasis of Paul's words here; the dead are not lost, but only sleep for a time. This is the message which was intended for our consolation, not the order of events, the literal sound of a trumpet, which side of the clouds we will be standing on. From the standpoint of contemporary scholars, the literal understanding of the Rapture is as good an image as any. But our hope lies not in the circumstance but in the resurrection itself.

GOSPEL: MATTHEW 25:1–13
Keep your eyes open, for you know not the day.

Jesus has moved on from his excoriation of the religious leaders and has left the Temple. At a question from his disciples, he has begun a new cycle of teachings on the matter of the end of the age. His images are dark and fearful: calamities, abominations, the darkening of the sun, the falling of the stars. In this passage, he continues a series of parables of destruction through the tale of the ten virgins.

Not knowing the arrival of the coming hour is common to all of these stories, as is the way all will be judged by their readiness in that hour. We may say in defense of the virgins who abandoned their post that they did the best they could, trying to repair their oversight quickly. This is not a defense that is acceptable in these stories. Even the fig tree will produce in the right season, Jesus says in this cycle. The servant who deserts his duties and abuses his power will be punished. The virgins who are absent at the critical hour will forfeit their right to the feast.

We might prefer more leniency in this matter. But Jesus does not provide any in Matthew's cycle of endtime teachings.

Questions for Reflection

- How can we make preparations for the coming of Wisdom?
- How do you understand the communion of saints, and our belief that the dead are not lost?
- How do you relate the treatment of the five belated bridesmaids to Christian responsibility?

Action Response

Prepare a dwelling place for Wisdom. Arrange to go on a retreat or day of recollection, or isolate a few hours to create an interior hermitage. Pray for the advent of Wisdom, and invite the Holy Spirit to give you the grace to receive her.

The Suddeness of Pains

FIRST READING: PROVERBS 31:10–13, 19–20, 30–31
Charm is deceptive and beauty fleeting.

To appreciate the proverbs regarding the Ideal Wife, you have to read all of them, and not just this clipped citation. All told, the Ideal Wife is a cross between my mother and Teresa of Avila (who wasn't married and didn't have eight children and so had time for the rest of these accomplishments). I would be happy to hear from anyone who has sighted this woman!

What is edifying about the worthy wife is that she is valued for who she is (compassionate, kind, wise, a woman of God) and what she does, and not for what she looks like. This is a countercultural notion in any age. The politics of beauty has so bound women hand and foot that they can scarcely make a move without being praised or blamed for a thing which is quite without real consequence. Imprisoned by the ideals of fashion and sexual politics, women exhaust hours and energy and health and money to offer, in the end, an illusion of themselves to a world which prefers illusion to substance.

To the unknown author of these proverbs, it was apparent that a woman is more than a rustle of silk and a pretty smile. For this insight, we owe thanks.

SECOND READING: 1 THESSALONIANS 5:1–6
All of you are children of light and of the day.

Here is the thing about the suddenness of labor pains: they *do* come on all at once, but they are *not* exactly unexpected. In fact, they are some of the most predictable pains life has to offer. So when Paul cites labor pains as a metaphor for the onset of the day of the Lord, he is saying two things: once they start, there's no escaping them; and, you do not really expect that this old pregnant world is going to avoid them, do you?

The new world will be born out of the body of the old. And we are children destined for the new, children born into the light of Christ. Of all people, we cannot feign ignorance about what is coming. God's reign is on the other side of every hour. We pray for this at every Eucharist, hope for this in every sacrament, witness to this in every act of justice. If it catches us by surprise, we must have been asleep these last 2,000 years.

GOSPEL: MATTHEW 25:14–30
"Come, share your master's joy!"

If I were one of the Twelve, I would be drained by this relentless teaching of Jesus about the final days. To read chapters 24 and 25 at one sitting is disquieting enough. Who among us received five talents, or two, and did as we were expected? Who among us received one and will prove to be a failure in our stewardship? My own stewardship is less decisive, more spotty. Some days I am playing the market for all it is worth, and other days I find myself, talents in hand, staring blankly out a window.

Is this going to be another lottery of hoping that God catches me on a good day and not a glassy-eyed one? Wouldn't it be a shame if God does not catch me at the Easter Vigil, when I am halfway to Rapture already, and finds me instead on an overwhelming day, when I have called in sick, pulled the covers over my head, and closed my eyes in ostrich-like defense? Let's hope not. For if so, as the disciples once asked, then who can be saved?

Questions for Reflection

• For both men and women: how has the politics of beauty affected your life and your relationship to others? How does your faith challenge this effect?

• What parts of your life are "awake" to the reality of God's reign? What parts are still asleep?

• Name your talents. Upon which have you made wise returns? Which ones still await investment for the reign of God?

Action Response

If, today, the suddenness of pains were to come upon our world, what one thing would you have wished to have done? Consider what steps could be taken now to bring that task to fruition.

The Truth about Sheep and Goats

FIRST READING: EZEKIEL 34:11–12, 15–17

The lost I will seek out, the strayed I will bring back.

To be sheep in God's pasture is a comforting idea. As Ezekiel paints the picture across chapter 34, sheep on God's land have nothing to fear and everything they could want. As it stands, however, we are sheep currently at risk in very foreign and unsafe territory. The problem is not the wildness of the land itself, but the unreliability of those we acknowledge as our shepherds.

As long as we wait for our government to make us just, as long as we abdicate responsibility to religious leaders or rule books, the courts or psychologists, the latest diet or the latest theory, we will be scattered in a place that is cloudy and dark. A few will grow strong and sleek while the rest of us languish.

The only true shepherd is the Lord, both Hebrew and Christian Scriptures agree. And when God comes to draw the flock together, the worst place to be found is on easy street.

SECOND READING: 1 CORINTHIANS 15:20–26, 28

The last enemy to be destroyed is death.

When the carpet is rolled up on time itself, Paul says, this is how it is going to go. First the faithful dead and living will be lifted up, then every power on earth will be smashed to bits. Then all will be subdued under Christ, including death. Then Christ surrenders to God, and God is all in all.

This is a mirror image of the Creation story, which is one of separation, delineation, and variation. The cosmic conclusion is reunion, the destruction of division, and the re-incorporation of creation by the Creator.

No more black and white, no more light and dark, no more Greek and Jew, male or female, slave or free. Nothing will ever be a life-or-death matter again for all eternity. Total unity as the Trinity knows it is something that we, born into separation the moment the cord is severed, will have to grow into. Imagine having no one to hate or to fear, nothing to need, and no reason to hide. This is something worth working toward.

GOSPEL: MATTHEW 25:31–46
Inherit the kingdom prepared for you.

You know the line: there are two kinds of people....Well, the Christian punchline is, yes, there are sheep and there are goats. You and I may appear more or less the same at first glance. But inside one of us may be a sheep destined for God's pasture, and in the other, a goat with a lot to answer for. I would hate to be divided from you. I would hate to be snatched up to a great place, knowing you are in an eternally worse one. I would hate it even more, to be honest, if it ends up the other way around! But how can we know if we will be together or apart, in a wonderful or abysmal state?

Jesus is not going to leave us hanging on this one. It is too important to gamble on, so he gives us the criteria right here, a role play for the exit interview. These are, in fact, the final exam questions in advance, so we can cram to our heart's desire. The answers are simple, as it turns out: compassion and justice. If we are just and compassionate with one another, we will all be revealed to be sheep. But if we take a look at the world, we know that we are not all sheep.

Group work is preferable on this final exam, so let's be church and share what we know. We can resolve to be people of compassion and justice. At the close of another church year, we do not know how near the day and the hour might be.

Questions for Reflection

• What powers or authorities shepherd you? How do you assess their responsibility?

• Does God being "all in all" comfort you or frighten you? What do we gain, and lose, in this union?

• Read through Matthew's depiction of the judgment of souls. If the exam were today, how well would you do?

Action Response

The end of the year is a time to tie up loose ends. The sacrament of reconciliation is a good place for binding and loosing. Pull yourself together and set yourself free.

Cycle B

On the Watch

FIRST READING: ISAIAH 63:16–17, 19, 64:2–7

Why do you let us wander, O Lord, from your ways?

If you have ever come to an awareness of sin in your life, you understand this lament intimately. Israel stands before God toward the end of a long exile, mindful of God's wonderful past works and knowing too the sins of the nation. In no way can the people claim to have earned God's favor. They are like withered leaves; their works are polluted rags.

When I disappoint one who loves me, I feel this same hang-dog misery. To fall short of love when all we have experienced is love must be among the most wretched moments of our humanity. And it is the very definition of sin. Israel reclaims hope by recalling the relationship: Israel is offspring, God is origin. Israel is clay in a gentle potter's hands. These ties are stronger than sin. And this close communion is the rope ladder thrown to us, too, in the midst of our failure to love.

SECOND READING: 1 CORINTHIANS 1:3–9

Wait for the revelation of our Lord Jesus Christ.

For Paul, everything comes through Christ Jesus: grace and peace, strength, prayer, and all other gifts. Testimony is to Christ, fellowship is with Christ. Our formula, "through him, with him, in him" comes from Paul's insistence that Jesus Christ is the vortex through which all that is redeemed must pass.

We commonly hear the name of Jesus invoked as a curse as much as a blessing. If we reclaim the name for blessing, our world may know once more its saving power.

GOSPEL: MARK 13:33–37

"Be constantly on the watch!"

Four weeks before Christmas, we hear a sober Gospel. We are preparing for a festive season; Jesus warns us of an appointed time. Can this be the same event? We are swept up in decorating, meal planning, gift buying, memories of past holidays. We are operating at the height of distraction. Jesus points simply and clearly to the future, warning us not to be lulled into inattention.

At the end of the year, it is natural for us to be looking back. As this season is such a powerful reminder of those we have loved and some we have lost, it is not surprising that we may lose ourselves in the past. The church selects these Advent readings to urge our attention to the coming of Christ and the kingdom, an event that belongs not to the past but to the here and now, its perfection yet to be revealed.

If we focus our gaze behind us we may miss the signs of the kingdom being born where we stand. And we may miss the chance to be a sign of the kingdom for others.

Questions for Reflection

• Where have you known sin in your life? What helped to reconcile you to God and others?

• How and when do you use the name of Jesus? Under what circumstances might you begin to use it with earnest reverence?

• What has your attention this Advent? How do you see God's kingdom being born where you are?

Action Response

Look for one sign of the kingdom of God every day this Advent season. Keep a list of these signs to remind you of the coming of Christ to which this season points.

Starting Over

FIRST READING: ISAIAH 40:1–5, 9–11
Make straight a highway for our God!

This passage comes from what has been called the Book of Consolation in Isaiah. It is meant to describe the return of the exiles from Babylon. The pain of long separation is ended. God's people are going home.

Starting over has a joyful character to it. A second chance to love better! What a relief it is, to be forgiven by a friend we have wronged, a spouse we have injured, a parent or child we have failed to honor. We have all known the pleasure of beginning again in a new place, a fresh situation, maybe sober at last or finally ready to make a genuine commitment to life in Christ.

You and I can make a pledge at any moment to a new deal. We can beat a straight path to God, know the protection of a strong arm and the comfort of tender words. This waiting season of Advent is seed time, planted down in darkness, preparing for a new life all of us have longed for.

SECOND READING: 2 PETER 3:8–14
The Lord wants none to perish but all to come to repentance.

You and I are not the only ones getting another try at something new. This world itself is passing—as the letter of Peter suggests, it is going down in flames—and what happens after that is something unlike anything we know now.

So what does total conflagration mean for us? Consider that everything you own, everything you have accomplished, all of your networking and politicking is going to go up in smoke. All we will have to clothe ourselves with in the new world is our love. No doubt some of us will be more scantily clad than others.

Before the end of time, while we still have time, we might want to consider how much of our energy is directed toward the new creation where the justice of God will reside. It is the only striving in our lives that is not in vain.

GOSPEL: MARK 1:1–8
"One more powerful than I is to come."

People came in droves to receive John's baptism. They came out to the desert from as far away as Jerusalem to hear John's condemnations and to embrace repentance. They drowned their old ways in the Jordan and rose up ready to begin again.

So what happened to all those reformed by John? One would expect these fervent followers to rise up and overthrow the lords of the temple, or topple the throne of Herod, or both. Herod, we know, was so terrified of John's power over the crowds that he had him imprisoned, and eventually beheaded. The testimony and authority of John was great indeed, we can be sure.

Some of those baptized transferred their allegiance to Jesus, as John recommended. Some had only gone out for the glamour and never really changed. Some fell away after the death of John, disappointed. Eventually, the excitement of the message and that day at the river faded from people's hearts.

Baptism and its testimony is not sustained by having been there, done that. The sign has to be carried forward, water and Spirit meeting in the testimony of our lives and choices.

Questions for Reflection

• What are the valleys and mountains in your life that need to be leveled to make the way straight for God?

• You have received advance notice that the day of the Lord is tomorrow. How will you express your love today?

• How does your life testify to your baptism, at home or work, with family, friends, and strangers?

Action Response

Consider your answer to the second reflection question. Choose one expression of end-of-the-world love that you can begin to express today. We know not the day nor the hour.

Expressing the Spirit

FIRST READING: ISAIAH 61:1–2, 10–11

The Spirit of the Lord God is upon me.

This was the fateful passage Jesus read in the synagogue in Nazareth (Luke 4) before he was chased out and nearly hurled off a cliff. It is a claim to Messianic authority, particularly if you follow it with the words, "Today this Scripture is fulfilled in your hearing," as Jesus did.

What does the anointed one of God bring into our midst? Good news for the poor, healing to those in pain, liberty to those who are not free, a day of having for the have-nots. This is a year of favor, if you are living in a world of hurt. It is described in the same breath as a day of vindication, upon those who have and hold and do not share.

The robe of salvation is worn by the one who wears the mantle of justice. Remembering the poor, in this and every season, is our participation in the year of favor and in the announcement of Isaiah's bold prophecy.

SECOND READING: 1 THESSALONIANS 5:16–24

Do not stifle the Spirit.

These no-nonsense recommendations from Paul make me wonder how often I stifle the Spirit without even thinking about it. Do I rejoice always, or even often? How often do I pray? Do I render constant thanks or constant complaints? Do I listen to the prophetic voices in my community or do they annoy me? Do I examine my ways, or go with the flow? Do I avoid proximity to evil, or do I dance with it from time to time?

The Spirit seeks a dwelling place in us; we have clear instructions on how to welcome holiness. Or we can make it hard for the Spirit by closing every window to grace and barring the door by our habits.

GOSPEL: JOHN 1:6–8, 19–28
"What do you have to say for yourself?"

Sooner or later we are all going to have to answer the question of the Levites: "Tell us who you are. What do you have to say for yourself?"

We can supply our names, occupations, relationships to others, the numbers and statistics that identify us. We can produce cards, bank books, degrees, awards. We can boast of our successes, even admit our failures. But we will never approach the originality of John's answer: "I am not the Messiah." It is the perfect answer! In John's humility is real understanding. It is not about me, or what I have done or where I have been. It *is* about Jesus, who is among us unrecognized.

Who I am as a Christian is properly defined by who I am not. John's role in history becomes the foundation for a real and healthy spiritual life for each of us.

Questions for Reflection

• What are you doing to announce Isaiah's year of favor to the oppressed?

• Use Paul's exhortations as a checklist. How freely is the Spirit moving in your life?

• How does John's self-understanding challenge yours?

Action Response

Give the Spirit full liberty in your life. Rejoice, pray, give thanks, and resist giving power to the Evil One by surrendering to negative voices and old habits.

The Mystery Is Manifest

FIRST READING: 2 SAMUEL 7:1–5, 8–11, 16

Should you build a house for me to dwell in?

David meant well, of course. He didn't want to think that he was enjoying more prestige and honor than God's holy Ark. The prophet Nathan was in agreement with the king initially. Then came the prophecy.

God does not choose to dwell in a house. God is content to be itinerant, wandering about in a tent, free to go before the people. (Later, in John's Gospel, we will hear that the word of God "pitched a tent and dwelt with us.") It is God who will build up David's house, establishing it for all time.

Wanting a secure place to put God is part of our finite, human urge to contain and control what is boundless. But no matter how often we try to define a place for God in our lives, God will escape it and seek more.

SECOND READING: ROMANS 16:25–27

The Gospel reveals the mystery hidden for many ages.

This is a doxology most likely added later to the letter to the Romans. It is a prayer in one long winding sentence, giving glory to the God who chooses to proclaim the Gospel to the Gentiles. It speaks about mystery and revelation, now and eternity. God alone who is wise can hold all these things together in one place.

We stand at the threshold of the celebration of great mystery. Virgin birth, eternity breaking into time, God taking on flesh are all manifest to us in the event of this inconspicuous child. The mystery hidden through the ages, known only in the voice of prophecy, comes now in tangibility and clarity. And better still: the mystery comes to us in utter vulnerability. Love walks with tender steps into our midst. Praise and glory are the only right response to the wonder.

GOSPEL: LUKE 1:26–38
Nothing is impossible with God.

Mary doesn't know yet that she is to be called Blessed Mother, Holy Virgin, for centuries to come. Right at the moment she is a God-fearing Jewish girl living in a backwater town, far from the people who matter and the places that count. She has been greeted by an angel, blessed and confided a great prophecy. It is a natural one by female reckoning: she will have a child.

But not just any child. This child will share the promises to David's house and be a ruler. He will be called Jesus, which means "God saves," and son of the Most High, which means...Mary has no idea what this means. She asks how. It is a natural question, and the angel gives a supernatural answer, about holiness descending, power and shadow, and a barren old woman becoming a mother at last.

Mary doesn't ask another question. She is God's servant, and accepts her part in the plan. In this season when love bears fruit, how long we will question God's way before we surrender to it?

Questions for Reflection

• Where is God's place in your life right now? Where else might God go if you were not an obstacle?

• Does the prayer of praise figure in your prayer habits? Compose a short doxology you can use as a prompt for praise.

• God has confided a great prophecy in each of our lives. What is yours, and how do you—can you—incarnate it?

Action Response

Consider a place from which you expect absolutely no life to emerge. Make that the place to offer your gift of love and hope this season.

Glory to God in the Highest!

FIRST READING: ISAIAH 9:1–6

They name him Wonder-Counselor, God-Hero, Father-Forever, Prince of Peace.

Imagine gathering up every souvenir of war and burning it, because war itself has come to an end for all time. The boots, the uniforms, the medals of honor, the tragic pictures of shattered bodies and weeping women, all banished from the world forever. Imagine the weapons of war dismantled and their metals put to use for peace and prosperity. Swords into plowshares: it's a dream as old as humankind.

Isaiah prophesies the coming reign of peace. It will mean judgment of the warlike ways of the world, and justice for those who were once oppressed. Light pierces the gloom of many lives, and the time of harvest never ends. It's a time that we long for, and God promises it is not just a dream.

The birth of a child makes this dream possible. Because this child has already come into the world, we now live on the brink of the reign of peace. We cannot enter that land with our swords, prejudices, lists of enemies, or gloomy hearts. Only the people who have seen a great light can come into this kingdom.

SECOND READING: TITUS 2:11–14

The grace of God has appeared.

When the grace of God appears, the rules change. Up until then, we live by the rules of the world, which go like this: look out for number one. Watch your back. Survival of the fittest. Help yourself.

When God's grace comes to us, conventional wisdom is no longer wise. We obey a new code: love one another. The last shall be first. Wash each other's feet. Bear one another's burdens. We love differently, we look differently, we behave differently, and the world around us is itself transformed. We become "eager to do what is right," instead of careening around doing what is wrong.

God's grace makes such a change in us, we don't simply struggle to do good, we desire good over evil. Our very being is changed, so that living "temperately, justly, and devoutly" isn't a cross; it's the blessing we seek and hope to bestow on those we love.

GOSPEL: LUKE 2:1–14
"I come to proclaim good news to you."

Good things come in small packages, especially in the birth of a child. A child is helpless, without language or skill or knowledge to protect its life. But it brings with it every possibility to recreate the world and transform the future for all of us. Genius, sainthood, art, or heroic love reside within each tiny new beating heart.

When it came to the new heart beating against Mary's breast, the future would be transformed in astounding ways. Caesar Augustus didn't know it, although he ruled an empire as far as he could see. The innkeeper of Bethlehem didn't know it, although he was a few yards away from the event. The news was revealed to shepherds, a rather humble lot: shabby, homeless, but faithful in the care of their flocks even by night. They were frightened to be visited at all, stunned by the presence of glorious beings. Yet glory comes to them, and brings tidings of great joy which will be sung down through the generations in gratitude for this night.

May the good news come to you, wherever you are, whatever your circumstances. May glory visit you and surround you with peace and joy.

Questions for Reflection

• What bars you from entering the reign of peace right now?

• Do you know people who are eager to do what is right? What makes them who they are?

• Describe glory. When have you seen it? Was it a place, a person, an event?

Action Response

Pray for pregnant women and expectant fathers. Lend a hand to parents raising their children under difficult circumstances. Be a source of comfort for your own children, and give consolation to the world's children through your charity.

Grace and Destiny

FIRST READING: SIRACH 3:2–6, 12–14

Revile not the old in the fullness of your strength.

The fourth commandment, right after honoring God, the Holy Name, and the Sabbath, proclaims the honor due parents. Just after God and before the rest of the world, we owe this debt to our mother and father. Ben Sira insists upon this kindness in the extended passage, even if the father has shame and the mother disgrace. This is a hard teaching, perhaps not for those who were raised by present and available parents but certainly for those whose parents were absent, neglectful, or abusive.

I have a friend whose father is a career alcoholic. He was rarely around when she was growing up; and when he was, it was not good. Honoring her father has been something she has had to do at a safe distance, even as an adult. Her honor takes the form of prayer, as she commends him often to the care and mercy of God.

Many of us may have been raised in situations that were less than holy. How much more is our kindness needed there, and our honor blessed by the Giver of every blessing.

SECOND READING: COLOSSIANS 3:12–21

Sing gratefully to God from your hearts.

Paul is intent on drawing a portrait of the ideal Christian community. He has followed a list of vices to be avoided with a list of virtues and orderly conduct to be emulated. We focus so often (and with some historical misgivings) on the latter list—a hierarchy of relationships between spouses, parents and children, and owners and slaves—that we overlook some timeless advice in the larger section.

One of the more curious items on the list is Paul's imperative to sing. Augustine was of the opinion that singing is praying twice, and every music director I know believes in the absolute value of congregational singing. But many of us are shy about singing in church, or anywhere outside of the shower. If you cannot sing in public, for vocal or emotional reasons, find a way to incorporate music and singing into your personal prayer. Music expands the spirit and helps us to express more than words can alone. Sometimes a good psalm chant will get you through the day.

GOSPEL: LUKE 2:22–40
"This child is destined to be…a sign that will be opposed."

The holy man and the prophetess are two of the many wonderful signpost characters in Luke's Gospel who recognize the grace at work in the life of a poor couple's child. Simeon has waited all his life for the Anointed One to come. Anna has fasted and prayed for decades in fidelity to her call to prophesy. Both of them receive the gift of a lifetime when Joseph and Mary dutifully enter the temple to present their firstborn son.

Not all of Simeon's predictions are easy to bear, and not all of those who will hear Anna's proclamations about the child will believe them. Grace and destiny unite to make the appearance of this child good news for the nations, but also a piercing reality for many, not the least of whom is the mother of the boy herself.

A family is holy when it does not doubt the relationship between grace and destiny, and commends itself to God's care. As church, we take this opportunity to commend one another as brother and sister to God's grace, which is close at hand.

Questions for Reflection

• If your parents are living, how do you fulfill the command to honor them? If they are deceased, how might you still honor the relationship?

• What item on Paul's list of Christian virtues is most important to you? Which one is hardest to hear and why?

• How do you contribute to the growth of holiness in your family or community?

Action Response

Jesus called those who follow the Gospel brother and sister and parent to him. Who are your spiritual family at this time in your life? Celebrate them as well as your natural family on this feast of the Holy Family.

Your Light Has Come

FIRST READING: ISAIAH 60:1-6
Rise up in splendor, Jerusalem!

Arise! Glow! These words give a more literal rendering of the double imperative with which the prophet opens this proclamation. Imagine the shining city, those beautiful necklaces of lights you see against the dark earth from an airplane. Imagine the beauty and splendor and excitement of your first glimpse of a grand city.

In the prophecy, all nations will come and bring tribute to build up this radiant society. We read this prophecy now as a sign of the reign of God, a reality that is among us and yet just beyond us, shining in the distance, beckoning us to come and be part of it. We know, too, that we are called the "light of the world" by no less a person than Jesus himself. If that radiant society is to be known, we have to become it. That city is built brick by brick with living stones.

SECOND READING: EPHESIANS 3:2-3, 5-6
We are all sharers of the promise.

Hundreds of years before the time of Jesus, Isaiah was prophesying that Gentiles would share in God's plan of salvation with the Jews. Yet the early Christian community was not entirely of that opinion. Peter had a hard time with that idea for quite a while, according to Paul. And "Judaizers"— Jewish Christians who wanted all Gentile Christians to be circumcised and to accept the law—were continually trailing Paul's mission, trying to claim the communities he left behind.

The idea of ecumenism is still relatively young in a church fragmented by the Great Schism with the Orthodox Church (eleventh century) and the ongoing fragmentation of the Reformation (sixteenth century). And interfaith dialogue progresses even more slowly between the Jewish community and the church which often sponsored the persecutions that haunted them.

Some friends of mine and I have started an interfaith supper, meeting once a month to talk about the riches of our respective traditions. In simple ways, we can all be part of the dialogue.

GOSPEL: MATTHEW 2:1–12
We have seen the star at its rising.

The astrologers traveled a long road to Judea following a star. Having reached that country, they naturally went to Jerusalem to make their inquiry. It was the greatest city in the land, and kings are to be found in places like that. Humble Bethlehem, just a few miles down the road, would not have been anyone's first stop.

The astrologers' inquiry reaches the ear of Herod, the present king of the Jews, who had proved to be the sort of man who would slay his own heir if he felt a threat to his power. Herod's advisors locate the birthplace of the child announced in the Scriptures. Herod then calls the astrologers into his presence and gives them the information they seek. He has his own agenda, of course, in sending them on their way.

God's agenda sometimes hijacks ours along the way. The astrologers needed the information only Herod could give them. Herod does not mean to cooperate with the divine plan…but he does. A convenient dream will send the astrologers home by a different route, and the child will be safe.

I am astonished how often my most dismal intentions become waylaid by grace into something redemptive. God knits us back into the plan, so that Christ can be all in all.

Questions for Reflection

• What have you done to carry the light of Christ to others today? What can you do before the sun goes down on another day?

• What are your feelings toward those who believe or worship differently than you do? How do these feelings contribute to or prevent dialogue with others who are "sharers in the promise"?

• How has God reworked your agenda in the past to make some good thing happen?

Action Response

Plan a festival of light! Bring the light of Christ within you to seven people this week. Write a card, make a phone call, visit, listen, share, make a donation, lend a hand. After each encounter, light a candle and pray for those with whom you have shared your faith.

Water and Spirit

FIRST READING: ISAIAH 42:1–4, 6–7
A bruised reed he shall not break.

I know a few people who come in peace, like the servant in this prophecy. They don't break so much as a bruised reed in passing. They don't speak ill of others and they don't participate in gossip, putting a stop to it with a gentle firmness that puts a room to shame. They are never abrupt with people or impatient with events. They do not make jokes that can hurt. Sarcasm and cynicism are foreign to them. They treat everyone with the same gentility, whether rich or poor, pleasant or rude. They reveal no prejudice. They work for justice and refuse acclaim.

Some people find these folks offensive, oddly enough, because of their unwillingness to give offense. People ascribe dark motives of pride or self-righteousness to them, or believe them to be secret hypocrites. Those of us who fear our own weakness and sin will be the first to quench a smoldering wick, attack a weaker person or group. The one who comes in peace is strong enough not to stand on the conquest of others.

SECOND READING: ACTS OF THE APOSTLES 10:34–38
"God shows no partiality."

Peter's presence in Cornelius' house was a wonder in itself. Cornelius was a Gentile centurion, and Peter was a law-abiding Jew. To enter the home of a Gentile made Peter unclean.

It was the sort of thing Peter would not have chosen to do but for the grace of God. Only the day before, Peter had a vision in which God told him not to think in the old categories: "What God has made clean, you are not to call profane." And the day before that, Cornelius had had a vision of an angel who invited him to find Peter. Each of them was responsive to the word they received. And so Peter proclaims the Gospel to the household of Cornelius, and all receive the outpourings of Spirit.

The Spirit prompts us beyond our categories and understandings. Grace takes us to places we've never dreamed of going, and into relationships we have studiously avoided. If we keep all the laws, we will be law-abiding citizens. But if we are called to be people of the Holy Spirit, we will be surprised again and again.

GOSPEL: MARK 1:7–11
"On you my favor rests."

John poured the water, God sent the Spirit. It is the usual cooperation we know as a sacrament. We perform the sign. God provides the grace.

Our cooperation in the event of grace in our world is a significant part of the story. Sometimes we sit on our hands, waiting for God to go to work. We forget the relationship of grace and free will. God waits for the invitation that only our action can provide.

Sacraments have become the language of invitation for Catholics. Also sacramentals, those little signs of reverence or faith that we take on, and prayer itself are a welcoming of God's desire to be with us and act with us. Catholic shrine-making has been a source of amusement or even offense to those who do not see the relationship between sign and response. But all those crosses and pictures and statues ultimately point us back to ourselves, to the indwelling presence that urges us into the partnership of grace.

Questions for Reflection

• Who are the peaceful servants in your community? What can you do to contribute to the work of peace and justice in your relationships?

• How has the Holy Spirit encouraged you beyond your understanding to a new vision?

• What signs or rituals do you regularly participate in to spur your acceptance of God's partnership in grace?

Action Response

In baptism we were each acknowledged as a beloved daughter or son of God. Help someone to know themselves as loved this week through your caring presence and service.

The Sign of the Ark

FIRST READING: GENESIS 9:8–15

This is the sign that I am giving for all ages to come.

Any water story points reflexively to the sacrament of baptism, and the ark that saves life becomes a symbol of what the sacrament does. Yet the water of baptism is as much a symbol of destruction and death as it is a cleansing, purifying source of life. We go under the water as into the flooded earth, and we are drowned to sin and the self-referencing ego. We have passed through the waters as through the tomb, and behold a new creation on the other side.

The story of the ark is about God's power over the corrupting forces of sin, taking creation by storm and washing it clean in a primal act of God. Of all the wonders of creation and the multitude of human lives, only a relative handful will survive. The eight members of Noah's family and the pairs of creatures will become like the loaves and fishes, multiplied again to fill the earth. God saves the faithful remnant, but the price is costly.

Seen through the sign of the ark, the death of the old way leaves ruins in its wake, on its way to the rainbow.

SECOND READING: 1 PETER 3:18–22

This baptism is…the pledge to God of an irreproachable conscience.

The stark phrase "Jesus died for your sins" has an echo of cruelty in it. The death in itself is cruel; but the phrase also seems to imply a cruelty in the human heart. And ultimately it suggests something duplicitous about God: that God is both so good as to sacrifice the Son and so juridical as to demand it.

The theology of Paul dealt with the dilemma naturally from the dispassionate perspective of atonement. The seriousness of the world's sin had become so monstrous by the time of Jesus that only a divine sacrifice could suffer the consequences of sin and remit its effect. The sign of the cross would become the sign of God's sacrifice and the world's wake-up call to forsake sin and cast our hopes upon the atonement of Christ.

Does this mean that "God was pleased to crush him with infirmity," as the suffering servant in Isaiah is crushed? Or is it the nature of love to choose the beloved, even at the risk of suffering, even, at times, at the cost of death? The argument in Peter's letter is about the goodness of Jesus more than the malice in us or the requirements of God. Jesus died for our sins to lead us to God. Our part is not simply to beat our breasts but to follow.

GOSPEL: MARK 1:12–15

He was with the wild beasts, and angels waited on him.

Mark's thesis for his Gospel is no better depicted than in these short verses. God's Spirit drives Jesus into the desert, where Satan is waiting. Between the Spirit and the devil for forty days, Jesus is portrayed as the companion of wild beasts and attended by angels.

What a startling scene! The cosmic dimension of the life of Jesus is a drama first revealed in the wilderness, but never far behind him. The Spirit is tangible. The demons know him by name. These forces we speak of almost metaphorically are in bold relief for Jesus, not simply a way of saying something. He is companioned, even haunted by them. And the way of Jesus from the desert to the cross is intersected continually by these powers at work to aid or destroy him.

His initial response to his time in the wilderness is to take up John's call to repentance. But he also adds a proclamation about the reign of God being fulfilled in the sight of all. Jesus has spoken with demons, and seen the kingdom. No wonder people heard him and were amazed.

Questions for Reflection

• If you were to be baptized today, with a fuller understanding of the call to die to the old way of sin and to live in Christ, what would you be surrendering now? What keeps you from surrendering it?

• The cross was a stumbling block to many in the early church. How is it still an obstacle for some today? Is it an obstacle for you?

• How has the Spirit been tangible for you? Where have you seen demons? What does the nearness of God's reign mean to you?

Action Response

Bring the kingdom a little nearer to your neighbor. Be just. Show mercy. Give forgiveness. Live peace. Walk humbly.

Not Sparing the Beloved

FIRST READING: GENESIS 22:1–2, 9, 10–13, 15–18

God called to him. "Abraham!" "Ready!" he replied.

Abraham said he was ready on that fateful day when God called to him. But he wasn't ready for what he heard. How could he be? God asked for the life of his son, the one born to him when he and Sarah were very old and beyond the hope of children. No parent would be ready for what he heard. It is hard to imagine the state of his heart, his hope, his faith in that hour.

But Abraham got the knife, got the boy, and went. The Lord and Abraham had been companions on a long journey of years and Abraham knew by now that God kept promises. God had promised him children, had granted him this miracle son. Abraham knew anguish now, and confusion, as he trudged up that hill. But he knew one thing more: trust. It had been a hard-won battle over the years, but Abraham had learned not to lie, not to cheat, but to trust.

We have all been on the journey of years. We have lied, cheated, scratched, and crawled to where we are. We have committed countless violences against each other, God's love, and creation itself to get here. God has been faithful. Yet the degree to which we count this journey a success is the degree to which we have learned to trust that God's promises are true. And the world will find a blessing in us when we, like Abraham, are ready.

SECOND READING: ROMANS 8:31–34

Will the one who did not spare the Son…not grant us all things besides?

It is possible for good people to do despicable things. A friend of mine once described himself as "a holy man who is also a rat." The self-knowledge in that phrase is desirable. In my mild-mannered Catholic life I have managed to generate astounding harm upon occasion.

This passage from Romans is good for the days when you feel like a rat and are sure you don't deserve to live. Nothing we can do puts us beyond the mercy and salvation of God. It may feel that way. From this side of sin, the damage control may be well nigh impossible. But God is for us. God did not spare the beloved. God justifies. Jesus intercedes for us. What more can God do to convince us that the plan is salvation, and not condemnation?

GOSPEL: MARK 9:2–10
"How good it is for us to be here."

Consider the subtle transfigurations you have witnessed. A frightened pregnant teenager suddenly looks like a madonna. A heartfelt letter from a friend begins to seem more and more like an epistle. A grassy field becomes a parable. A beggar is Christ. As your eyes focus on one thing, your heart finds another. "The world is charged with the grandeur of God" for those who have eyes to see.

The three great friends of Jesus saw their friend on the mountain one minute, and the glory of God the next. They had been listening to him and watching him for a long time now. They had seen miraculous healings, demons expelled, crowds moved to astonishment by his words. And now, staring at him, they saw light, authority, and the favor of God. Was this something new, or had it been there before? Had their eyes gotten adjusted at last to the vision of Jesus, leaving their blindness behind them?

Since the three did not know what to say on the mountain, Jesus tells them not to say anything at all as they descend. So much can be lost in the transmission of a vision. And a transfiguration is too powerful an image to risk losing it in speech.

Questions for Reflection

• When in your life have you been challenged to trust what you could not understand?

• In light of the abundance of God's mercy shown to you, whom do you still dare to judge?

• Explore moments of transfiguration you have known. How have they changed your way of seeing?

Action Response

Think of someone who drives you crazy, someone you are in conflict with, or some group you experience negatively. Pray for a transfiguration in your way of seeing.

No Other Gods

FIRST READING: EXODUS 20:1–17

You shall not carve idols for yourselves.

Consider what goes into the carving of an idol. First you have to choose a material—wood or clay, stone or metal? Then you have to find the appropriate tool to make the features, sharp or blunt. You have to decide what your God ought to look like: fierce or kind, majestic or simple, watchful or indifferent. You take great care in fashioning your idol. This will be, in the end, what you serve for a long time.

The first commandment forbids the carving of idols, and it is the first commandment we learn to break. When we set our hearts on anything apart from the reign of God, we have already chosen the material for our false god. We carve it with our injustices, our lack of charity, our greed. No matter which features we choose, the face we carve invariably ends up being our own likeness.

If we obey the First Commandment, the others will follow. If we disobey it, it will be all too easy to ignore the others.

SECOND READING: 1 CORINTHIANS 1:22–25

We preach Christ crucified.

The God of the Hebrew Scriptures forbade the making of images of the divine. The Gospels supplied us with the only image we need: the face of Jesus. Carved of flesh and blood like ourselves, this image is born into weakness and capable of suffering and dying. It's an odd God. Nobody would sit down to carve such an image of divinity. No one would have ever spontaneously created a crucifix.

This image of God was a stumbling block to the religious community of the time, seeking the usual theophany of almighty power, God's strong right arm outstretched. The Gentile world, admiring human achievement, ridiculed the apparent human failure of the cross. When the early church chose to preach Christ crucified, they held up a face of God that few could recognize. Yet the cross continues to be the image of God that draws millions to worship and to praise.

GOSPEL: JOHN 2:13–25
"Zeal for your house consumes me."

This story has always prompted two strong reactions in me. The first is: who is *this* Jesus?, and comes from the part of me that has gotten used to the nice guy, wouldn't-hurt-a-fly Jesus I heard about in parochial school. That is the Jesus who is *so* good, they kill him (which is a strange thing to teach a child, if you think about it!).

But the Jesus in this story does not fit the soft image at all. He goes wild with conviction. He destroys property, beats people and animals. When concerned citizens challenge his actions, he gives a mystical answer. Who is this muscular Jesus, this holy man with teeth? Even the Beatitudes sound beefier in light of this revelation.

My second response to this passage is from the gut. I do not think I ever fully trusted the other Jesus of the pale cheek: the victim Lord who is trying to teach spirituality and take care of the sick when he is caught in the crosshairs of a power play between the temple and Rome. That Jesus seemed too innocent. That Jesus could not have wrestled with the Devil in the desert and come up the victor. That Jesus could not have borne the cross with such strength and command. But this Jesus could. He is a man who could be crucified, and a man someone might very well want to kill.

Questions for Reflection

• Consider the idols that tempt you. What are they made of? What are the tools you use to carve them?

• What kind of cross or crucifix is displayed in your church, home, office, or car? Contemplate the images. What does each say about "Christ crucified"?

• How do you feel about people in our contemporary church who behave with zeal? What makes their behavior like Jesus', or different from his?

Action Response

Find an image of the cross or crucifix that you particularly like, or make one. Keep it visible during Lent as a constant meditation on the face of God.

FOURTH SUNDAY OF LENT

A World So Loved

FIRST READING: 2 CHRONICLES 36:14–17, 19–23

Early and often did the Lord...send messengers to them.

In this chronicle of the last days of the kingdom of Israel, the thread finally snaps. The nation has become heedless of its covenant with God, and from the princes to the priests to the people, the abominations mount. The Chaldeans overrun Jerusalem and the people are driven into exile in Babylon.

God had sent messengers in the form of prophets "early and often," but no one had been listening. It is one of the curious details of the Hebrew story that the messenger they finally do heed is the enemy. And by the hand of their enemy comes deliverance: Cyrus, the next king of Persia, will send the remnant of Israel home.

Can God speak to us through the enemy? It is an unsettling thought, but many of the saints swore by their enemies as their best teachers. If you are looking for a real lenten challenge, try hearing what God might be saying through the enemy.

SECOND READING: EPHESIANS 2:4–10

This is not your own doing; it is God's gift.

Imagine yourself at the drawingboard for the plan of salvation. Plan A reads: "Flood the earth and drown all sinners. Build a craft to save the just (not very large.)" There's a red circle with a line through this one.

Plan B: "Give them a precise, exacting law and let them save themselves, if they can." So Paul of Tarsus, the perfect Pharisee, has a winning ticket after many centuries. Anyone else?

Plan C: "Send them prophets, early and often. If they repent, they're in. If they don't, they're deadwood for Gehenna." Well, that's good for a handful of prophets, a king or two, some widows.

The floor is littered with plans. Finally, you find Plan Z: "Save them Myself." According to Paul, that was the plan God settled on. We did not earn it. We do not deserve it. It is not about us, it is about God's plan to save us, no matter how furiously we plan on being lost.

GOSPEL: JOHN 3:14–21
The one who acts in truth comes into the light.

Jesus says we love the darkness, and it's true. There are certain rooms in my life not even wired for electricity. Oh, I don't mind highlighting my religious involvements. I keep my finances pretty clean; my business dealings are not too shady. My relationships with family and friends and others? Well, some can bear a lamplight, others a candle, still others look best by flashlight. And then, of course, there's the place where I keep my skeletons. But it's too dark in there—let's move on....

Jesus came into the world to be the light of the world. Light tells the truth, about our age, what we are doing, who we are with, who is missing, what the story is. Light shows all the seams in our lives, where achievement meets failure, and promise meets pain. We may not want to see so clearly; but the presence of Jesus in our midst demands that we do. As we raise the new Paschal candle in our assembly in just a few weeks, we will see where we are, who is here and who is missing. We will listen to the story again, and be challenged to keep that light held high into the future.

Questions for Reflection

• Who or what are the enemies you face? What is God saying to you through them?

• Have you ever been saved from harm? How did you feel? How does God's gift of salvation compare with that experience?

• Who is missing in your parish: the old, the young, families, single people, the disabled, the poor? Are the reasons for this circumstantial or deliberate?

Action Response

Invite one person who is missing from your local community to come to Mass or services with you between now and Easter.

The Hour Has Come

FIRST READING: JEREMIAH 31:31–34

All, from least to greatest, shall know me, says the Lord.

There are two kinds of rules: the kind imposed on us from the outside, and the ones that spring up from within. Rules imposed from outside us bind us in varying degrees of commitment. They are the easiest rules to ignore when no one's looking and penalties can be avoided because our investment in them is all that gives them currency.

But interior rules are of another order. They are our moral instincts, our personal code of honor. It doesn't matter who is looking or how little reprisal we can expect. We identify with them; they are who we are. To break an interior rule is to lose connection with ourselves and to feel lost.

Jeremiah insists in this oracle that the Lord's new covenant will spring up from the heart of the people of God. It will not be like the law of Moses which came down from on high and was eventually ignored. The law of love would be as close to us as our next heartbeat, and to violate it would be to break our own hearts.

SECOND READING: HEBREWS 5:7–9

Christ offered prayers with loud cries and tears to God.

The unknown writer of the letter to the Hebrews assures us that Jesus was heard in the hour before death, because of his reverence. God was able to save Jesus from death, certainly. But God chose to save Jesus *out* of death, to raise him up from death. God did not circumvent death, but launched straight into it and acted through it.

If it had been God's purpose to save Jesus from dying, an angel could have been dispatched as in the story of Isaac, to stay the hand of the executioner. But as Jesus himself said, in order to prepare a place for us, he had to go there first.

GOSPEL: JOHN 12:20–33

"The hour has come for the Son of Man to be glorified."

Some Gentile converts to Judaism have come to the city for Passover. They find out that Jesus, who has been much in the news lately, is also in town. What luck! They go to Philip, who is from Bethsaida and therefore probably bilingual. He turns to Andrew and together they go to Jesus.

Jesus is aware that the hour on the cosmic clock is the hour of glory. He knows because the Gentiles are now seeking him out, one of the prophetic signs of God's reign foretold in the Scriptures. The hour of glory, he makes rather clear, is also the hour of his death. It is an hour from which one might prefer to be saved, but Jesus cries out for God's glory instead.

A voice gives assent. People argue over what they heard: a clap of thunder? Or the voice of an angel? The crowds do not hear what is apparent to Jesus. Shortly after this revelation, he withdraws from their midst for the last time. Some believe in him. Most do not. But even those who have believed will not forsake human esteem to follow him. Like the Gentiles, they were there while Jesus was still the best show in town.

Questions for Reflection

• List some of your interior rules. Are they part of your unwritten covenant with God? What would be the cost to you to break one?

• Read the agony in the garden scenes in Mark, Matthew, and Luke. Which treatment of Jesus' suffering, including John's stoic portrayal in the Gospel passage for today, is most powerful to you?

• What "grain of wheat" in your life might fall and die to become more?

Action Response

Where in your life might it be inconvenient to see Jesus? Invite him to be there; let him prepare a dwelling place.

Emptying the Self

FIRST READING: ISAIAH 50:4–7

God opens my ear that I may hear.

Take a few moments to read the four Servant Songs in Isaiah, of which this passage is the third (see Isaiah 42, 49, 50, 52–53.) Christian scholars have seen the mission of Jesus mirrored powerfully in these oracles. In the first two, the call of the servant is benign and noble-sounding. The servant of the Lord will bring forth justice as the world awaits his teaching. Called from birth to serve God, the servant is gentle, unwilling to break a bruised reed. He is a polished arrow in God's quiver, a light to the nations.

But in the third song, the message turns darker. The servant speaks eloquently, but he is rejected. He does not turn back, even as he receives beatings, is spat upon, and humiliated. And in the final oracle, death comes for the servant. The same kings stand speechless, not in honor this time but in horror. The servant is offered as a sacrifice for sin. He is buried in ignominy. Yet that is not all. The servant will have his reward, and many will be blessed through his surrender.

These four songs provide an unpopular sense of what God's anointed one (Messiah) might do, and were therefore largely rejected by those who awaited redemption. But it is clear that Jesus looked into the portrait of the servant and recognized his own way.

SECOND READING: PHILIPPIANS 2:6–11

He did not deem equality with God something to be grasped at.

Paul follows the trajectory of Isaiah's servant in this hymn to Christ the Lord. Jesus as the word of God from the beginning of time has the form of God, but lets it go to take on our likeness. The noble one becomes the humble one, a thing we seldom see in our world. He goes down into humiliation and death and is lifted up to unsurpassable glory.

We who do not empty ourselves can only marvel at his example. We are very full of ourselves, our activities and our plans. From time to time something will empty us, in one way or another, but we will not voluntarily give much away.

But really, nothing is ours; our lives are full of people and things we have gotten used to having around, that's all. The practice of self-emptying may not be easy, but it is the path down which life is taking us just the same.

GOSPEL: MARK 14:1—15:47
The Son of Man is going the way the Scripture tells of him.

Peter was arguably the best friend Jesus ever had in this world. On the way to the Mount of Olives, Peter swears: "Even though all are shaken in faith, it will not be that way with me.... Even if I have to die with you, I will not disown you." We know he is in earnest. Yet at Gethsemane, Jesus points out that Peter can't even stay awake with him for one hour. And he flees with the others a few moments later.

But you have to hand it to Peter. He finds his way to the high priest's courtyard and waits nearby for news. Just like his noble words earlier, this brave act is belied almost at once by three betrayals of Jesus. When the cock crows, such self-knowledge is bitter enough to make a fisherman cry.

And so Peter vanishes. He is not the one to help Jesus carry the cross, not there while Jesus is crucified and jeered at. He is not there when his Lord dies and not the one to declare, "Clearly he was the Son of God!" It is left for outsiders and a few women with nothing to lose to do these things. The real hope in Peter's story is that he still gets the keys. Despite the many times our discipleship falls through, our friendship with Jesus is not forfeit.

Questions for Reflection

• The servant of the Lord is also the ideal model for discipleship. Compare yourself to this portrait. How alike are you?

• Consider a time when life has emptied you. What did that experience teach you?

• Imagine you are Peter, living through the events of the Passion reading. What would you say to Jesus when you meet again? How do those words resemble your prayers of contrition in this season?

Action Response

Choose a way to empty yourself this week. Lighten your purse with charity. Listen instead of talking. Give your attention rather than seeking it. Be humble when you would normally be proud.

Witnesses

FIRST READING: ACTS OF THE APOSTLES 10:34, 37–43
We are witnesses to all that Jesus did.

To Peter, it all comes down to testimony. He offers this address in the home of Cornelius, a Gentile. You've heard the news about Jesus, he tells them. It would have been hard news to miss in those days. "I and my friends are witnesses to all that you've heard," Peter insists. He is not only a witness to the life and ministry of Jesus but has also seen him and eaten with him after his resurrection. Those who have done so share a commission to witness to Jesus as "judge of the living and the dead." All the prophets testify as well that sins are forgiven through his name.

Count the number of times Peter says witness. Once the frightened denier, he is now the bold testifier to the Gospel. Through the bitterest experience, he has learned that the most important job of a disciple is to profess publicly in word and deed that Jesus is Lord. No one's testimony could be harder won than his.

SECOND READING: COLOSSIANS 3:1–4
Set your heart on what pertains to higher realms.

It is Easter. You made it. Whatever your little self-denials may have been this season, you can lay them down now and relax. Some things have become new habits, like a regular time for prayer or curbing the impulse to indulge some behavior. These forty days may have led you to some new resolve in your life that you can take with you into the new season and beyond.

But whatever the exterior journey has been, Paul reminds us in this letter that the point is always Christ. The Colossians were focused on the outward trappings of piety and purity, and got caught up in angelology and rules and regulations. But you have died to all of that, Paul says earnestly. Set your heart on Christ. It is too easy for us to become caught in a personal quest for holiness or perfection and forget what is essential. It is better to be a sinner searching for Christ than a saint who does not know him.

GOSPEL: JOHN 20:1–9
"The Lord has been taken from the tomb!"

In Journalism 101, there is an exercise in scene-of-the-accident reporting: taking the same facts, write four reports of the same accident. Slant each one a different way. The truth, you realize quickly, is not in the facts. It is in finding the correct interpretation.

The empty tomb is a study in interpretation. In John's Gospel, the facts are reported one at a time, like clues to a mystery. In the darkness, Mary Magdalene sees the stone rolled away, and runs to get the others. All she knows is that the body of Jesus is gone. The disciple who is with Peter arrives at the tomb next, and sees the wrappings on the ground. Finally, Peter arrives and notes also that the head covering is neatly rolled in place. The first disciple enters the tomb, sees, and believes.

Believes what? The writer states plainly that they did not understand about rising from the dead. John permits the hearer of this Gospel to become the unnamed disciple, to consider the facts and make an interpretation. Do you believe? And what is it you believe?

When we each arrive at the empty tomb on Easter morning, our witness is required of us.

Questions for Reflection

• Do you deny Jesus, not with your lips but with your actions? Think of a place in your life where your fear, unforgiveness, or indifference overshadows your faith.

• Is Christ the center of your life, or are you? Support your answer. What would you have to change to set your heart on higher realms?

• What do you believe about the events of Easter Sunday? How do you witness to what you believe?

Action Response

Find life where there is only death. Revisit a ruined relationship, an unhealed memory, and ask God to grow new life in the barren place.

Get the Story Straight

FIRST READING: ACTS OF THE APOSTLES 4:32–35

None of them ever claimed anything as his own.

The Greek term *koinonia* means the bond of responsibility believers in the Gospel share toward one another. It isn't such a rare idea. Religious communities strive for it. Parishes within each diocese commit to it. And families, the most fundamental of society's institutions, are bound to it. Koinonia should not seem such an amazing ideal as it does.

Yet we read these words from Acts and are in wonder at the utopian sound of it all. We know our families don't resemble Norman Rockwell paintings. We know every attempt at building a utopian society, from the communes of the sixties to entire political systems, has not succeeded. Every group dedicated to social justice houses its own injustices.

Yet just because our families, our parishes, and our governments are not idyllic does not mean we abandon them. Nor should we throw up our hands at the ideal and say cynically, "That's just not the way the world is." That *is* the way of the reign of God. The closer we can match the spirit of Acts, the closer the kingdom will come.

SECOND READING: 1 JOHN 5:1–6

Who, then, is conqueror of the world?

To the writer of the Johannine tradition, the one who conquers the world is the one who knows the truth of the Gospel. Writing around the end of the first century, this writer was combating some new heresies that would continue to haunt the church even to our times. One is that Jesus was not the Messiah of Israel or the Son of God. The other was the opposite: the idea that Jesus was surely God, but hardly one of us.

John calls three witnesses to testify to the truth of Jesus Christ: the water, the blood, and the Spirit. The water of Christ's baptism called forth the voice of God: this is my beloved Son. The blood poured out on the cross was human blood, as painful and costly as the bloodshed of any of us. The Spirit at work in the community assures us that the life of Jesus "remains" (John's favorite word) and lives in us until the end of the ages.

These three witnesses remain in the church. Our baptism, Eucharist, and the Spirit alive in our community continue to be the testimony the world depends on to know the truth about Jesus Christ.

GOSPEL: JOHN 20:19–31
"Receive the Holy Spirit."

When Luke tells his story of Pentecost in Acts, Jesus is already returned to the Father. The point of the story is how the church begins its powerful ministry of preaching and witness. At the descent of the Spirit, the disciples are led to proclaim the Gospel in the streets. Three thousand are baptized that first day.

But John's audience is a church under persecution, and they have gone underground. The quiet reception of the Holy Spirit behind locked doors mirrors something of their situation, just as Luke's account was meant to inspire like activity in his.

John's story concludes with the singular plight of Thomas, the one who was not there. Faith comes harder for the one who did not see for himself. When we call Thomas the doubter, we should remember that he stands in for all of us "who have not seen" and struggle to believe. Through faith, each of us can answer, "My Lord and my God!"

Questions for Reflection

• With whom do you live *koinonia*, the life in common bound by responsibility? Your family? Friends? Coworkers? Parish? What are the responsibilities you bear for one another?

• Think of the testimonies of water, blood, and Spirit in your own life. How do they speak to you as a believer?

• How do you react to Thomas: positively, negatively, or sympathetically? What keeps you from believing, and what helps you to believe?

Action Response

Call a meeting with your family or primary community. Make a list of what works well in your life in common, and what needs work. Allow each person to choose one way he or she can contribute to greater harmony.

THIRD SUNDAY OF EASTER

The Witness Begins

FIRST READING: ACTS OF THE APOSTLES 3:13–15, 17–19

"God raised Jesus from the dead, and we are his witnesses."

To appreciate Peter's speech, consider the background. Peter and John had been on their way into the temple for daily prayer. A man crippled from birth is sitting in his usual spot and asks Peter for spare change. Peter admits he is broke but will give what he has: the name of Jesus Christ. At that, Peter seizes the man and drags him to his feet, whole.

As the man dances about, an astonished crowd gathers. Peter takes this opportunity to disown all personal authority in the healing. Instead, he preaches about Jesus, the Servant of God, the Holy and Just One, the Author of Life. He accuses the people very harshly for their part in putting Jesus to death. It is this Jesus who has caused the wonder they now see.

Peter and John are taken into custody by the temple guard for this speech, by the way. And so is the beggar. It is wonderful to see the change in Peter, no longer afraid to own Jesus but willing to proclaim his name at any cost. Some thirty years later, Peter will be crucified for speaking that name.

SECOND READING: 1 JOHN 2:1–5

The one who claims, "I have known him," without keeping his commandments, is a liar.

The term "justification by faith" is often used in the great theology wars. Defined simply, it means that faith and faith alone can save us. It is no good trying to purchase paradise with good works, donations to God's favorite charities, or winning God's favor by being good people.

Few Christians would deny justification by faith, but some have interpreted it radically, saying faith is all you need and what you do after that does not count for anything. John begs to differ here. To say you know Jesus and to live like you don't simply makes you a liar. John uses the argument also defended in James (see James 2:14), that sure knowledge of Christ is revealed by the one who also keeps his commandments. If our lives do not profess Christ, then we can save our breath professing him in words.

154

One can only presume that John is writing this because such people are moving within his community, saying, "Lord, Lord," and living like the pagans. Justification by faith is the great gift of God's generous love. It was never meant to be a license to sin.

GOSPEL: LUKE 24:35–48
"Recall those words I spoke to you when I was still with you."

Jesus tells his disciples that the law of Moses, the prophetic tradition, and the great prayerbook the people have been using for centuries all spoke of his coming and its meaning for human history. This is one of the reasons that Catholics don't simply use the Christian Scriptures (New Testament), but include the Hebrew Scriptures (Old Testament) among the books of our canon.

If we really want to understand who Jesus is, we have to know the whole story of salvation. The scriptures of our lives open up to us in the same way. Things happen through the years, seemingly random and unconnected. The only common point of reference is that they happen to us. And then one day we look back and see God's fingerprints all over our story, clear and undeniable. A moment of grace is given to us, and we see what God was saying to us all along.

Questions for Reflection

• Often we are "broke" when people ask for help, money, time, or sympathy from us. Peter gave what he had. What do you give to those who reach out to you?

• Faith alone will save us. But how do people recognize you are a person of faith?

• Where do you find the fingerprints of God? Tell a story of when God moved powerfully in your life, even if you didn't see it at the time.

Action Response

Choose three stories in the Bible which are personally meaningful for you. Reread them this week and meditate on the significance, beauty, or hope they hold for you.

A Life Given Freely

FIRST READING: ACTS OF THE APOSTLES 4:8–12

This Jesus is "the stone rejected by you the builders which has become the cornerstone."

The image of the rejected cornerstone was a popular proverb. Although it first appears in Psalm 118 in celebration of Israel's triumph in battle, early Christianity adopted it as a metaphor for the crucifixion. Jesus, rejected by his own people, is revealed to be the savior of the world.

A thing is valued, in the end, not for its worth in itself but in the way it is built into the whole. An execution, if anything, has a negative value, and crucifixion is a shameful, painful death, not to be prized or praised. Jesus, executed as a criminal against the state and the temple, regarded as a blasphemer and friend of the devil, is discarded as a man with no value, a life that is in the way, as Caiaphas almost said.

Ironically, Jesus is not *in* the way but in fact *is* the Way, not a blasphemer but the Truth, not dead but the Life for all who will hear the Gospel. As Peter explains this to the elders of the Sanhedrin, one can imagine he is not reaching sympathetic ears. They will let him and John and the beggar go, not because they believe Peter but because they are, typically, afraid of the crowds. The cornerstone, as Paul once observed, remains a stumbling block.

SECOND READING: 1 JOHN 3:1–2

Dearly beloved, we are God's children now.

John uses the term "world" in a technical way. The world is anything that is opposed to the Gospel. The children of light, the Christians, have been separated out from the darkness which is the world. That separation caused great sacrifice and could mean the forfeiting of life itself. But only life in the world, of course, which is passing.

I wonder how the words of John sound to us, separated by twenty centuries. We find ourselves, for the most part, in harmony with the world. We consider ourselves good citizens, the very champions of family values, and do not think of arraying ourselves for spiritual battle. The war is over, and we are ready to sleep through the turning of another millennium.

But that would be a mistake, I think. There still is a world in opposition to the Gospel and its law of love, justice, and peace. The war is far from over, and we dare not find ourselves the strange bedfellows of cozy values that harden our hearts to the poor one at our door.

GOSPEL: JOHN 10:11–18
"No one takes my life from me; I lay it down freely."

The Pharisees, to whom this teaching is directed, recognize themselves in the image of the hired hand who abandons the sheep when danger is imminent. It is not a flattering image, which is one of the reasons they are eager to see Jesus killed. But Jesus warns them here and elsewhere that his death, the one thing they both agree on, will come on his terms, at the chosen hour, for his Father's purposes. Their role in this matter is decidedly peripheral.

Even while offering us the gentle and pastoral metaphor of the good shepherd, Jesus has his gaze fixed on the horizon and the cross. We might paint him with the lost sheep draped around his neck, a kindly smile at his lips. But in John's portrayal of Jesus, being the good shepherd means countering the wolf and being torn to pieces. For the sake of those who are his own in the world, Jesus has come to be glorified through this very act.

Questions for Reflection

• What are the "rejected cornerstones" in your life? Why were they rejected, and what made their value apparent?

• Using John's understanding of "world" as anything opposed to the light of Christ, what belongs to the "world" that is an obstacle to your faith today?

• Do you like John's Gospel the most or the least of the four Gospels? What makes you feel differently about it?

Action Response

Examine the current cornerstone of your daily life. Does it support or contradict the message of faith? Observe how it functions in your life for a few days, and make a discernment on its value to your life as a Christian.

Trimming the Fruitful Branch

FIRST READING: ACTS OF THE APOSTLES 9:26–31

They even refused to believe that he was a disciple.

The Jewish community in Damascus who saw the upstart Christian follow-ers as a threat had been expecting Saul to come and reassert the authority of the temple with his mandate. Imagine their surprise when he showed up in town entirely blind, led by the men who had come with him from Jerusalem. And then a Christian named Ananias visited with him, restored his sight, and baptized him. Saul, once the hope of the orthodox crowd, was now preaching Christ in the synagogues of Damascus!

So they sought to kill him as a traitor, and he fled to the Christians in Jerusalem. And were they happy to see him? No. They did not believe him any more than they believed the reports they had heard about his so-called conversion. If Paul had not been fortunate in gaining the trust of Barnabas, chances are he would have been shunned on both sides.

Conversion is not a simple matter of transferring allegiance. Any person who has ever made a strong life choice can tell the story just as well. You may change dramatically, but the people around you may not adapt to or support your decision. Friends and loved ones are often the last people who will give you permission to change. The conviction that you are choosing the light may have to sustain you for a long while.

SECOND READING: 1 JOHN 3:18–24

Little children, let us love in deed and in truth and not merely talk about it.

There is a constant underplay in John about the futility of verbal testimony alone. We cannot "merely talk about it," but we have to become the word we speak. God is love and we must love and that is the root and heart of our testimony. Even believing in the name of Jesus Christ is paired immediate-ly with loving one another (verse 23). If we are justified by our faith alone (again, that's Paul's term for salvation by faith), then our faith is evidenced by its incarnation "in deed and in truth."

Maybe you are thinking this is all very obvious. Well, it is. It is like the child's game of matching faces with the appropriate description. Even small children know a joyful person is indicated by a happy face, and a sad person by a crying face. Believing Christians should be as self-evident. Our piety—defined by the church as right relationship with God, self, others—should be clear across our lives.

GOSPEL: JOHN 15:1–8
"My Father has been glorified in your bearing much fruit."

Have you ever tried to prune your life clean of the deadwood? Our lives are full of stuff, events, and folks that don't do us any good as disciples of Jesus. During his Last Supper discourse, Jesus says God prunes away the barren branches altogether and even trims clean the fruitful ones to make them more fruitful. In order to be counted among the fruitful, there is much we can do—or perhaps stop doing.

For years, I was doing too many things. Many of them were good things, at least potentially. Then a day came when I was given an opportunity to do a great good—but there was a price. I had to cut my present commitments down by about eighty percent and decide what was really important. In order to be more fruitful, I had to be seriously pruned.

The process of pruning can be painful, but the life it yields is the life God has promised us. The fruitful as well as the unfruitful branch need cutting from time to time. Springtime is a good season for the procedure.

Questions for Reflection

• Do the people in your life support you or resist you in your attempts to change and grow? How and why?

• Where in your life are you loved? Where in your life do you show your love?

• Have you ever made a decision to prune your life free of useless stuff, events, or folks? Have you ever been pruned involuntarily? What were the results?

Action Response

Mark one branch in your life for cutting, another for trimming. Get rid of the old self, make way for the new.

The Love Command

FIRST READING: ACTS OF THE APOSTLES 10:25-26, 34-35, 44-48

"I begin to see how true it is that God shows no partiality."

The first followers of Jesus were, like Jesus, observant Jews. A naturally closed and wary community (for very good historical reasons), they could not imagine that God was interested in the life and times of non-Jews. Those who accepted the message of Jesus were mostly convinced that what he said and did was for them. The Gentile world had no share in it.

Some were willing to consider that Jesus could be a phenomenon for non-Jews. But those who became Christians had to become Jews as well, circumcision, law, and all. Paul spent his entire ministry fighting this mentality, arguing that Gentile Christians were under no obligation to become Jews.

Today, we see these tensions as of historical interest. Jews and Christians have gone their separate theological ways. Catholics since Vatican II have even adjusted to the idea that Protestants have a crack at salvation. But even as ecumenical and interfaith dialogues have softened the "us" and "them" in the obvious groups, we still find categories of persons to shun. And we insist God does too. Historically speaking, this policy tends to backfire.

SECOND READING: 1 JOHN 4:7-10

Love, then, consists in this: not that we have loved God, but that God has loved us.

Here is the best answer to give someone who wonders why we should not shun categories of persons, as in the previous discussion. The decision to love is not ours, it is God's. We are not loved because we are acceptable to God. God loves us which makes us acceptable. Anything that is of love comes from God, and there is no love apart from God. So "everyone who loves is from God and knows God," even if they are not our kind of people.

Jesus was not about to waste time rounding up those who were already doing God's will. He spends a surprising amount of time preaching to and against the scribes, Pharisees, and Sadducees. He knew that converting even one of them was a victory of major proportions, since the damage each of these teachers could inflict on the populace was so great. I wonder who

Jesus would direct a campaign against in our day. We might be startled not to find any of the groups we rail against on his list.

GOSPEL: JOHN 15:9–17

"It was not you who chose me, it was I who chose you."

Jesus offers his disciples his love, joy, and friendship—all this, only hours before he is to die. The depth of that love will soon be revealed on the cross. The intensity of that joy will be felt when they see him again, and he breathes over them the gift of his Spirit. The meaning of his friendship will be made known in the unfolding of the years, in the companionship of the Spirit which remains until the end of time.

The first disciples knew they had not chosen to follow Jesus, not really. Jesus extended the call and they came voluntarily enough. But their decision to come was based on the initiative of the one who asked. Had Jesus not extended that personal invitation, most of these fishermen would still be fishing.

The call to follow Jesus comes from Jesus himself, his compelling life, his passionate death, his startling summons to new life in the kingdom. Each of us was chosen and called, personally, to be disciples. Whether we "go forth and bear fruit," however, is up to us.

Questions for Reflection

- Make a list of groups that fall under the general categories of "us" and "them" in your community. How might the fact that they are included in God's plan of salvation change your relationship to "them"?
- Consider: God loves you before you do a single thing to change your life. What is your response to that kind of love?
- Jesus calls you to come and follow. Who in your life has supported you in understanding that call?

Action Response

Cross the lines between "us" and "them" this week. Take a public stand, give a donation, defend "them" against slurs in conversation, pray for "them" and their needs. And start calling them "us."

ASCENSION

Signs Like These

FIRST READING: ACTS OF THE APOSTLES 1:1–11
"Wait for the fulfillment of my Father's promise."

Waiting would be easy if not for mortality. The fact is, we all have a set number of years to our lives, and all sorts of plans as to how we would like to spend them. Waiting is not high on anyone's list. We want to go, we want to do things, we have places we would rather be.

After the resurrection and the reappearance of Jesus, the disciples are understandably rarin' to go. They are ready to take the world of Judea by storm. They want to race back to Galilee and tell the rest of the story to those who had their doubts. But Jesus says: wait. He knows they are not yet ready. Something is missing in their grasp of the story, and the missing piece is crucial. The Advocate has not yet made a home in them, and anything they might say would do more harm than good to the mission.

New adult Catholics, still in the period of formation after Easter, or renewed Catholics of many kinds often fall into the same trap. They want to become priests or sisters; they want to become missionaries to Africa; they want to convert their families to the same zeal they are experiencing. To say "wait" sounds like discouragement, when it is simply prudent. When the Spirit calls, the time will be right.

SECOND READING: EPHESIANS 1:17–23
God grant you a spirit of wisdom and insight to know him clearly.

How do you get to know someone better? You spend time with them, of course. You do things together, build up a common frame of reference, a mutual history. You share stories of your life. You dream together about the future. You open your heart.

How do we get to know God better? It is much the same process. The stories of salvation history tell us about God's story, at least so far as human eyes and ears can apprehend it. In the stories of Jesus most of all, we can see and hear what God has longed to share with us through all time. God loves, has compassion, forgives, and delights in us. God wants us to be happy, and is willing to shepherd us along the way of true happiness, if we will walk in the way of love and truth. The Spirit of wisdom is ready to lead us to the "wealth of God's glorious heritage," the perfect world we know as the kingdom of God. God's reign is a peace we can know right now.

GOSPEL: MARK 16:15–20
"Signs like these will accompany those who have professed their faith...."

I admit, I have not seen demons expelled by the name of Jesus, snake-handlers, or poison-drinkers. I have been in places where ecstatic speech is spoken, but the phenomenon was not given to me. I have seen some people healed by the power of prayer, but many more who remained sick and did not recover. Signs like these are very rare in the church, after twenty centuries.

But I have seen signs of the power of faith that are just as miraculous to the people who experience them. I have seen alcoholics stop drinking and reunite with their long-suffering families. I have known people whose lives are darkened by depression lift up their faces and see the light. I have seen those injured by the memory of a difficult childhood freed from the burden of the past and able to receive a future of happiness. I have known those tortured by a life of sin rescued from their demons through the power of love.

Signs like these happen all around us. We need to believe in them, testify to them, and live them out courageously. If ascension means being lifted up, then all of us know what that is like. And we all know someone who needs to be lifted up through our efforts.

Questions for Reflection

• What have you learned through the practice of waiting? About yourself? About the world? About God?

• What efforts do you make to get to know God better?

• Tell a story of when you have been lifted up. Who needs to be lifted up in your community?

Action Response

Wait on the Holy Spirit. This kind of waiting is not passive. It is not about sitting on your hands, but lifting them up in prayer and confidence. Pray for a release of the Spirit in you, in your parish, in your community, upon the world.

SEVENTH SUNDAY OF EASTER

That All May Be One

FIRST READING: ACTS OF THE APOSTLES 1:15–17, 20–26
"O Lord, you read the human heart."

This lectionary passage is a real fill-in-the-blanks. If you read the deleted verses in Acts, you find an alternative rendering of the death of Judas to the one we are used to in Matthew. If you look at Psalm 41:10, you find out what David's prophecy regarding Judas was. And if you look all over the New Testament, you find out that Matthias was…was….

You will find that Matthias was not mentioned before or since his election to the Twelve. But a lot has been written about Matthias nonetheless. An apocryphal work, "The Acts of Andrew and Matthias," tells of his being captured by cannibals while preaching to them about Jesus. (Don't worry, Andrew rescues him.) A Gospel of Matthias is mentioned in writings by church fathers, and "The Traditions of Matthias" is another writing that was likely used by a certain group of gnostics.

For a fellow hardly mentioned in the Scripture, he has quite a heritage. What we are told of him canonically is that he and the other fellow were chosen for the lottery because they were both with Jesus throughout his ministry. This leads to the most interesting question of all: if these two were with Jesus all along, and we never heard of them, how many more anonymous followers of Jesus were there?

SECOND READING: 1 JOHN 4:11–16

God is love, and the one who abides in love, abides in God.

The writings of John are the impassioned letters of a lover. If you have never been in love, never spoken the involuntary poetry of one lost to passion and union with the beloved, then John's writings sound like mad ramblings. He says the same things over and over again, when the whole passage could be reduced to one sentence: God is love, and we should be likewise.

If you have experienced the indwelling love of God inspiring your heart to love beyond human limits, then reading John is a pleasure of recognition. If you have not yet had this experience, then reading John is a mystery. Fall in love with God? Live in God's love and let God's love live in us, the way lovers exist as one soul, dwelling one within the other? Anyone who has ventured this close to the mystery knows this is the inevitable next step.

GOSPEL: JOHN 17:11-19
"I do not ask you to take them out of the world, but to guard them from the evil one."

This is the great Prayer for Unity that Jesus offers during his last evening with his friends. It is Jesus' great hope for us, the church, that we may be one, united as Jesus is to his Father. To be "catholic" means to be of one spirit throughout the world. It is our testimony, and also our hardest task.

Jesus speaks about "the world" again, using John's technical term for every spirit opposed to the Gospel. He prays that his disciples do not give in to the "evil one," the spirit of darkness that draws us into selfish disregard of the love command and our responsibility to God and one another. We are called to be children of the light and the new day.

The curious thing about the Prayer for Unity is that Jesus does not pray for the disciples to be taken "out of the world" and preserved from contact with it. Jesus knows that the proper place of the disciples is in the world, witnessing against it with their faithful example, just as he did. Those still caught within the world and its reign of death need the church—that's us— to shine our light and help them find their way.

Questions for Reflection

- Many disciples whom we do not hear about were part of the story of Jesus' ministry. What are the implications of that for groups within the church whose service is anonymous or unrecognized?
- Reflect on the experience of being deeply in love. How is this like or unlike your relationship to God?
- What does the unity of the church mean for you? Do you think it is threatened in our day by the spirit of dissent?

Action Response

In some aspect of your life, your testimony to the "world" is needed. Think of one thing you can do to make it clear which side you're on. Someone may be seeking your witness.

All Heaven Breaks Loose

FIRST READING: ACTS OF THE APOSTLES 2:1–11

There came a noise like a strong driving wind which was heard all through the house.

We need Pentecost to happen again. We need Pentecost to happen in every household, in every assembly, wherever two or more are gathered. We need Pentecost to drive us into the streets compelled to speak of the things of God. We need the Spirit, the forcefulness, the commitment, and the wonder to fire the heart of the church again.

And then again, we really don't. That same Spirit is available to us, in every hour. We are temples of the Holy Spirit, and God's Spirit dwells in us like a perpetual tongue of fire. This Spirit blows through the church searching for a heart willing to be transfigured by grace. But most of the time, we close our doors, and blow out the light. We do not want to be changed.

What if we welcomed into our lives a personal Pentecost? What if the sacred wind blew through our lives and took away our attachments to the old way of being, and the fire burned within us to bring Christ to the world through love? What if we were driven into the streets, the marketplace, the parish, the homes of friends, as witnesses of what we say we believe? The church, the real church of Pentecost, is waiting to be born in us all the time.

SECOND READING: 1 CORINTHIANS 12:3–7, 12–13

All of us have been given to drink of the one Spirit.

The community at Corinth was particularly impressed by those among them who spoke in tongues, and they decided only these people really had the Holy Spirit in them. Yet Paul spends a good part of this letter affirming the other gifts that testify as well to the presence of the Spirit in a person of faith. He points out that some are called to be apostles, sent out to preach the Gospel. Some have the gift of prophecy, others can teach. Some can do "mighty deeds," as Jesus said his disciples would do. Some have the gift of healing, or service, or administration.

We are not supposed to get hung up on thinking one gift is definitive for

Christians to have. But it is easy to envy the ministry of others and say, "They are really living the life of the Spirit," or "God really works through them most of all." Paul says "no" to this kind of mental hierarchy. Whatever gifts we have, if we exercise them in the ministry of love, are as vital to the church as any other.

GOSPEL: JOHN 20:19–23
"As the Father has sent me, so I send you."

The contrast between Luke's version of the sending of the Spirit and John's is remarkable. Where Luke shows us fire and excitement, John emphasizes peace and forgiveness.

Peace and forgiveness. An inseparable bond exists between the two. The unforgiving and the unforgiven live without peace, mutually tied to the sin which divides them. Peace requires forgiveness, and forgiveness restores peace. Even as Jesus gives his disciples the gift of peace, he bestows the power of binding and loosing sin through forgiveness.

Our willingness to forgive others sets them free to live at peace again. Our desire to hold them bound is a refusal of the gift of Christian peace. The celebration of the church's anniversary at Pentecost is a time for both Luke's vision and John's. We must be that church aflame with the Spirit of the resurrection. And we must also be the community of forgiveness. This is the peace the world cannot give. If it does not come from us, from whom will it come?

Questions for Reflection

- If a sacred wind blew through your life, what would be blown away? If a holy fire was lit in your heart, what would you be led to do?
- Which gifts that Paul mentions most closely reflect your personal gifts? How do you use them in the service of the church?
- Reflect on experiences you have had of being forgiven, or being able to forgive. How is this peace central to the mission of the church?

Action Response

The fire of Luke, or the forgiveness of John: choose the Pentecost God is calling you to express. Invite the Holy Spirit to be manifest in you, and be willing to follow.

TRINITY SUNDAY

The Road Out

FIRST READING: DEUTERONOMY 4:32–34, 39–40

"Did anything so great ever happen before?"

The Book of Deuteronomy is written as Moses' last sermon. He delivers it before Israel will follow Joshua across the Jordan and into the Promised Land. Moses is not going. After forty years of carrying these people, he is about to lay his burden down and be gathered to the Lord.

So Moses tells the Exodus story again, to be sure the people have got it right. Exodus means "the road out." The people have been led out of Egypt, out of slavery, and out of ignorance. They have a new home stretched before them, new freedom, and a law to teach them God's will. They have seen the signs and wonders. They have been delivered. They have everything they need. All they have to do is remember what they know.

But very soon, the people of Exodus will forget their God, their law, and their history. They will choose the road back in, the one that returns to the slavery of sin and idolatry. And they will lose their home and be sent into exile. Moses' final exhortation will become, along with the Book of Psalms, the favorite texts of rabbis for centuries to come, including Jesus. Remember what God has done for you. Know and fix in your heart the One who is your Lord.

SECOND READING: ROMANS 8:14–17

The Spirit gives witness with our spirit that we are children of God.

What does it mean to be a child of God? Jesus said we have to become like children, and he did not mean cuddly and innocent. We have to be willing to learn from scratch. We have to be willing to be taught and led. We have to trust in God as children must trust their guardians for their very survival. We have to be willing to rejoice in our weakness, as Paul says elsewhere, "for in weakness power reaches perfection."

Well. That's a hard way to go for people who pride ourselves on self-sufficiency, independence, and strength. The freedom of the children of God is the freedom to rely utterly on God's power lived out through the Spirit. For many of us, becoming this kind of child is not comforting. Slavery to self-reliance, even if it makes us orphans, is something that gives us the control we have grown used to.

GOSPEL: MATTHEW 28:16–20
"And know that I am with you always, until the end of the world!"

This reading puts the trinity in Trinity Sunday, with the baptismal formula established for all time. The Father who creates, the Son who redeems, and the Spirit who makes holy are revealed in this image of "unity in community." God is one, and acts as three. Catholics are comfortable in this mystery.

To explain the mystery of the Trinity, I once tried to use the image of Neapolitan ice cream: three flavors in one box. All equally ice cream, but distinct in themselves. Some people were offended by the banality of the comparison. Others did not know what Neapolitan ice cream is. And many people immediately tried to assign the flavors, certain that the least important should be strawberry and God the Creator must be chocolate.

This attempt taught me why the church would rather refer to the Trinity as a mystery. And so I am happy to accept today that the Trinity, in whatever way that Divinity exists within Trinity, will be with us on the road out, to the end of time.

Questions for Reflection

• When have you had a clear perception that "the Lord is God and there is no other" in your life? How do the circumstances compare to those of Israel in the desert?

• If being a child of God means learning from scratch, what one thing might you have to unlearn?

• Which revelation of God is most powerful for you: Creator, Redeemer, or Sanctifier? Has this choice changed for you over the years?

Action Response

Draw a map of your journey through the years. Consider where you may have taken the road out to liberation, or where you might encounter that road in the future.

Covenants of Blood

FIRST READING: EXODUS 24:3–8

"All that the Lord has said, we will heed and do."

Covenants of ancient times had three main qualities: they were made between unequal parties, they were serious, and they were bloody. Since covenants were often made between a king and his people, they were treaties that brought some sense of benefit or ownership to the king while offering protection to the people. They were not about trivial matters but lifelong commitments of responsibility and allegiance. And the blood?

Blood was the sealing factor in the covenant. Blood meant "take my life if I break this oath." It was a very sobering moment in the covenant ceremony. As the people stood before Moses and received the sprinkling of blood at Mount Sinai, they must have remembered the earlier blood of the Passover lamb in Egypt. And they could not have been ignorant of the message of their circumcision. The blood tie between Israel and the Lord was marked in the flesh of every male among them. If this covenant were broken, someone would pay for it with his life. At Mount Sinai that day, could anyone have dreamed it would be the Lord?

SECOND READING: HEBREWS 9:11–15

Christ is mediator of a new covenant.

The economy of salvation is not quite the same as our local economy. It is not about supply and demand, or the rise and fall of interconnected factors. It is simplistic to say: the blood of Jesus was required to wash away our sins. Redemption, the notion of bartering for a pawned item, did not include Jesus as a puppet for God's purposes. Only an ill-examined theology would claim that God required the death of God to achieve the divine purpose.

The story of Jesus is the story of freely chosen love. God surrenders Jesus to earth to walk with us and to give us what we seem to need: a hands-on experience of divine intent. In Jesus we learn that God knows, loves, listens, heals, forgives, guides, encourages, welcomes, and waits for us. And we learn something crucial in the surrender of Jesus to death. There is no limit to this divine love. It goes with us to death, and takes us beyond it, saving us from its cold effect. Jesus shows us what God's love does, pouring himself out without self-interest or selling out.

The story of Jesus is no grim tale of cause (our sin) and effect (the cross), but a passionate story of love given without counting the cost.

GOSPEL: MARK 14:12–16, 22–26
"The Teacher asks, Where is my guest-room where I may eat the Passover with my friends?"

Blessed be the door that opened on the Lord's supper. Blessed be the room that sheltered these friends in the final hour. Blessed be the innkeeper who made the room ready. Blessed be the bread and the wine which they shared. Blessed be the ears that heard, the lips that ate and drank, the hearts that struggled to understand.

Blessed be all who continue to share in this meal of grace. Blessed be the doors of our churches, opening for two thousand years despite persecution and schism. Blessed be these houses of faith, built at great cost by people of faith willing to shoulder the burden. Blessed be all those who make this supper ready, from the servants of the liturgy to the priest who speaks for us. Blessed be our Eucharist, our communion of Body and Blood. Blessed be our ears that hear God's word, our lips that dare to eat and drink. Blessed be our hearts that struggle and hope and need and believe.

Questions for Reflection

• What are the serious commitments you have made with your life? How do they compare with Israel's understanding of covenant?
• Is there a difference between saying sin caused the cross, and Jesus chose the cross?
• What does Eucharist mean in your life?

Action Response

Choose one of the serious commitments you have made in your life and rededicate yourself to this commitment, investing in it with flesh and blood.

Answering the Call

FIRST READING: 1 SAMUEL 3:3–10, 19

"Here I am. You called me."

The boy Samuel can be forgiven for not recognizing the voice of the Lord. He had been brought to the holy place of Shiloh as a Nazirite by his mother Hannah shortly after he was weaned. The priest Eli in charge of the tabernacle at Shiloh was not much attendant to the Lord's voice himself. Eli was a weak man with sons who had caused great offense at the holy place without being punished. So Samuel had not learned to discern a call from the Lord in that house.

Once he became the listening servant, Samuel never made that mistake again. Listening to God's voice and attending to the word spoken is what obedience means. Samuel became a great prophet because he learned how to listen.

We live in a distracted society. A thousand voices from the world around us seek our attention and our submission to their bidding. There are idols waiting to be worshiped everywhere we look. Recognizing the call of the Lord through this confusion is not so easy. But those who practice the way of obedience will learn how to distinguish God's voice from any other.

SECOND READING: 1 CORINTHIANS 6:13–15, 17–20

So glorify God in your body.

Paul's protest against casual sexual union is a clear and powerful statement. If we are whole people, the creatures of God in both body and spirit, then we cannot separate the acts of our bodies from the deeper spiritual implications. We cannot be united to Christ in spirit while uniting our flesh in thoughtless liaisons. It is the old teaching about two masters: we cannot hope to go in two opposing directions. In a finite humanity, we have to make a choice.

Either God is glorified or sinned against by the use we, as members of one Body, make of our bodies. Sexual union was intended as a means to make two lives one reality. That power is profaned in casual couplings where no real meeting and communion are intended. Sacred vessels are not to be used for profane purposes. That story is as old as the Bible.

GOSPEL: JOHN 1:35–42
"We have found the Messiah!"

It is always intriguing when a piece of biography slips into a story about the disciples. Here we meet Andrew, disciple of John the Baptist, about to make an historic change of allegiance.

Andrew is a follower type, but a very discriminating one. He has a brother, Peter, who probably stole the limelight when they were children, outrageously impetuous and quick to speak up. So Andrew developed a quieter style, attaching himself to John's band and being near enough to the inner circle to be one of two companions John travels with. When John points to Jesus with great fervor and excitement, Andrew walks away from John cleanly, to become one of those who will ever be known as the Twelve.

Andrew gets a few bit parts recorded in the Gospels after this, but perhaps his most significant accomplishment was in knowing who to follow. After spending one evening with Jesus, he is ready to cast his lot with him. He immediately goes home to get Peter, another fateful decision. The story of Andrew gives the church reason never to underestimate the resources of follower-types.

Questions for Reflection

• Which contemporary voices make claims on your allegiance? How do you know when a call is from the Lord?

• How do you honor your body as a temple of the Holy Spirit?

• Who are your spiritual leaders? Who looks to you for example?

Action Response

Learning to listen obediently is an ongoing process. Regular spiritual direction, prayer partnerships, or days of reflection and retreat can help to sharpen the skill of discernment. Escape the din of many voices and find some quiet time to listen to the voice of the One who loves you.

This Passing World

FIRST READING: JONAH 3:1-5, 10

All of them, great and small, put on sackcloth.

You know you are reading a parable when the caricatures are this obvious. Nineveh was such an evil city that God made up the divine mind to destroy it in forty days. But one fainthearted prophecy from the reluctant prophet Jonah and the citizens repent, wearing sackcloth from the king down to the cows, dogs, and parakeets. Now *that* is some kind of conversion.

God is sufficiently impressed to call the whole demolition off, and we can learn much from this small section. God is not set on divine judgment and retribution, but on seeing justice done. God would prefer not to have justice over our dead bodies. Our show of contrition is enough for God to relent. God's desire is to save Nineveh, and not to lose it.

God approaches the sinner with the hope of salvation. We who are sinners know that's a good thing. But the Christian extension is always that we must approach one another with that same hope of conversion, and not condemnation. It is easy to be Jonah, and tell everyone else about God's wrath: it is tougher to be the messenger of God's forgiveness.

SECOND READING: 1 CORINTHIANS 7:29-31

The world as we know it is passing away.

Let it all go. Walk away from attachment. Relationships, conditions, possessions, and any circumstantial realities are on their way out. What is coming has nothing to do with this world, and our worldly concerns are a waste of time, which is short. When Paul says things like this, we feel frustrated, as no doubt the Corinthians did. Our relationships are important to us, gifts that make life rich and full. Our material conditions and possessions are the context of our days and it is simply not possible to ignore them.

Paul presumed that Jesus was returning in short order. If I thought Jesus was due in a few hours, I might rewrite these paragraphs—or more likely, abandon them altogether. Still, the spirit of Paul's urgency carries the truth that our lives are not ultimately about our lives. "It is no longer I who lives but Christ who lives in me," as Paul says in Romans. We cannot stumble sleepily through our routines like unbelievers. The time of our testimony is short, and the world is in need of our light.

This is the time of fulfillment.

Four men woke up one morning as fishermen, and went to bed that night as disciples of an extraordinary prophet. Zebedee was short the help of two sons, and Peter's wife was not going to see much of her husband for awhile. What had happened?

Mark provides a terse account of the call of the disciples. Just as John the Baptist disappears from the scene, Jesus shows up and takes up John's message about the coming of God's reign. As Jesus walks along the shore of the sea, he invites people to join him in the work he is about to do. There is no job description, no salary, and only one promise: you will catch bigger fish. Maybe to a fisherman, that is all you have to say.

Maybe they were all young and bored; maybe they saw Jesus as a way out of their dead-end lives in Galilee. But there is also a sense that these folks were not possessed by their routines and the normal need for security. They were free to move, and they could travel lightly. Those seem to be the prerequisites for discipleship.

Questions for Reflection

- Are you more likely to judge or to forgive? Whom are you most likely to judge, and who is hardest to forgive?
- Make a list of ten aspects of your life that consume much of your attention and energy. Which of these interfere with a Christ-centered life?
- Why do you follow Jesus? What traits make you a good disciple?

Action Response

When this world passes away, what will be the hardest thing for you to surrender? Consider ways you can begin to relinquish your hold on that circumstance of your life.

A Prophet Among You

FIRST READING: DEUTERONOMY 18:15–20
"I will raise up for them a prophet like you from among their kin."

Prophets make lovely additions to the Bible, but you certainly don't want one in your own neighborhood. No sir! Prophets wreak havoc on the status quo. They are no fun on committees, they don't understand local politics, they don't wipe their feet before entering privileged rooms, and they are never polite. Overall, prophets cause problems.

But still, we like to have just a few—somewhat marginalized and carefully controlled—prophets around. They torque the national agenda just enough to keep Big Government in line. They are available to speak to our personal consciences in tender hours when we feel a desire to clean house, just a little. They occasionally come in handy when we happen to agree with them.

And if they get out of line and become really dangerous to the system as it stands, never fear. They will probably be assassinated or done away with by the proper authorities. Prophets don't have very long careers, and they have no insurance, only the power of oracle and God's eternal promise.

SECOND READING: 1 CORINTHIANS 7:32–35
I do want to promote what is good.

Some conservative folks will love this reading, and liberals will put their hands over their ears. It seems to promote the spirituality of celibacy over and against that of married life. It might imply that a life of holiness is available to priests and religious that is simply not an option for married people. We suspect this has something to do with sex, or the lack thereof; ways of the flesh and ways of the spirit are not reconcilable.

But Paul is more interested in time than in sex when he extols the choice of single life. After all, it has given him more time to put at the service of the Lord. He also believes that Jesus is returning shortly, so starting a family now is poor timing. Paul does not claim to speak for God here, but only for himself. The way he is called to serve the Lord is clearly assisted by a life of celibacy. Yet we have all known many holy women and men who fully served the Lord within the context of the home and the marketplace.

GOSPEL: MARK 1:21–28
"I know who you are—the Holy One of God!"

In urban areas, it is not uncommon for people who are mentally ill to haunt our churches. At my parish, a woman sits out front every week wearing all the colors of the rainbow, talking to herself nonstop and holding out her cup. Inside the church, there are occasional outbursts during the Mass, as someone wrestling with inner demons shrieks, speaks, or wanders the aisles, staring at us all with vacant eyes.

One week, a man who was deeply disturbed kept repeating the Mass parts after the priest from the back of the church. He started out softly at first, a faint echo of the presider. By the time of the Eucharistic prayer, he was loud, even belligerent, adding profanity to the responses and mocking the service. I felt angry, offended, though I knew the man was not rational.

And then something wonderful happened. At the sign of peace, a woman left her pew and extended her hand to the man. He took it, and then another person appeared behind the woman, and then another. Pretty soon dozens were gathered to extend peace to this troubled intruder, and the man began to weep openly. He sat down, and a small child went out to him and sat on his lap, instinctive to the sound of tears. The Mass continued, and the man never spoke another word.

Questions for Reflection

• Who are the prophets of this generation? How do they challenge us?

• Describe the holy people you have known. How was their faithfulness to God present in their lives, whether vowed, single, or married?

• Have you ever known a person who defeated their "inner demons"? What demons have you wrestled with over the years?

Action Response

Find an opportunity this week to exercise the call of the prophet. Bring peace where there is division, challenge established injustice, offer kindness unreasonably.

No Stranger to Demons

FIRST READING: JOB 7:1–4, 6–7
I shall not see happiness again.

Almost anyone who has ever asked the question, "Why do people suffer?" spends careful time mining the Book of Job for answers. Although this is a book with many answers, it does not have the answer most of us are looking for, the one that makes sense of human suffering. Certainly there is no sense or justice in Job's suffering. He is terribly afflicted by material loss, personal grief, and physical suffering. His pain is worsened by the rejection of his wife and the insistence of his pious friends that all of this misery is because of what Job "has done or failed to do."

Job knows this is nonsense. He is furious, and cries out for death. He screams at his friends; he demands God's response to his suffering. He acts like we do when the pain is too great to bear. And he gets a response. A voice from the whirlwind speaks in eloquent language about why Job's questions are inappropriate and spoken in ignorance. It's the same response we give a child fearful of the dark: hush. Trust me. You have nothing to fear.

And then God lifts the curse of Job's darkness, and his world is restored to wholeness. Job is not a prophet, a guru, or a Messiah. He is a fellow traveler like us, our one true representative in Scripture, who dares to ask what we hold in our hearts. And his quest is favored with inspired authority.

SECOND READING: 1 CORINTHIANS 9:16–19, 22–23
I am ruined if I do not preach the gospel!

Paul is obsessed with the message of the Gospel; his phrase is "under compulsion." He was a zealous Pharisee and is no less consumed as an apostle for Christ. He is also a chameleon for Christ (see deleted verses): a Jew for Jews, a Gentile for Gentiles, weak for the weak. As a Jewish man of Roman citizenship, he will play either card to gain an audience for his message.

Paul was an early believer in the idea that the medium is the message. He was not going to let the medium of his life prove to be a stumbling block for the Gospel.

He would not permit the demons to speak, because they knew him.

Imagine the life of Jesus as Mark sees it, with God for a father and on speaking terms with demons. No wonder he was intensely faithful to prayer. He rises early and goes to a lonely place which rebounds with spirits, both the shrieking and the celestial kind. The uncomprehending friends track him down and tell him everyone is looking for him. Jesus must be thinking: "You mean everyone *else*." There is no *alone* for him. There is merely the seen and the unseen.

When he is discovered by his friends, he declines the invitation to go back to where he has become, after one day, a celebrity. Let us move on, he says, to do what I have come to do. And he moves on from synagogue to synagogue, preaching and exorcising demons. He is engaged in a twofold battle, to shatter the authority of hell and to open people's eyes to the cosmic dimensions that he sees.

Mark's Gospel aims at revelation, and we hear no details of what Jesus is preaching and teaching in these towns. What is important is who he *is*, as revealed in his baptism at the start of this chapter. The demons know very well who he is. But do even his closest disciples suspect the power of his name?

Questions for Reflection

• When have you raged against suffering or injustice? What answers were you able to find in prayer?

• Consider Paul's role as "chameleon for Christ." What would Paul have to become to convince you of the urgency of the Gospel?

• If Jesus were to come to your house today, what demon might you ask to be relieved of?

Action Response

You may not be the type who would stand on a street corner and shout about Jesus. But choose a place, a situation, a relationship in your life where you are willing to explore the passionate side of your call to faith.

Unclean, Unclean!

FIRST READING: LEVITICUS 13:1-2, 44-46

"The one who bears the sore of leprosy...shall cry out, "Unclean, unclean!"

Pity the leper of ancient times. A variety of afflictions of the skin—as well as molds affecting cloth or the walls of buildings—fell into the category of biblical leprosy. Swelling, scabbing, discoloration, rashes, and hair loss could all make one suspect of the disease. Imagine being driven out of town and away from your family for a case of eczema. The safety of the community was protected by the law, not the rights or interests of an individual.

Most people didn't die of biblically defined leprosy. But they could die or at least languish in their separation from the community. Life outside the camp was haunted by hunger, hunted by wild beasts. And then there was loneliness, which dilutes the will to struggle and survive.

Biblically defined leprosy still exists around us. Many people are estranged from the camp, not welcome to sit at our tables or invited to share in our stories. Count the lepers who are effectively outside of your community, and consider how to welcome them in.

SECOND READING: 1 CORINTHIANS 10:31—11:1

Whatever you do, you should do all for the glory of God.

The Corinthians had a community that operated like many a parish I have seen. There were two tiers of membership: the insiders and the outsiders. The insiders got invited to the best parties and had the most privileged spots in the assembly. They were invited to join the favored committees. The outsiders got to clean up after the parties, fill in for the insiders when schedules became too demanding, and got drafted for the most grueling service needed by the parish.

Paul tells the Corinthians, in finely restrained outrage through most of this letter, that such divisions have no place in the church, not at the Lord's supper and not among their membership. Everything they do should give glory to God, and not offense. And there is no quicker way to offend God than to cause harm to the least of the sisters and brothers.

GOSPEL: MARK 1:40–45
Jesus touched him and said, "I do will it. Be cured."

Jesus understood that people needed community more than they needed a cure for what ailed them. Often, in fact, community is the cure for what ails us. That is why the church was founded on the idea of community. Even Jesus did not travel alone, nor did he send his disciples out in fewer than twos. He promised "wherever two or more are gathered, there I am in the midst of them." Church is not a solo act. We need each other.

Jesus cures a lot of lepers in the Gospels, maybe because there are a lot of lepers, or maybe because their condition was a particular grief for him. Or maybe lepers were the most aggressive seekers of a cure, since the penalty of exclusion was unbearable.

Whatever the case, Jesus does not simply heal them but points them in the direction of the proper authorities who regulate their return to the community. In the same way, real communities of caring and inclusion are the greatest sign of God's presence among us. Community is not an extra in the life of faith. It is the heart of the matter.

Questions for Reflection

• Who fits into the category of lepers within your community? How does your parish welcome them?

• Are there insiders and outsiders at your parish? In your neighborhood, office, family?

• Is your parish a real community, or a Sunday assembly? What are the significant communities to which you belong?

Action Response

Welcome an outsider in. Invite someone to lunch who normally gets left out. Share some extra minutes talking with a neighbor who lives alone. Call a relative who is estranged. Stretch your community at the borders.

He Was Nothing But "Yes"

FIRST READING: ISAIAH 43:18–19, 21–22, 24–25

It is I, I, who wipe out, for my own sake, your offenses.

We like to play God in our own little fiefdoms, but really being God is hard work. Think of the endless deadlock of wills: the divine will pleading and guiding us along the way to full humanity, pitted against the human will to make its own way at the expense of others. Consider the endless outpouring of divine love to the stubborn, resisting, hard hearts of mortals. Think of divine forgiveness standing as an eternal offer to people who refuse to forgive the smallest offense from their sisters and brothers.

Yet God remains God. God continues to do "something new" even while we cling to our well-worn grooves. God traces a road through desert sand, curls a river through a barren place. God continues to generate creation for the sake of an uncreative and unoriginal lot like ourselves. God may have rested on the seventh day, but picked up the task again on the eighth. The divine work, it seems, is never done.

SECOND READING: 2 CORINTHIANS 1:18–22

Jesus Christ…was never anything but "yes."

Word play can be a lot of fun, but only if you speak the language. We read the Scriptures now in English, but the letters of Paul were written in Greek, and the word play he employs is often Semitic.

What Paul is doing in this extended passage (verses 15–24) is toying with the idea of "yes" in a variety of forms. The root of yes is the same root, in Paul's native tongue, as the root for faith, security, amen, and firmness. Paul has been accused of vacillating in his purpose, since earlier he had promised to visit with the community and was detained. He assures them he did not say "yes" and mean "no." He goes on to say that Jesus was a man who meant "yes" and was as good as his word in laying down his life. He then exhorts the community to be "yes" too, to address their amen to God.

Being the people of the Great Amen means we will be constant in our purpose, meaning what we say when we profess our faith and drink from the Lord's cup. It is all too easy to say "yes" with our ritual actions and mean "no," or perhaps "maybe." But the people of "maybe" worship another God.

GOSPEL: MARK 2:1–12
"Stand up! Pick up your mat and go home."

Talk about a commanding "yes." Jesus forgives a man's sins in full sight of a crowd, and when they are offended, he throws in a healing of paralysis on the spot. Jesus affirms the eternal life of this suffering man, and affirms his mortal life as well.

Amen. Amen. We can hear the man puffing all the way home, dragging the mat which had been his prison since his injury. Amen. God is good. Amen. God has freed my arms and legs, freed my years, my future, my possibility. Amen. And God has forgiven the sin of my heart, the burden of my soul that I have carried all this while. God took from me the burden of heart, mind, and body, and offers me a freedom few have known. All of you, walking and limber, able and strong, you think you are free, but you do not know what real freedom is. Amen. I know. My heart is free to love, to give and to receive. My hands are free for service, and after a long season of standing still, my life can now go forward. Amen. Praise God.

Questions for Reflection

• Where is barrenness in your life, and how might God be creating a river there?

• Make a list of ten ways you say "yes" to God in the way you live your life. How else might you say "yes"?

• When have you known the freedom of forgiveness? How has it freed you to move forward?

Action Response

Say "yes" to God's gift of forgiveness. Accept that God wants to do something new in your life, and lead you through the desert on a safe path. Seek God's forgiveness in the sacrament of reconciliation, or offer your forgiveness to someone who has been waiting for it.

You Are a Letter of Christ

FIRST READING: HOSEA 2:16, 17, 21–22
I will lead her into the desert, and speak to her heart.

First love is a powerful experience. It captures all the senses, and defines the meaning of beauty, the possibility of happiness, the hope of pleasure. We wait for the coming of the beloved, and rejoice at the sight of the one who holds our fragile dream in hands seemingly immortal.

The prophet imagines God as the lover trying to elicit the memory of first love from a spouse gone cold and faithless. Remember when you first loved me? Remember the things we said, the vows we exchanged, the trust we had in one another? Remember the good times we shared, and how wonderful it was, when love was new?

Memory is a powerful tool in the life of faith. The one thing Jesus asks us to do in the Eucharist is remember. When we remember the love of old, it lives again in our hearts. And what is alive can grow and bear fruit.

SECOND READING: 2 CORINTHIANS 3:1–6
You are a letter of Christ which I have delivered.

You go to the mail box, not expecting much, pulling out the usual catalogs, solicitations, and a bill or two. And then you see it, the handwriting that sets your heart dancing. It is a letter, addressed to you from a friend. A real letter!

The pleasure of a real letter may pass from the earth with this generation, now that the telephone and e-mail have made penmanship a lost art. But just as a letter or phone call or electronic note from the right person can be the great consolation of the day, so we can personally deliver good news from God on whichever doorstep we may arrive. We are living letters, consolation in the flesh, good news in person. Wherever we go as Christians, we bring Christ with us. Do people experience your arrival as good news?

GOSPEL: MARK 2:18–22
"New wine is poured into new skins."

Jesus uses an argument as old as Ecclesiastes and as contemporary as a song from the 1960s: to everything there is a season. Turn, turn, turn.

When Jesus is accused by the pro-fasting league of not teaching his disciples the proper pieties, he assures them he is not against fasting per se. (He might have added that he had pulled off some pretty spectacular fasts earlier in his career.) It simply is not time to fast right now. What is appropriate for one occasion is not for another. In the same way, old patches belong on old clothes, and new wine is properly poured into new skins. There is no blanket formula that works for every occasion.

That's why we have so many feasts and seasons in the life of the church. We celebrate birth, and remember our dead. We mourn and fast, and also anticipate and rejoice. We sing *Te Deum* and Alleluia. We cannot remember Easter morning and forget Good Friday afternoon, or vice versa. To everything there is a season.

Questions for Reflection

• What were some of the powerful early memories you have in your life of faith? How do they hold you fast in faith?

• Whose arrival brings good news to you? To whom do you carry the good news in your heart?

• Which feasts or seasons of the church are most meaningful for you at this time of your life? Have they changed as you have seen the advance of many seasons?

Action Response

Choose a day in which you will pledge to bring nothing but good news to those around you. Be a messenger of good news to your family, your coworkers, your neighbors, and strangers you meet along the way. Bring no gossip, nothing divisive, just a letter from Christ, in so many words.

Preserve or Destroy?

FIRST READING: DEUTERONOMY 5:12–15

"Take care to keep holy the Sabbath day as the Lord commanded you."

The Sabbath was originally designed to be a gift from God. People need rest, and so even God models the Sabbath rest in the story of creation. But human beings found a way to make the Sabbath more work. The original commandment would eventually have more footnotes than a college term paper. The Sabbath would be morphed into a headache of rules and obligations so elaborate, one could dishonor the Sabbath and not even mean to.

Sabbath rest is fast disappearing from our society. Working mothers, full-time employees finishing degree programs, moonlighters, and plain old workaholics are quickly becoming the largest percentage of our society. So much is going on that it is hard for us to keep up with it, much less consider stepping back from it for twenty-four hours each week. Yet the need for rest is not only human, but a sacred obligation. How we can honor the Sabbath in an era than moves like lightning is a dilemma many of us have yet to resolve.

SECOND READING: 2 CORINTHIANS 4:6–11

We are struck down but never destroyed.

When Paul catalogues the list of afflictions in this letter, he is not using the royal "we." He means he and Barnabas, specifically, who are having some bad times out on the road of apostleship. And he also means we the church, who suffer with Christ in carrying out the mission to which we are called. These frail earthen vessels of ours carry a light greater than ourselves, and we are destined to go much farther than they can carry us.

But some of us may not feel so very afflicted, or think our small inconveniences for the faith amount to much in the way of persecution. Just wait. Those who are faithful in small matters will be put in charge of larger ones, Jesus taught his disciples. If we remain faithful over the course of a lifetime, we will find ourselves, like Paul, at the point of being struck down. Happily, we are guaranteed in advance not to be crushed.

GOSPEL: MARK 2:23—3:6

"Is it permitted on the Sabbath...to preserve life—or to destroy it?"

Jesus could accept fear on the part of his disciples, or doubt like Thomas', or even denial like Peter's. But the one thing that earns his ire is the closed-mindedness of the Pharisees who come to set him up to disobey the law. They don't come to see if he is teaching in error, or to see what he might have to say for himself when challenged. They come to watch him fall. They have already judged him in their hearts.

The scene of this healing, then, lacks the tender encounter of many other stories where Jesus is moved by compassion for the sufferer. Jesus shouts at the man with the useless hand to come forward; there is no indication that he sought a healing from Jesus. Jesus addresses his remarks angrily to the Pharisees watching him like vultures, while the man with the withered hand stands uncomfortably in the spotlight. When the healing takes place, Mark does not waste a word telling us of the man's joy, the crowd's wonder. Immediately, we are plunged into the plot against Jesus. Because Jesus chose to restore life here, his life is already forfeit. And all because he blessed a man on the day of blessing.

Questions for Reflection

• How do you preserve the spirit of Sabbath rest?

• Compose a short list of your afflictions and doubts. How have they been (or are they being) answered in your life?

• Consider some ways you have known people to keep the spirit of the law without the letter: unmarried couples more faithful than married ones, unbaptized people being more just than churchgoers. What does this teach you about God's grace?

Action Response

Consider Sunday a day for blessing. Bless others with your kindness, charity, attention, compassion. Never be too busy on a Sunday to extend a healing touch or word.

The Conquest of Evil

FIRST READING: GENESIS 3:9–15

"Because you have done this, you shall be banned."

We all play the blame game. We have developed a culture based on suing somebody for every misfortune we suffer. The wounded ego defends itself against the insinuation of error: I'm not wrong—you just don't have all the facts! It's Mom, it's society, it's circumstance that made me do it.

The man and the woman in the creation story each find scapegoats to deflect their participation in guilt. Eve is the first person to use the alibi: the devil made me do it. God punishes the serpent, but the others are not exonerated. Each one freely chose to form the mosaic of guilt that we call original sin.

One of the tests of Christian maturity is the quick recognition of our own sin. I have heard priests say that often people come to confession to rationalize or defend their actions rather than to admit guilt. How can we seek forgiveness if we have done nothing wrong? We cannot receive God's forgiveness when we pretend we are beyond the need of it.

SECOND READING: 2 CORINTHIANS 4:13—5:1

What is not seen lasts forever.

We'll be seeing a lot of Second Corinthians in the upcoming weeks, so a moment for context is not wasted. It is considered the most personal of Paul's letters, and for this reason can be confusing. Paul has a volatile relationship with the residents of Corinth, a seaport town with all of the usual problems: sailors, prostitutes, fast living. In his first letter he writes some famous words about the need for unity and acceptance of different gifts. He assures them love will hold the church together.

The second letter has a more urgent tone. Evidently love is not working. Paul is beside himself and tries sarcasm, assigning guilt, and even boasting to get the people to come around. He does not organize his thoughts too precisely, and we can only guess at the underlying causes for his frustration.

In this excerpt Paul's concern is that this "earthly tent" which so fascinates the Corinthians is passing. If they would lift their gaze higher they might glimpse what lasts forever. Even those of us who live in stable and landlocked towns can benefit from his advice.

GOSPEL: MARK 3:20–35
"How can Satan expel Satan?"

The argument Jesus advances reminds me of what I heard once in a psychology course. Paranoia is untreatable, so the argument goes, because the therapeutic method is based on forming a relationship of trust. Paranoids cannot trust, therefore they cannot be helped.

I wonder if that is what is meant by the unforgivable sin. Nobody really knows what it means, to blaspheme against the Holy Spirit. How can the all-merciful God refuse the forgiveness of one sin? That one sin stands alone like the tree in the Garden, the one fruit we dare not eat, lest we die.

This sin of calling the Spirit of holiness itself an agent of Beelzebul is what triggers Jesus' pronouncement. Maybe the unforgivability of this sin lies in its nature, like the untreatability of paranoia. If God looks like the devil to you, if you cannot tell the difference between a great act of love and outright hostility, then how can you be loved? If you refuse the forgiveness and salvation offered to you with outstretched hands, where else will forgiveness and salvation come from?

Questions for Reflection

• What kind of blame is easy for you to admit to? What are you more likely to rationalize?

• What attractions hold you to the "seen" world? What do you long for in the "unseen" realm?

• Have you known anyone who cannot discern holiness from evil, the "morally blind"? Do you think they are lost?

Action Response

Practice taking responsibility for your actions at once. Refrain from defensiveness, do not rationalize or offer mitigating circumstances. Discover the freedom of genuine confession.

The Unreasonable Kingdom

FIRST READING: EZEKIEL 17:22–24
It shall put forth branches and bear fruit.

The key to understanding this passage is in the word "too." Earlier in chapter 17, the Lord proposed a riddle to Israel concerning a certain eagle who snips off the top of the cedar. The oracle refers to the exile of the Jewish royal house to Babylon. But the Lord, too, can take and plant the people at will. Just as the future of Israel seemed lost in the great exile of 587 BCE, so will it be recovered when God transplants the royal house back to Zion.

The covenant with the house of David is not ended. What is humbled can be exalted again, what seems to triumph can be brought down. This reversal of fortunes so popular in the prophets will be heard again in the teachings of Jesus. There is no such thing as "hopeless" in God's dominion. Even the despair of the cross is not the end of the road.

SECOND READING: 2 CORINTHIANS 5:6–10
We walk by faith, not by sight.

Paul writes a lot in this letter about the afflictions he and his companions have suffered for the sake of the Gospel. Earlier he mentioned that something bad happened to them recently in Asia, which is never spelled out. Because of this trauma, it is understandable to hear Paul say again and again that it is preferable to be out of the body and at home with the Lord. Paul's body has taken some hard knocks.

Imagine Paul's life as a Pharisee: correct, admired, a cakewalk for a man with such steely discipline. Now compare it to his life in the Lord: hounded, accused, reviled, chaotic. He must have held fast to the image of the tribunal of Christ and the recompense he would receive. That image is less comforting for those of us who know we have not done all we could to walk in faith. We are so easily seduced by the glamour of the world in our sight.

"This is how it is with the reign of God."

The reign of God is not at all like a sensible kingdom of earth. We build our kingdoms on certain rules: hard work equals profits. Earn your keep. Bigger is better. Jesus says an unreasonable thing. The reign of God is like planting seeds and then losing complete control of the process. Life happens and it is no thanks to us. When the harvest comes we get it all. What kind of system is that?

It's like the folly of the church: baptizing infants who make no profession of faith, marrying couples who are not practicing Catholics, absolving sinners who will go out and sin again. What a strange use of grace, some say. There should be more rules, higher standards, more proof.

Jesus seems to disagree. The reign of God is a small seed planted into darkness, promising nothing. From obscurity and irrelevance comes more than we suspect. The process does not belong to us, only the decision to begin.

Questions for Reflection

- What if the reversals of God's reign came upon the world today? Where would you find yourself?
- If you were not a Christian, would your life be any different?
- When has a small seed planted in your life produced great things?

Action Response

Plant some small seeds. Be kind to those who "don't deserve it." Forgive wantonly. Be more generous than is sensible. Break the rules in favor of people.

Holding Back the Sea

FIRST READING: JOB 38:1, 8–11

Who shut within doors the sea, when it burst forth from the womb?

The Book of Job makes for great Bible study. It asks a crucial question: why do people suffer? And it ponders the answers of religion, rejecting all of them. In the end, we are left with the Voice from the Whirlwind, who gives a majestic and poetic reason why we fail to answer the question.

It's a matter of authority, power, and mystery. An inferior thing cannot pass judgment on a superior thing. As writer Huston Smith has said, it's like a tribunal of dogs passing judgment on the human use of mathematics. What tests can they apply? The sniff test? And if the sniff test fails, does that mean math is untrue, or the dogs are inadequate in their testing? Understanding of mathematics belongs to humans. Understanding of suffering belongs to God. If suffering is a mystery to us, that is only because the authority to command it is not ours.

SECOND READING: 2 CORINTHIANS 5:14–17

The one who is in Christ is a new creation.

I know a man who is advanced in the way of holiness. He tells me he has a kind of bifocal vision about the people who come to him for spiritual direction. He can see who they are, in the limitation that sin has placed on their lives. And he can also see who they are called to be, in the freedom of the children of God. He can see all the way to the new creation. He has "kingdom eyes."

Paul urges us to assume that kind of vision. We tend to look critically on others, seeing where they fail to live up to our standards. It is harder to see people, especially ourselves, through God's eyes, as beloved creatures. Using "mere human judgment," we condemn humanity. Even before we see, can we believe in the new creation?

GOSPEL: MARK 4:35–41

"Teacher, doesn't it matter to you that we are going to drown?"

Here is the ultimate sniff test: it looks like we are drowning, it feels like we are drowning, therefore we must be drowning! The disciples wake Jesus up after trying hard to keep the faith in a storm. They are just a little accusatory in their tone. And Jesus first calms the storm, and then casually rebukes his students.

None of this is particularly surprising. In Mark's Gospel, the crowds seem to "get" Jesus, while the disciples never do. What is amazing is that, after the calming of the storm, the disciples wonder among themselves, "Who can this be?" They seem astonished at his power. If they did not expect him to do just what he did, then why did they wake him up?

I suppose they expected him to save the boat, and not stop the storm. I suppose they expected a more normal kind of salvation. They who could not see that there is no danger while Jesus is in the boat cannot imagine the extent of his authority.

Questions for Reflection

• Read the entire speech from out of the whirlwind, chapters 38–41 in Job. What does Job learn about God's authority?

• How does it affect you when people look at you according to your potential instead of your faults?

• When have you believed you were "drowning" only to find yourself in the arms of safety? What does this teach you about faith?

Action Response

Wear your "kingdom eyes" for a week. Look at your family, coworkers, the rich, the poor, and yourself as free to live according to the new creation. Do what you can to share what you see with them.

THIRTEENTH SUNDAY IN ORDINARY TIME

Fear is Useless

FIRST READING: WISDOM 1:13–15, 2:23–24
God does not rejoice in the destruction of the living.

The Book of Wisdom has a very contemporary ring to it. It was written about one century before the time of Jesus, yet it includes passages we associate with him, like the condemnation of the just one (2:12–20). Because the book is part of the wisdom tradition which sprang from the experience of the Jewish community outside of Israel, it does not concern itself with the politics of kings or the temple. The love of wisdom is equated with a life of justice or discipline. So wisdom is not so much about knowing things as it is about doing things.

The Jewish tradition did not originally include a theology of afterlife, and this later development was not unanimously accepted in Jesus' time. The Pharisees taught it; the Sadducees belittled it. The life-affirming spirit of Wisdom rejects death as the irregular element in the world, and sees restoration of life after death the only logical response of the God who "did not make death," and formed us to be imperishable. In light of what we know, it seems like a pre-Christian moment. The leap between Wisdom and Christianity is an Incarnation away.

SECOND READING: 2 CORINTHIANS 8:7, 9, 13–15
Christ made himself poor though he was rich, so that you might become rich by his poverty.

Catholic charities are among the finest organizations of their kind. With education or medical care, famine relief or aid in war-torn areas of the world, Catholic missionaries are on the scene and effective. In our own country, Catholic agencies fight poverty, addiction, homelessness, and the isolation that afflicts the sick and aging. Our record as the open hand of Christianity is one reason to be proud to be Catholic.

But we really are not doing anything praiseworthy when we assist those in need. Jesus once likened our obedience to God's word to the behavior of the servant who follows the orders of the master. At the end of a long day of faithful service, all the servant has done is what is expected. We follow the

Lord who emptied himself of divine privilege in order to become one of us. When we are generous with our surplus, we are not being heroic, just faithful.

GOSPEL: MARK 5:21–43

"Fear is useless. What is needed is trust."

The woman was understandably afraid. She had been ill for many years with "women's trouble," and had been so long deemed unclean by the flow of blood that she no longer went out in public at all. No one could touch her, not even her husband or her children. She was as taboo as a corpse, and lived like a ghost among her own people.

Yet, when news reached her that the Healer was in town, she left her home and went out into the streets. She knew that if she were recognized, she would be severely treated. But hope! Hope like a bird took flight in her, and she made her way, face covered, pushing and squirming through the shoulders as the flow of blood was jarred from her again and again. Her fear urged her to return to her home, but faith moved her forward to grasp the Healer's cloak.

Later, Jesus would be reminded of her as the delegates would come to Jairus and beg him to send Jesus on his way. "The girl is already dead," they would say. With the image of the courageous woman before his eyes, Jesus told Jairus, "This fear is useless. You must have faith."

Questions for Reflection

• What makes people wise: what they know, or what they do?

• How many ways have you found to give from your surplus, in money, time, presence, and love?

• When has faith overcome your fear? What were you seeking then? Is fear an obstacle to what you need right now?

Action Response

Be not afraid: be generous! As the missionaries often say, prayerfully consider what you can give from your surplus—and then resolve to give double that amount. Trust that God will supply you with everything you need.

"Spirit Entered into Me"

FIRST READING: EZEKIEL 2:2–5
They shall know that a prophet has been among them.

Apocalyptic writing is mysterious by design. Visions and oracles—seeing things that most people don't see, hearing what most people don't hear— are the prophet's domain. But apocalyptic goes beyond what we might call normal prophecy into symbolic language. Though the words are audible, they produce the feel of "speech in tongues." This hidden speech has to be translated for it to be discernible.

Ezekiel has many such experiences, and his book is full of beating wings, spinning wheels, and fantastic creatures. In each of these encounters, he feels the movement of God's Spirit within him. And he makes the move from apocalypse to revelation, from experiencing the unseen to speaking God's word fearlessly. When Spirit enters into him, you know he is either a madman or a prophet.

SECOND READING: 2 CORINTHIANS 12:7–10
When I am powerless, it is then that I am strong.

Paul is no stranger to revelation himself. Though Paul does not claim to be a prophet, he has had a vision or two that turned his life around like a top. Scholars have spent some time making educated guesses about Paul's "angel of Satan" and what his "thorn in the flesh" might have been. Was it an illness? Was it lust? Was it a deformity or spiritual imperfection?

What is more valuable to consider, perhaps, is our own thorn in the flesh, the thing that keeps us from developing spiritual pride. People are imperfect in many minor ways but we all know the one thing that causes us particular problems. It could be anger. Unforgiveness. Prejudice. Greed. Fear. Or something else, known to you alone. Paul's experience tells us that God seeks to use the very thing that tries to crush us as an instrument of grace. Then we will know, as Paul did, how God makes the powerless one strong.

"Where did he get all this?"

Spirit was in him. That was not the issue. Yet Jesus could not do much in the neighborhood of Nazareth. A few who were sick enough to need to believe in his miracles were cured. But Jesus was so distressed by the lack of faith, he stuck to teaching.

There is a reciprocal relationship between the giver of grace and the getter. It is like trying to sow a garden on cement. The seeds just bounce off and dry up. No matter how persistent the sower, nothing receives the seed. So Jesus taught in the villages surrounding Nazareth instead, preparing the ground for the sowing. When he found faces lit up in the message they received, he would know it was time for planting again.

How often do I present myself as hard ground, and lose to the wind the seeds I have been given? How often have miracles passed me by, as I questioned the source of grace?

Questions for Reflection

• What criteria do you use to judge between madness and prophecy?

• What is your thorn in the flesh, and how does (or can) God use it for divine purposes?

• What is the most fertile part of your life? What is the most barren? How can you till the barren soil to make it ready for God's word to be planted?

Action Response

Get apocalyptic! Draw if you're courageous, make a collage of pictures if timid. Gather some symbols that speak to you of God's revelation present in your life. (It doesn't have to make sense to anyone else. That's the beauty of apocalyptic images. It's your private revelation.)

Go, Prophesy

FIRST READING: AMOS 7:12–15
"I was a shepherd and a dresser of sycamores."

Unlike Elijah, Isaiah, and others who seemed to have no life before their time in God's service, Amos had a life. Maybe his prophecy is the bleakest one in the Hebrew Scriptures for that very reason. He was a prophet by force, and not by inclination. He goes from the south to prophesy to the people of the north. He gets the job done and is finally expelled from the north. One presumes he went back to the farm and got on with his life.

Amos is so relentlessly dark in his prophesying that he gets parodied within the Bible. The Book of Jonah is a satire on prophets like Amos who hate their call. But we can find a soft spot in our hearts for this conservative fellow who followed the prompting he received. We know moments in our lives when the spirit of prophecy overcomes us. We have to testify to the truth even though it is unwelcome, embarrassing, and unpopular. We speak our peace, maybe dreading the whole business. But sometimes the truth has to come from someone, and that someone is you.

SECOND READING: EPHESIANS 1:3–14
God chose us…to be holy and blameless in God's sight, to be full of love.

Paul says "chosen" and "predestined" so many times in this passage, he sounds like a Calvinist. Also God's "will" and "favor" are invoked, as well as "the plan" and "the decree." So what is the plan? Paul is not mysterious: it is the union of all things in the heavens and on earth under Christ. Reality used to be an us-and-them proposition of Jews and Gentiles. It used to be heaven against earth. But now these irreconcilable opposites have been bridged by the generosity of Jesus. The ancient opposition is over, and peace has been declared. And this was the goal of God before the world began.

Paul's original audience was chosen to be the first to hope in Christ. We who come along after twenty centuries are no less welcome to participate in the task of reconciliation. Our world is shattered in many more pieces than two, and never has the need for reconciling opposites been more deeply felt.

GOSPEL: MARK 6:7–13
They went off, preaching the need of repentance.

Imagine you are one of the Twelve. You have been with Jesus for awhile, heard his teaching, watched his miracles. Now he sends you off with only one companion to do the same. He gives you authority over unclean spirits. (You, called to cast out demons?) He tells you not to take a suitcase, or a sandwich, or money. (Empty-handed, without your VISA card?) Don't take a change of clothes, and make no reservations. Just go gently into the unknown, and be open to the Spirit.

It is amazing to think of that journey. It is even more incredible to think it would really work! Mark reports that demons were cast out, and cures were granted. These neophyte missionaries were successful.

I don't think this means we should quit our day jobs and take up exorcism, though heaven knows this world has its share of demons. It does suggest that, like our brain power which goes largely unused, our spiritual resources are vastly underutilized. We test our faith so little, we have no idea what would be available to us if we stepped out into the wind of the Spirit.

Questions for Reflection

• When have you been called upon to witness to the truth? What did you learn from the call to prophesy?

• Name the broken elements of your family or community that need to be reconciled so that Christ can be all in all.

• What was the greatest test to which your faith has been put? How was it resolved?

Action Response

You have been chosen to be part of the plan to unite heaven and earth under Christ. Choose one way you can participate in the great plan of reconciliation, and make it your mission.

Shepherds

FIRST READING: JEREMIAH 23:1–6

Woe to the shepherds who mislead and scatter the flock.

Jeremiah was the son of a priest of Anathoth, so it was daring for him to take on the shepherds of the people. Maybe he was a typical minister's son, rebelling against the hypocrisies he sensed in the system. He takes on both kings and prophets with equal vigor, and speaks ringing condemnations that draw danger from every side.

But is there anything worse than a leader who chooses against the protection and welfare of the people? Remember, this was in the days before democracy, when leadership was not a mere matter of living up to the public trust. Leaders of any sort were seen as elected by divine decree. These people had God to answer to, not simply their constituency. Their failure to exercise proper authority was not much short of blasphemy.

God promises to raise up a final leader from the house of David who will be God's justice. This new shepherd will have lasting care of the sheep, and an authority without end.

SECOND READING: EPHESIANS 2:13–18

Christ reconciled us in one body through his cross.

In the first-century Jewish mind, there were two camps: Jews and non-Jews. When Christianity started, all Christians were Jews. It did not occur to anyone that what Jesus had to offer was for anybody else. Paul's efforts among the Gentiles were fiercely objected to and even actively fought by many. "Judaizers," people trying to make Gentile converts into kosher Jews, followed Paul's missionary path.

It took a generation for people on both sides to understand that what was happening was not a movement that would stay within Judaism but would become something new. Meanwhile, Paul was trying to weave a theology gracious enough to receive both groups. This is behind his words to the community at Ephesus.

Today, Paul's message continues to fuel efforts to reconcile opposing groups. Christ is our peace. He is the peace we share at Mass, the peace that feeds ecumenism and interfaith dialogue. He is the peace we need to reunite our homes, our communities, and our world. He is the peace we need to seek above all in our hearts.

GOSPEL: MARK 6:30–34
Jesus pitied them, for they were like sheep without a shepherd.

The apostles have returned from their first missionary efforts very excited. They had followed his command to teach and heal, and it worked! But Jesus knows the cost of this mission, and the need to rest and pray. He draws them tenderly aside from the limelight.

The crowds pursue. Of course they do. What with all the miracles happening around Galilee that week, it is a wonder Jesus' band got out of town at all. The people want more. Then, as now, there was no dearth of sick people, or people whose lives were not working. And there are always plenty of people curious about the latest craze. So Jesus and his friends are mobbed before their retreat has begun.

Jesus responds with pity. The desire to teach wells up in him. This crowd is so needy, hungry, hurting, ignorant. There is so much they do not understand, even in the midst of miracles. The desire to teach them overwhelms his need for rest. In a world marred by sin, the Good Shepherd cannot look away.

Questions for Reflection

• Who are the unfaithful shepherds whom Jeremiah would rail against today?

• Have you ever reconciled with a long-standing enemy? What led to the peace?

• What sights draw out your compassion? What do you then do with your compassion?

Action Response

We are all shepherds of those who come under our care. Look upon those in need of your care with the loving eyes of Jesus.

Bread for the People

FIRST READING: 2 KINGS 4:42–44
"Give it to the people to eat."

The backdrop of the Elisha story is a raging famine. The people are going hungry, and some fellow brings an offering of the first fruits of his grain to the prophet. Elisha sees the matter as clear-cut: God does not need this offering, but the people do. So he orders the servant of the Gilgal shrine to distribute the loaves. We who are accustomed to how bread gets multiplied in the Gospel are not surprised, but the servant is. A food miracle follows the word of the prophet and a hundred people can eat, with bread left over.

Count the miracle bread stories in the Bible: manna in the desert, Elisha's barley loaves, Jesus and the 5,000, not to mention the Last Supper. Bread means life, and the bread from heaven means life for all. God does not need our Eucharist, but we do. That is why the church continues to hold this supper until the end of time.

SECOND READING: EPHESIANS 4:1–6
Live a life worthy of the calling you have received.

Theologians have a term for the kingdom of God: "realized eschatology." *Eschaton*, from the Greek, is another name for the end of the world and the new creation God has promised. *Realized* eschatology means that the reign of God Jesus talks about is not just "kingdom come" but kingdom coming in every hour. What we are waiting for is already here, in the Spirit working through us. Or, as Jesus put it, at hand.

What also needs to happen, of course, is "realized *ecclesiology*." Ecclesiology is the Greek word for what pertains to the church. If the reign of God is going to be realized, then the church has to get real. We who are church have to behave like the church. We have to look like Jesus. If we do not look like Jesus, then we fail in our mission to be the body of Christ. Then the kingdom does not get realized, and the old creation of sin and death continues to reign.

Paul tells us how to look like Jesus, how to live a life worthy of our call to be church. It takes humility (oh no, not that), meekness, patience, forbearance. All of that requires putting our pride aside. It means real love, the courageous kind that stands up for what is right; putting justice before personal comfort or gain; putting ourselves at the service of life. People with this kind of rugged, real humility have walked on this planet. We can do this.

GOSPEL: JOHN 6:1–15

Jesus took the loaves of bread, gave thanks, and passed them around.

This is the only miracle story that is told in all four Gospel accounts. Evidently everyone agreed what happened that day was important.

In John's version, there are dueling responses to the same dilemma: Philip's and Andrew's. When Jesus asks how the people are to be fed, Philip says it is flat-out impossible. Now remember, Philip is a disciple of Jesus. He has seen a few miraculous cures, heard some extraordinary teaching. A stranger might say it is impossible and be forgiven. But Philip's lack of faith is staggering. Then Andrew pipes in, Andrew who once was a disciple of the Baptist. Andrew has the advantage of a career disciple: he knows that something is up. So he points out what little food is apparent, and wonders what good can come of that.

And that is all it takes. Once again it is the mustard seed of faith, the grain of wonder, that Jesus can use to produce food for a multitude. The difference between Philip's and Andrew's response may seem minuscule to us, but it's light-years to Jesus. The difference between no faith and mere doubt is earth-shaking. Doubt is soil in which a seed of faith can take root.

Questions for Reflection

• As a Christian, whom do you feed? As a Christian, how are you fed?

• Name people you have known who have the look of Jesus in their lives. What is the difference between you and them?

• How has God used your doubt to bring you to faith?

Action Response

Put yourself at the service of life. Feed the hungry. Defend the helpless. Care for children. Remember the elderly. Respect the planet. Take care of yourself.

A Spiritual Way of Thinking

FIRST READING: EXODUS 16:2–4, 12–15

The Israelites asked one another, "What is this?"

At a recent breakfast, a woman confessed over a cup of coffee, "God has done so much for me, and still I keep asking for more. God has given me blessing after blessing, and still I am afraid to trust."

She is not alone. Most of us, with some embarrassment, identify with the complaints of the Israelites in the desert. After the miraculous ten plagues visited upon Egypt, and the parting of the Red Sea, it does not take the community long to forget and be aggrieved. "I wish God would have killed us outright in Egypt!" the people say to Moses. We hear the same lament later from Job, who says, "Why was I ever born?" Why are we given life, happiness, hope, only to risk them in times of distress?

God sends quail at night, and manna in the morning. God proves love and fidelity once again. The people don't know what to make of it at first, having grown accustomed to their doubts. It takes us all a long time to become accustomed to faith.

SECOND READING: EPHESIANS 4:17, 20–24

You must no longer live as the pagans do, their minds empty.

In the fourth grade, I was punished for talking during a lesson by having to write 150 times, "Empty vessels make a lot of noise." That line comes to mind when I listen to Paul's refutation of the pagans. They are given over to every kind of boisterous excess, but they are empty in head and heart. Paul admonishes the community not to live "in the futility of their minds, darkened in understanding." To the educated Greek, the insinuation that the life of the mind was futile would be outrageous. But Paul insists that all understanding is dark when alienated from the life of God.

Some years back, while a student of the liberal arts, I found the need for "a fresh, spiritual way of thinking." As I studied ethics, philosophy, the nature of the good, and the theory of knowledge, there always seemed to be a God-shaped hole in the debate. When I tried to incorporate that piece into my papers, my professors insisted, "You cannot posit God. You cannot take that position." Finally one kind mentor recommended that I consider studying theology, where I could "posit" God without seeming anti-intellectual.

Once posited, God assumes the entire space of the debate. All things in fact take on God's shape, as we ourselves become new people in God's image.

GOSPEL: JOHN 6:24–35
"What must we do to perform the works of God?"

Jesus had the crowd pegged. They ask for a sign like Moses performed when he gave the people manna in the desert. This is a double affront, as Jesus has just given the multitude miraculous bread, and also because the people attribute to Moses what came from God. Jesus assures them they are looking for the wrong kind of bread, the kind that does not last. So they ask for the bread that lasts, and Jesus offers himself.

Though Thomas Aquinas would later suggest that one can come to faith through reason, faith is not a "reasonable" thing. Faith is often described as a leap, a crossing through air, a movement over the gap that separates the worldly concern from the eternal. For the crowds to accept Jesus as the bread from heaven, they would have to lay down their expectations of who he is and what bread is. They would have to be willing to cross over into faith, and leave the material values behind.

Questions for Reflection

• How has God been faithful to you? What are the signs of God's care in your life?

• When have you been challenged to take on a spiritual way of thinking? Has this helped you to become a new person in God's image?

• Name some worldly hungers that you feel pulled by. What spiritual food does God give to fill you?

Action Response

Spend a week making decisions from the spiritual side of your mind. Before each decision, large or small, ask which response is better aligned with God's kingdom.

Bread from Heaven

FIRST READING: 1 KINGS 19:4–8

"This is enough, O Lord! Take my life."

Elijah has had a prophet's career: occasional glorious moments of bold proclamation followed by long seasons of persecution and doubt. At the moment, Jezebel the Queen has promised to slay him in revenge for the slaughter of her Baal prophets at Mount Carmel. Elijah goes into the desert and prays for death by God's hand. He has had enough.

When the angel appears, Elijah is ordered, not invited, to eat and drink. What seems a kindly comforting visitation is in some measure a command to get a grip on his nerve. He has a journey to make, the angel tells him, and he'll need strength to get there. This is not food for the poor, but bread for the journey.

Our own Eucharist is like this, food en route to the kingdom. It is no end in itself but is intended to get us where we are going. Too often we share this meal and go nowhere. Elijah's story reminds us we have a long journey ahead.

SECOND READING: EPHESIANS 4:30—5:2

Get rid of all bitterness, all passion and anger.

Stephen Crane, who wrote *The Red Badge of Courage*, was also a poet. In one of his poems the narrator comes upon a girl eating her heart. When asked why she is doing this, she says, "I eat it because it is bitter, and because it is my heart."

Too often we consume ourselves in just this way, as Paul warns the Ephesians. We spend our passion in dark ways and have little left in the service of love. Paul is the premier example of a person whose passion is entirely surrendered to love. Consider the fruit of his life: the Gentile mission of the church. If not for his great love poured out on foreign peoples, Christianity might have remained a small sect within Judaism, or died out altogether. God chose Paul, madman lover, to take the message to the ends of the known world.

It is common to see people whose passions are tied up in nursing old wounds, fueling old rages, or maintaining a traditional hostility. We who are at the service of the Gospel can do no less than to lay our passion at the feet of Christ.

GOSPEL: JOHN 6:41–51
"They shall all be taught by God."

The murmuring against Jesus grows louder. Chapter 6 is called the crisis in John's Gospel, because the Bread of Life discourse that Jesus is proclaiming makes the people increasingly uncomfortable. What is this man saying about himself? Just who is he claiming to be?

Jesus dismisses their protests. He remembers the phrase of both Isaiah and Jeremiah, that the day would come when no mediation between God and humanity would be necessary. God would speak to the human heart with a new law written intimately there. There would be no need for sages and prophets to bring the word of God from mountaintops, for all would have access to the truth.

That day arrives with Jesus. That bridge was built with his cross. The new law written on our hearts is the law of love. Once more, Jesus offers himself to the crowd, acknowledging that the only way to reach him is through the open heart drawn by God. We can hear the muttering crowd grow angrier, their hearts clamped shut. They want no new law, they want no challenges to their complacency in righteousness. Though Jesus shouts above them words of life for the whole world, all they hear is the death of their familiar way.

Questions for Reflection

- Reflect on where your own life's journey may be taking you. How does the Eucharist feed you on this journey?
- Where is the energy of your passion most vital? Where does your passion need to be freed for service?
- What part of you must die in order for new life to come?

Action Response

Reread Paul's "no" list: bitterness, senseless passion, anger, harsh words, slander, and malice. Target one of these for release from your life. Look at Paul's "yes" list: kindness, compassion, and forgiveness. Pray intensely for one of these gifts to be given to you.

Wisdom's Table

FIRST READING: PROVERBS 9:1–6

"Forsake foolishness that you may live."

Compare Lady Wisdom with Dame Folly in Proverbs 9:13–8. Both offer their hospitality liberally, yet one is the pathway to life and the other the door to the underworld in disguise.

Why don't more choose the invitation to Wisdom? Perhaps Wisdom has a bad rap as a choice that is less hip. Younger people have perennially been led to believe that being drunk, doped up, or on the wrong side of the law is a cool place to be. Adults get no gold stars here, either. They have been persuaded that power, sex, wealth, and prestige are where it's at.

Wisdom is not hip, not likely to follow the fads. Wisdom is a careful listener, not a big talker. Wisdom has no high profile, but vanishes quietly from the scene. I guess you do have to sacrifice hipness to the cause of Wisdom. But it's not a bad choice, considering that if you choose Folly, you forfeit everything.

SECOND READING: EPHESIANS 5:15–20

Sing praise to the Lord with all your hearts.

Paul joins the Wisdom chorus with his live-in-the-light passage which ends here. He says "make the most of the present opportunity," not knowing how soon the world will draw to a close. It is good advice even for those of us who live as if we have more inside information than Paul had.

I used to volunteer at a shelter for pregnant teenagers. Some of the girls there made the most of the services being offered to them. They were eager to learn, to shoulder the responsibilities that faced them. Others abused the opportunity. They behaved like the teenagers they were, evading the rules, not being serious about working the program. They ended up back on the streets, and we saw them again in weeks or years.

Even we who are in less critical situations often botch the opportunities presented to us. A way to "do right" opens before us, and we walk on by.

GOSPEL: JOHN 6:51–58

"The one who feeds on this bread shall live forever."

John's mystical images unravel the intellect. They play mind-games with those who like their Christianity a little more civilized. Right after this speech, many of the disciples around Jesus gave up and went home. This was too much to take. "Bread of life" is one thing: but eating flesh, drinking blood? What separates the words of Jesus from the ancient practices of those who believed consuming the heart of a defeated warrior gave them courage?

During this second year of the church's three-year cycle, we spend four weeks contemplating the Bread of Life discourse in John. Each time, we have the chance to consider our own relationship to this table. Those who would follow Jesus would share this Body and Blood and trade it for their own in persecution.

If it cost us our lives to share in the Eucharistic meal, would we still partake?

Questions for Reflection

• Who is the wisest person you have known? What revealed their wisdom?

• What opportunities have you taken recently to grow in the Spirit of God? What opportunities did you pass by?

• Explain your relationship to the Body and Blood of Christ. Share a story of when it was most meaningful to you.

Action Response

Receive the Eucharist thoughtfully this week. Share both your meals and your attention consciously with others. Contribute to a meal program for the disadvantaged.

To Whom Shall We Go?

FIRST READING: JOSHUA 24:1-2, 15-17, 18
"Decide today whom you will serve."

After Moses died, Joshua led the people out of the desert, across the Jordan and into the land that was promised. When he realized that death was near, he gathered the people to make a choice. Would they serve the Lord, who brought them all this way, or the gods of the land? The people swore to follow the Lord. Joshua pressed the issue a second time. "You may not be able to serve the Lord," he tells them later in chapter 24. But the people vow obedience to their God.

So Joshua takes a rock and calls it a witness before the people, laying it at the base of the sanctuary established in that place. We have such milestones that testify for us: our baptism, confirmation, and each Eucharist proclaim our willingness to follow the Lord. The community of faith to which we belong testifies for us. By sign, word, and membership, we testify for ourselves. Still we know Joshua's warning is true: we may fall short of our witness if our lives do not also cry out the faith we profess.

SECOND READING: EPHESIANS 5:21-32
The one who is in Christ is a new creation.

This controversial passage has both conservative and liberal Christians trembling in either passion or anger. How can we continue to employ an admonition that supports an unequal relationship between women and men?

Many try to rewrite the text speculating on what Paul might have said if he were teaching today; a more honest approach is to consider his intent. Paul seeks order in the church. Husbands must love their wives and care for them; (reading further in this passage), children should not be provoked needlessly; masters should not bully slaves. These were brave words in the first century, though the rest of the text sounds dissonant to contemporary ears.

The tension between the need for order and the changes demanded by the new creation remains within the church.

GOSPEL: JOHN 6:60–69
"This sort of talk is hard to endure!"

How can anyone take this kind of talk seriously? the people asked one another. Jesus spoke the mystical reality of his mission and self-offering, and many who had followed him did not associate with him anymore.

I wonder myself if I would have stayed: "I am the living bread come down from heaven"? I might have cheered when Jesus took on the temple authorities; attached myself fervently when the boy's fever was lifted, and the sick man walked after almost forty years. I would have tried to listen to teachings about the hour that was coming, and the relationship of the father and the son. But I might have reached my limit with the Bread of Life discourse. It seems so wild, so graphic and yet intangible.

Peter's words in this hour are characteristically brave. He says all of the right things, has the right vigor and certainty: Lord, we are not going anywhere. We are staying put. Apart from you there is no life, only the trickle of days and then darkness.

But Jesus knows there is a devil among the Twelve, and even the most faithful response is capable of turning into denial.

Questions for Reflection

• Besides the sacraments, what are some of the milestones which serve as markers of faith in your life?

• Reflect on this Sunday's second reading. Do you think Paul's words were meant to be taken literally? Can you see them as a commentary on the nature and role of service in Christian relationships?

• How would you have responded to Jesus in chapter 6 of John's Gospel? How do you respond now with your knowledge of the Eucharist?

Action Response

Think of the people you know who were "scandalized by religion," because of divorce, ill treatment by church members, hypocritical example, or inability to reconcile religious talk with the world they saw. Pray for them on their journey, and offer them acceptance.

Act on this Word

FIRST READING: DEUTERONOMY 4:1–2, 6–8
"This great nation is truly a wise and intelligent people."

Browse through Deuteronomy, from chapter 12 onward. You get the sense of a meticulous society, especially in passages like chapter 21, "The Expiation of Untraced Murder," in which the blood is accounted for by pacing off which town is closest to where the body falls. Every sin is to be accounted for and no guilt is to be unreconciled. There are twelve curses for those who do unspeakable things, like mislead a blind man, as well as blessings for obedience to God's word.

Moses tells the people that adherence to this way will lead to life, not to mention the esteem of other nations who marvel at this perfect society. Unfortunately, there is no way to know if this might have come to pass. This wholly reconciled and law-abiding community never materialized.

The church has chosen to follow a new way to life, not as perfect people but as sinners who count on God's forgiveness. Sinners are people who do not obey God's law meticulously, and sometimes do unspeakable things. But the God of mercy redeems us in our contrition and makes us worthy to be called God's own.

SECOND READING: JAMES 1:17–18, 21–22, 27
Humbly welcome the word that has taken root in you.

The letter of James is a peculiar piece of literature. As far as scholars can tell, it was not written by either James mentioned among the Twelve. It is a very Jewish letter, more in line with the Wisdom writings of the Hebrew Scriptures than anything found in the New Testament. Yet it is written in excellent Greek, unlike most of the crude Greek found elsewhere in the Bible.

As in Wisdom tradition, James shows a practical concern for what faith does, not what it says. He exhorts taking care of widows and orphans, the "poor little ones of God" so often evoked by the prophets. A society's response to justice and God's law would be measured by its relationship to

God's little ones. If the people were to be "first fruits of the nations," and offer "pure worship without stain," they would have to produce the actions behind these lovely words.

GOSPEL: MARK 7:1–8, 14–15, 21–23
You disregard God's command and cling to human tradition.

The battle between Jesus and the Pharisees is about anything but hygiene. Jesus is not opposed to washing your hands before meals, or washing the dishes (sorry, kids). Jesus is protesting empty rituals of purification that have no deeper significance.

We all have ways of washing our hands of the guilt we share. We tell little white lies that leave no tracks. We put people down and say, "Just kidding." We don't vote or get involved in politics because it is too messy. Like Pilate, we wash our hands of unpleasant responsibilities, and believe we are clean.

Run-of-the-mill wicked designs come out of hearts that seem quite neat and orderly to the eye. Lots of churchgoing folk harbor malice in their hearts. And shouldn't this be a cause for our concern, when Jesus tells us every sin begins in our hearts?

Questions for Reflection

• Christian practice has been to call ourselves sinners while knowing we are the saints of God. Which name are you least comfortable with? How do you know yourself to be both sinner and saint?

• How do you put actions to the faith you profess at home, at work, in the community?

• Examine the contents of your heart. What there is harmful to your discipleship? How can you empty what is not pure from your heart?

Action Response

Time to act on the word. Who are today's "widows and orphans," some forgotten group in your community or society at large? Contribute from your time, concern, and resources to the poor little ones of God.

Be Opened!

FIRST READING: ISAIAH 35:4–7

Be strong, fear not! Here is your God…who comes to save you.

The Negeb was an arid stretch of desert in the southern part of Judah. It was not a place of much hope or life, yet Isaiah foretells a time of great transformation for this desert. He compares the salvation of this barren land to the return of the exiles from Babylon. Both may seem unlikely events, but the God who can make a desert bloom can save the people from captivity. Be strong! Isaiah urges. The blind will see, the deaf will hear. Fear not! The lame will dance and the mute will sing. The great reversals of fate are in God's hands. The desert will have abundant water.

Each one of us has circumstances in our lives which we consider irreversible. A job in which we are hopelessly stuck. Relationships irretrievably broken. Depression that seems a permanent part of the landscape. Money trouble that will never go away. Yet the prophet proclaims that God seeks to make the barest desert into a place of blooming flowers.

SECOND READING: JAMES 2:1–5

Have you not set yourselves up as judges?

Discrimination is an almost inescapable aspect of group dynamics. Among church people, discrimination is the most distressing, since we are required under the law of love to receive "the least of these" with particular favor. Yet I have served on RCIA teams that wanted to exclude the homeless from candidacy; worked at receptions where poorly dressed people were not welcomed. I have struggled myself with those who are not gifted with pleasing personalities, wanting to keep them out of the groups I was in. The poor, the crazy, the smelly, the boring, the whiners, the nonstop talkers: it is all too easy to find ourselves setting up walls to keep out the marginal folks.

Every teaching of Jesus makes the last come out first, the poor one ahead of the rich one. Jesus ate with undesirables, chose smelly fishermen as his closest companions. He did not say: the kingdom of God is not for whiners and the boring. Jesus said the kingdom was a dragnet, and everything at the bottom would be raised to the light.

GOSPEL: MARK 7:31–37
"He has done everything well!"

Jesus goes into Gentile territory and brings his message to those who have no share in Israel's God or heritage. Evidently they had advance notice of his accomplishments, because they bring out to him a man who might otherwise have been hidden away. Jesus senses the man's discomfort in front of the crowd, perhaps, because he draws him aside and performs a healing. But the crowds are not about to allow this quiet miracle to remain quiet. What they had heard about Jesus is true: he does all things well.

As in our own time, we often hear the reactions of the crowd, but not the more private response of the individual. I want to gather up all those who were healed by Jesus and ask them, apart from the roar of the crowd, "What has happened to you? How has this changed you? What will you do now?" We know that crowds are fickle. They shout for Jesus today and against him tomorrow. Their astonishment is a passing thing. But what happens inside the person touched intimately by Jesus is another story. This is the story that remains largely untold in the Gospels. It is the story we can tell in the unfolding of our own conversion.

Questions for Reflection

• What part of your life resembles a desert? How might God cause that place to bloom and become a holy way?

• Who is favored in your community? Who is despised or overlooked?

• Imagine you are the deaf and impeded one called to be opened by Jesus. Explain what has happened to you. How has this changed you? What will you do now?

Action Response

Think of one marginalized group or individual in your community who might benefit from your welcome. Resolve to be more inclusive and respectful in your dealings with all who seek a place in the human community.

What's in a Name?

FIRST READING: ISAIAH 50:4–9
See, the Lord God is my help; who will prove me wrong?

Someone once called my aunt a noble woman because she had faithfully suffered a great deal in her life: a difficult marriage with an alcoholic, several stillborn children, and poor health later in life. With undisguised bitterness in her voice, she advised me, "Whatever you do, don't be noble."

After reading the Songs of the Suffering Servant in Isaiah, of which this passage is one, many might be tempted to say the same thing. In a succession of verses, the servant is mistreated, libeled, beaten, and eventually killed for his fidelity to the way of the Lord. No wonder that those who prophesied about a coming Messiah conveniently overlooked these verses. Nobody wanted to be so noble.

Jesus, however, took them very seriously, and was willing to be noble for the sake of humanity. Every generation is blessed to have one or two souls who are willing to follow the way of truth-speaking with real courage, and many of them will surrender their lives for what they hold dear. But I think there are other people who, with less visibility and little thanks, manage to live a small, heroic fidelity of their own. These too deserve our gratitude.

SECOND READING: JAMES 2:14–18
"You have faith and I have works—is that it?"

As early as the first century, some Christians were arguing one stereotype over another, until James puts an end to the charade. During the Reformation, Catholics were seen as the salvation-earners by the Protestant churches, not believing in the power of Christ's cross to relieve the world of its burden of sin. Instead, Catholics were out there "earning" heaven through good works, or at the worst, trying to buy their way out of hell.

Meanwhile, Catholics accused, Protestants were making too little of their relationship to the world. All they had to do was "believe in the name of the Lord" to be saved. They could rest on their laurels after that. Once saved, always saved. Where was personal initiative or accountability in that?

The fact is, no one with real faith would fail to live a life of good works. And Jesus himself said of those who were not followers in the normal sense but who imitated his example, "Who is not against us, is for us." We can't separate each other into the "faith" vs. "works" camps. In an incarnate faith like Christianity, one leads naturally to the other.

GOSPEL: MARK 8:27–35
"Who do people say that I am?"

People thought a lot of things about Jesus. Many compared him to the prophets, the Baptist, and Elijah, but others saw him in the same vein as those magicians and philosophers from the East who often came to town with their strange science and stranger ideas. Some probably thought he was like rabbis they had heard before, or the better doctors of Jerusalem.

And then, some had less enthusiastic ideas. People said he was irreligious, a blasphemer, no keeper of the Sabbath and no respecter of authority, a troublemaker who would one day turn Jerusalem a shade darker with more spilt blood. When Peter finally offers his best guess, "You are the Messiah," Jesus does not seem particularly pleased about that, at least not in Mark's version of the story. The term "messiah" had come to mean so much, and so little, in Israel's long history.

Who Jesus is for us becomes the real question of the Gospel. Who we are willing to let him be in our lives becomes the central matter of our faith.

Questions for Reflection

• Have you known people whose fidelity in the midst of suffering made their witness heroic ?

• Are there areas of your life in which faith has led you to action? Are there areas in which action has led you to faith?

• Give Jesus a name in your life. Is he Lord, savior, king, friend, teacher, healer, or something else?

Action Response

Address Jesus in your prayer throughout the week with different names. Each day choose a new answer to the question, "Who do you say that I am?" and live out the relationship that follows for that day. What do you learn about who Jesus is?

The Way of the Wise

FIRST READING: WISDOM 2:12, 17–20

Let us put him to the test that we may have proof of his gentleness.

Wisdom literature is largely a philosophy of contrasts: the wise one versus the fool. The just one in contrast to the evil one. In fact, we are all sometimes wise and sometimes foolish, sometimes just and sometimes prone to sin.

In the Book of Wisdom, the argument is advanced even further. Sometimes the just suffer precisely because they *are* just, and evil cannot tolerate such a witness. And sometimes the good person is put to death, as in the case of Jesus. So how can Wisdom literature claim that the just are blessed by God?

The Book of Wisdom suggests that God's justice is served in the life to come. This is a novel idea in the Hebrew Scriptures. A theology of afterlife is hardly touched on until the writings of Wisdom and the Maccabees. By the time of Jesus, the Pharisees have a well-developed theology of the afterlife.

As we look at the evening news, we have to agree that good and evil are not rewarded fairly in this world. If God is just, then real justice must be something we will see in the kingdom.

SECOND READING: JAMES 3:16—4:3

Wisdom from above is first of all innocent

James makes all of the usual connections: wisdom leads to justice, justice to peace. He also reminds his audience that desire is at the heart of all sin and leads to endless rounds of conflict. It is in every sense the original sin. Sin originates in our desire for more.

The whole of capitalism would collapse tomorrow if we could not be lured by the prospect of more. Don't you want a newer car? A bigger house? This year's clothes? The latest thing? Our original wound of sin drives us to pastimes like "going shopping," which is another name for arousing covetousness. We see, therefore we want. By any other name, shopping arouses one of the seven deadly sins, simple greed.

Greed leads to envy, and anger…why, you could probably work up a batch of deadly sins on one trip to the mall! James contrasts this downward spiral with the fruits of wisdom: innocence, peace, tolerance, sympathy, kindness. The interior conflicts aroused by desire are at rest in the one who seeks wisdom. The wise seek God's way, which is another kind of more.

GOSPEL: MARK 9:30–37
"Whoever welcomes a child such as this for my sake welcomes me."

We can imagine the conversation the disciples must have been having about who is most important. Peter is saying, "I'm the first to act! I'm right at his side every time!" John points out that it is he who reclines his head on Jesus' chest at supper. Andrew says, "I was one of the first to follow. Peter wouldn't even be here if not for me." Judas says, "He trusts me with the purse." But Matthew keeps the books, and is taking good notes for what might be a prophetic parchment one day. They all have their reasons to think they are most vital to the mission.

Jesus puts an end to this nonsense by saying the most important one is the one who seeks to be least important. Then he draws out a child by way of example. What an irrelevant person a child was seen to be! A child was an economic liability, a helpless person in need of defense. But Jesus says: Value this person as you would me.

The sight of that child's uplifted face made all their arguments fall away.

Questions for Reflection

• Where do you see signs of justice in your community? Where are the signs of injustice?

• How has desire made you unwise? How does wisdom calm the desire for more?

• Who do we consider valuable according to the standards of society? Around whom would Jesus wrap his arms and stand in our midst?

Action Response

Where in your life are you a leader? In your family, at school, at work, among friends? Practice being the servant of all. Enter your group as one available to welcome the humblest person as you would Christ.

Whose Side Are You On?

FIRST READING: NUMBERS 11:25–29
"Would that all the people of the Lord were prophets!"

Who knows why they did not go out to the Tent of the Presence that day? Eldad and Medad obviously were not excluded by God, and they were on the list of elders. Maybe they were sick, or someone needed their help. Whatever kept them in the camp did not keep them from receiving the portion of God's Spirit allotted to them. Yet some found the prophesying of these two distressing. It was not right for them to share in the gift of prophecy.

Sometimes we get more caught up with the source of a prophecy than with the discernment of its message. I remember really liking a series of little television ad spots about family togetherness, and then blanching when the tagline read: Church of Jesus Christ of the Latter-Day Saints. Would the message be more true if the Catholics had sponsored it?

In the same way, sometimes the right rubber stamp does nothing to lessen the inauthenticity of a message. We probably do not need to go all the way back to the Crusades to think of something the institutional church has sponsored that was not particularly holy. God's Spirit blows where it wills. As soon as we think we've got it in a bottle, it is sure to turn up someplace else.

SECOND READING: JAMES 5:1–6
See what you have stored up for yourselves against the last days.

You do not want an address in a first world country when this reading comes up. Yet it does not tell us anything we do not already suspect. The one who has the most toys at the end doesn't win, spiritually speaking.

Of course, a lot of us are in this for the short haul, with emphasis on what we can haul. We do not climb the corporate ladder with our thoughts on heaven. We do not buy a more comfy couch thinking about our spiritual life. Likewise, most of us do not withhold workers' wages, nor did we consciously kill a just person.

But the question is never: how bad are we? The question is: how good are we? If our lives are predominantly about getting ahead, we can be sure someone is being left behind. If we are focused on what will make our lives more comfortable, we can be sure someone else is made less comfortable. Wherever it is we think we are going, we have to stop and consider the shouts of those harvesters which reach the ears of the Lord.

GOSPEL: MARK 9:38–43, 45, 47–48
"Anyone who is not against us is with us."

John brings to Jesus the same saga Joshua brought to Moses: someone not of our company is speaking in the name of the Lord, with the same success. Jesus points out, I imagine dryly, that anyone expelling demons in his name is likely on his side. It is an argument he used with those who questioned his own power over demons: might he be in league with Beelzebul? Jesus countered: Beelzebul is having a bad day if he is casting out his own demons! Good fruit comes from good hearts, and rotten fruit from rotten hearts. It is a simple enough formula to understand.

Jesus moves much further than we would like in this argument. He says whatever leads us into sin is not worth possessing. The extreme examples he uses are gory but sincere. If we cannot stop our eyes from causing us to sin, we have less need of the eye than of ridding ourselves of the sin. Few self-mutilations occur in parishes after the Twenty-Sixth Sunday in Ordinary Time, so one must presume we have found other ways of avoiding the sins that most attract us.

Questions for Reflection

• When have you heard the right prophecy from the "wrong" source? How did it affect your ability to receive the message?

• How good do you want to be? How might you measure how good you already are?

• Think of a time when you may have become involved in serious sin. How did you "cut it off" from your life?

Action Response

Think about your answer to the second reflection question: how good do you want to be? What keeps you from answering that call? Resolve to "cut off" one aspect of your behavior that keeps you from being as good as you are called to be.

The Suitable Partner

FIRST READING: GENESIS 2:18–24

"This one, at last, is bone of my bone, and flesh of my flesh."

In the first creation story in chapter one of Genesis, man and woman are created simultaneously, in the image and likeness of God. That story emphasized how much the first people were one with God, alike to God in a way that was tangible as well as functional. They carried the divine image and the mandate to co-create the world through human history.

The second creation story in chapter 2 is about how the first people were one with each other. They shared flesh and bone, were made for the purpose of companionship and partnership. The plan was beautiful. But like the garden itself, it was not invulnerable to sin.

Sin created division between the Creator and creation. It caused friction between the man and the woman as well. Because of sin, love would be hard work, requiring real commitment and a spirit of reconciliation. Two can still know the joy of being one body, a holy partnership. With forgiveness, the beautiful plan can still be realized.

SECOND READING: HEBREWS 2:9–11

Jesus was made for a little while lower than the angels.

Jesus "tasted death" for our sake. We tremble at the idea of our death, but Jesus took it on in order to know our humanity completely. We shrink from mortality, but the one who did not have to die chose to die so that we would not walk there alone.

Imagine what it meant for Jesus to become a companion of death, so that we might become the companions of eternal life. What's more, the writer of Hebrews tells us that we have become, along with Jesus, the children of one loving God. Jesus "is not ashamed" to be our brother, but chooses to welcome us into his holy family. We all know of families who have hidden away or disowned their less admirable members. For Jesus to desire such close kinship with us is nothing less than amazing.

GOSPEL: MARK 10:2–16

"They are no longer two but one flesh."

More Catholics have been lost over the matter of divorce than just about any other issue. Jesus is clear about his stand, derived from Genesis. But both the teachings of Moses and the actions of the church have sometimes wavered on this issue. Jesus says two lives joined by God cannot be taken apart. Yet we stand by and watch marriages crumble every day.

Two people contract a marriage for a variety of efficient reasons: to legitimate a sexual union, to beat loneliness, insecurity, financial solvency, to please someone else. When holes in the contract appear, after a year or five or forty, people head for the doors and that's it. Many of those relationships should end and few of us doubt it. So the church's unyielding stance, borrowed from Jesus, can seem unrealistic.

Annulment is one way the church has found to say: these two lives did not come together for a holy purpose to begin with, in the way Jesus speaks of or the teaching of the church intends. It has to be a deliberate partnership inspired by the love of God and nourished by fidelity. It has to include the element of mutual forgiveness. Otherwise, in the eyes of the Catholic Church, what is lost by divorce is not a sacrament at all.

Questions for Reflection

• Name three lessons you have learned in love, whether with a spouse, child, parent, or friend. How do these reflect the beautiful plan of love in Genesis?

• Jesus, your brother, is coming to spend the weekend with you. What is in your heart that you want to share with him?

• How has your life been touched by divorce? Who has shown you the love "joined by God" that Jesus calls us to, and how?

Action Response

Identify those relationships in your life that are "suitable partnerships" of love and faith. Think of family members or others in your community, parish, or circle of friends, with whom you are joined by God to bring love into the world.

God's Word Is Alive!

FIRST READING: WISDOM 7:7–11

I chose to have Wisdom rather than the light.

It sounds like a riddle: what is more valuable than power, riches, and light itself? Wisdom! Too often, we get wisdom mixed up with knowledge, and fool ourselves into thinking an Ivy League education is in order. We know that people with degrees can have lives as unsuccessful and unhappy as anyone else's, so knowing a lot obviously is not the answer.

To the writers of the Hebrew Wisdom tradition, wisdom means more than being schooled in human learning. The spirit of wisdom is a gift from God, bestowed through prayer. It is guidance into the ways of God that will lead to a splendor that human wealth cannot provide. All good things come to the one who keeps company with wisdom. And without wisdom, all riches are folly.

In the Christian tradition, Jesus is later identified as the Wisdom of God. With his Gospel in our hearts, we are wealthier than kings, more powerful than death. The light of Christ is better than a thousand suns, and enables us to look into the human heart with clear sight.

SECOND READING: HEBREWS 4:12–13

God's word penetrates and divides soul and spirit, joints and marrow.

We live in a time in which the written word is more and more dismissed. Maybe newspapers will disappear and books will become more rare. But the power of words will never fade as long as there are people to speak them. Think of the words of leaders throughout history which still echo their truth and authority to this day. Think of the words of those who are close to you that you hold dearly or painfully in your heart. The power of words to transform hearts and lives is in no danger of losing its effectiveness in our world.

How much more authority does the word of God hold for us, in its truth, beauty, and majesty? The manifold word which God utters is at once creation itself, the story of Scripture, and Jesus, the incarnation of God's love, spoken tenderly into our midst. We ourselves are words of God being spoken into our communities. What are we saying to those who hear us?

GOSPEL: MARK 10:17–30
"With God all things are possible."

The story of the rich man is two stories, really: the dialogue between the earnest man and Jesus, and the ensuing conversation between Jesus and the disciples. The rich man has kept all the rules and knows there is more. He seeks Jesus out for the greater challenge to go deeper in his walk with God. But his face falls when he learns the cost. Following Jesus is one thing; giving up his possessions is another.

The disciples at first see this test as too hard, If this is the standard, who can be saved? Peter perceives the parallel between the admonition to the rich man and the way of the disciples: "What you ask of him is what we ourselves have done!" They indeed left their nets, their homes, their way of life to become his followers. And Jesus promises Peter that one who has surrendered the old life in favor of the Gospel will be rewarded a hundredfold with property, family, persecution, and eternal life.

Did somebody say persecution? If we read beyond this passage, we find the disciples amazed and afraid at this speech. No kidding! So Jesus once again explains what the Son of Man must suffer. Discipleship has its price, and we are all like the rich man who finds it set just a bit higher than what we expected to pay.

Questions for Reflection

• Who is the wisest person you know? What makes them wise?

• Make a short list of some of the most powerful words ever spoken in your life. What is the most powerful statement in the Bible to you? How is it like the words on your list?

• What are the riches in your life that might be hampering your call to deeper discipleship?

Action Response

Be conscious of the power of words this week. Listen to the words you speak to others, and take care to be an incarnate word of God's love to everyone around you.

Drinking from the Lord's Cup

FIRST READING: ISAIAH 53:10–11

Through his suffering, my servant shall justify many.

Martyrs, both secular and religious, have a hold on our imagination. When we encounter people willing to die for their convictions, we have to ask ourselves: is there anything I am willing to die for? Is there anything I hold more precious than my own life?

The servant of Isaiah described in this last of the four Songs of the Servant is a particularly heroic figure. He does not give his life for a loved one or for a grand ideal, but as a sin offering. Willing to die, not for good but in reparation for evil? Those who originally contemplated the scroll of Isaiah must have had as difficult a time with this passage as we do. Yet Jesus saw himself in the role of Isaiah's servant, and set about to fulfill the prophecy.

The servant is promised long life and descendants, neither of which Jesus had in a natural sense. But Christ lives in the church, and we are all heirs to his kingdom in the Spirit. Christ lives in the world to the extent we are willing to give him breath and being in ourselves.

SECOND READING: HEBREWS 4:14–16

Let us confidently approach the throne of grace.

We share in the life of Christ because Christ has shared in ours first. This is a fundamental Christian belief, that the life of Christ is available to us because God took on flesh and knew mortality in Jesus. God knew the frustrations of human limitation, not being able to control events or foresee the future. (The Gospels vary in their understanding of how much Jesus could control and predict, but Mark says Jesus could work no miracle in Nazareth without the cooperation of faith, and John's account says plainly that he did not know the hour until it arrived.) God knew rejection, loneliness, weariness, hunger and thirst, fickle friends, and sorrow deep enough to shed tears.

In Jesus, God came to know the full horror of physical suffering and death. All of this is the human condition which God gladly bore so that we might in turn know life in the kingdom. Clearly, we get the better part of the deal. Confident in such love, we can approach God for our heart's desire.

GOSPEL: MARK 10:35–45
"From the cup I drink of you shall drink."

You have to admit, James and John had a lot of nerve. They asked Jesus to make sure they would share in his glory and be properly rewarded for their fidelity. If this scene were vaudeville, we might see Jesus smacking his forehead with his hand. He has just told the rich man to give up all of his possessions if he wished to be a disciple. And then he reminds his disciples a third time of his coming passion. And James and John, oblivious to the warnings, are still looking for the payoff.

So Jesus says: you are looking to share in my life? You really want a share in what's coming to me? Well, then, drink from my cup. Oh sure, they said reflexively. In the simplicity of their greed, they are not hearing the consequences of their assent. And Jesus assures these naive followers that they will indeed share in his fate—though they scarcely imagine the fine print on the contract they are eager to sign.

We drink from the cup of Christ and hope for everlasting life. We forget this is a cup of blood, and that the way to glory is the cross.

Questions for Reflection

• For what might you be willing to give your life? Is your faith on the list of things you might die for?

• Which elements of your humanity cause you the most trouble (e.g., anger, impatience, limited energy, being misunderstood)? How did Jesus deal with these or similar conditions?

• Have you ever behaved like James and John, more interested in what you can get from religion than in what it costs to be a disciple? How has that affected you now?

Action Response

Where is the cross of Christ being carried in your community? Share a drink from the Lord's cup, and help someone bear their cross.

Receiving Our Sight

FIRST READING: JEREMIAH 31:7–9

I will gather them from the ends of the world.

Consider the scene Jeremiah has drawn for his fellow Jews who have languished in exile in Babylon. The Lord will return the people to their land. After a generation of loss, everyone is going home.

And I do mean everyone. Jeremiah sees the blind and lame, those most likely to be left behind, as being brought back in the midst of the people. No one will be counted as unworthy or unvalued. Pregnant women and those with small children will be part of the stream of those moving homeward. Those with special needs are welcome on this journey. The Lord will personally smooth the road so that no one will stumble along the way.

We read this journey now as a forerunner of the road to the kingdom. God's consolation and guidance companion us on this road. We have the living water of baptism to quench our thirst along the way. We have an obligation to help those for whom such movement is difficult, and we keep pace with the weak, not with the strongest among us.

SECOND READING: HEBREWS 5:1–6

Even Christ did not glorify himself with the office of high priest.

I admit it: I seek the esteem of others and bask in words of praise. If there is glory to be had, I would like a slice of it. A big slice, please.

The writer of Hebrews points out that the most glorious office in the land, that of high priest, is appointed by God's design and not according to human merit. What is more, the high priest is humbled by the task of offering sacrifice for the people's sins, knowing he is a sinner as well.

Sitting in the glory seat does not make a person glorious, but simply chosen to be there, for God's greater good. Even Jesus received the role of eternal high priest at God's decree alone. If Jesus does not presume to glorify himself, we walk on uncertain ground when we seek glory for ourselves.

"Get up! He is calling you!"

I worship in a large city parish where the Mass is often interrupted by someone making a disturbance of some kind. It could be someone drunk or on
drugs, mentally ill, or perhaps just needy and desperate. I have heard that
the papal Mass at Easter has been interrupted in the same manner, so even
the pope has days like ours. The sizable crowd around Jesus responds to
Bartimaeus in the same spirit most of us are inclined to at these times: they
want to shut him up, so that the holy experience they are having is not
marred by his lament.

But Bartimaeus will not shut up. Needy desperate people seldom do, as
they have nothing to lose. And since "the Lord hears the cry of the poor,"
Bartimaeus is summoned into the presence of Jesus. Jesus asks him what he
wants, and the blind man is not shy or coy: he wants his sight given to him.
He knows Jesus can do it. And Jesus, always grateful for the incredible faith
of the poor, says faith has granted his heart's desire. And he sends him on
his way.

Bartimaeus, however, does not go on his way, but goes in the way of his
Lord. Given eyes to see, he changes the course of his life in the favor of the
one who is life. Now there is a person with real sight.

Questions for Reflection

• On the road to the kingdom, who is being left behind in your community? What can be done to include them on the journey?

• What kind of glory is available to you in your community, work, or
relationships? Do you seek it, advertise it, or simply accept it?

• Think of a time when your eyes were opened by faith. What did you
come to see that you did not see before?

Action Response

Get one step closer to the kingdom this week. Include someone who
is normally left behind by inviting them to lunch, to church, into the
conversation or activity from which they have often been excluded.

Not Far From God's Reign

FIRST READING: DEUTERONOMY 6:2–6
"Hear, O Israel! The Lord is our God, the Lord alone!"

After giving the people God's Ten Commandments, Moses summarizes them in one brilliant phrase, "You shall love the Lord, your God, with all your heart, and with all your soul, and with all your strength." If one keeps that commandment, the others are already obeyed.

Many of us would rather keep any commandment but that one. This reminds me of a preaching class I taught at a local seminary. After many weeks of giving each student both oral and written evaluations on every homily they preached, they complained to me that they were not getting enough feedback. Stunned, I asked them what more they could want: "I have told you every strength you have demonstrated, every phrase I have admired, every structural method that worked well for you."

"But you never tell us what we are doing wrong," they protested. Oh. They found it more helpful to know what to avoid than to know what to do. In the same way, we might find it easier to approach religion like a checklist, striking off each item to our credit, and then finding some free time at the end of the day just for ourselves. But faith is a relationship, not a job. We are never properly outside our relationship with God.

SECOND READING: HEBREWS 7:23–28
Jesus has a priesthood that does not pass away.

The ancient office of priesthood was first and foremost one of mediation. People, being sinners, could not comfortably or without peril approach God directly. Priests were sinners too, of course, and there was some real peril in the performance of their duties. There are stories all through the Bible of priests getting zapped for handling sacred things without the proper reverence or permission.

Still, when a priest was cautious enough and pious enough, he could perform a great service on behalf of God's people in reconciling them to the Holy One through the sacrificial offerings. The author of the letter to the Hebrews argues that the priesthood of Jesus surpasses and replaces the need for human mediation. Jesus is the perfect high priest because he is not a sinner, and can most perfectly represent us to God. That is why the Eucharist is called the great sacrament for the forgiveness of sin. Through Christ, we are reconciled with the Holy One in the sharing of this meal.

GOSPEL: MARK 12:28–34
"You are not far from the reign of God."

Once in a while, a professional minister of Jesus' day managed to "get it." There were followers of Jesus among the Sanhedrin, like Joseph of Arimathea and Nicodemus. And there is the unnamed scribe here, who comes to listen to Jesus with an open mind and goes away with the best reference of anyone in history: "You are not far from the kingdom."

That is, of course, true for all of us. We are as close to God's reign as our purest impulse, and as far from the kingdom as our most selfish act. The reign of God is at hand, Jesus tells us, and we can be in it with a simple act of will. Most of the time, we don't will it. We prefer to live in the world where we can be sovereign, at least within the confines of our hearts. In God's reign, which is not so far from us at any moment, God is at the center of things, and we are willing to let God be God of heart and soul and mind and strength.

Questions for Reflection

• How do you demonstrate your love for the people in your life? How do you show your love for God?

• What is the role of the priest in our assembly today?

• Consider the various roles you play in your daily life. How many of these roles do you play out within God's reign, and how many exist solidly within your own domain?

Action Response

Choose one relationship in your life that is farthest from the ideal of God's domain, and make some effort this week to move it a little closer to the ideal. Pray to be given the grace to stop being in charge of this relationship, and to let God be God there.

Places of Honor

FIRST READING: 1 KINGS 17:10–16

The jar of flour did not go empty, nor the jug of oil run dry.

Things were bad enough after her husband died, and she and her son were plunged into poverty. But now this: another mouth to feed, from God no less. The widow must have wondered if her prayers were being mocked.

As she carefully explained the situation to the prophet, a small flutter of hope might have brushed her. Would God act on her behalf at last? Elijah asks her to believe in God's promises, and she does. And no one goes hungry in her house through the remainder of the land's famine.

Often, we who have much more are able to believe in God's promises much less. Maybe depending on our own efforts for so long makes us jaded in our faith in anything but ourselves. Faith, like any other attribute, must be exercised if it is to be used. We cannot draw on dormant faith in crisis and expect it to be there for us. Like something left in the attic too long, it may lose its capacity to serve.

SECOND READING: HEBREWS 9:24–28

Christ entered heaven itself that he might appear before God on our behalf.

Catholicism cultivates a sense of sacred space. We consecrate the ground where churches are to be built, and we believe a True Presence inhabits our tabernacles, sacraments, and rituals. We believe a True Presence dwells among us as well, wherever two or more are gathered.

We borrowed the sense of sanctuary from the Hebrew tradition of a place where God protects the sinner from the destruction due for sin. Our sanctuaries are still places of refuge and comfort, where holy words are proclaimed and a holy meal is laid for the guests of the Lord. We are also charged to provide sanctuary to those who are needy and seek our help.

Christ is ever-present to God and so needs no formal meeting ground to act on our behalf. We, however, still need holy ground, a sense of holy times and places, to call us to the encounter and remind us that God is ever-present to us.

GOSPEL: MARK 12:38–44

"Be on guard against those who like marks of respect and places of honor at banquets."

It is easy to target the modern priest for being the parodied character in this teaching, especially because the scribes held a similar role in the assembly that Jesus is using as an example. Our Sunday homilist, who reads his own epitaph in this Gospel, is wiser than the scribes whom Jesus is observing within the temple, who are oblivious to his criticism.

But none of us can safely point a finger on this issue of seeking places of honor and marks of esteem. We all like our efforts to be recognized and acknowledged in some compartment of history. I remember in graduate school how some of my fellow students would run to see the latest copy of *Who's Who* to see if they were somebody yet. I know spouses who rush home to tell their partners what a fuss the boss made over them today, or parents who brag to anyone who can stand it about their children's achievements. We want very much to be important in someone's eyes.

Jesus points out the poor widow who discreetly slips two coins in the temple treasury box as the most "important" contributor of all. What she has done has no merit in the world's assessment, but that makes it all the more valuable in the eyes of God.

Questions for Reflection

• What helps you to believe? What hinders your faith?

• What places and times help you to encounter God and become mindful of the holiness of every place and every hour?

• Make a list of what makes you important in the eyes of the world. Then make a list of the contributions that God values. Which list is longer?

Action Response

Get down and get humble! Try to do one good deed every day that escapes all attention except the Lord's.

The Time of Distress

FIRST READING: DANIEL 12:1-3

At that time your people shall escape.

Time for a second look at this passage from Daniel. The prophecies of Daniel are apocalyptic, which means "hidden." Daniel is not the author but the hero of this book, written during a period of persecution for the Jewish people two centuries before Christ. The moral of these stories is always that the faithful will persevere even in times of great distress.

The archangel Michael appears elsewhere in Daniel, Jude, and Revelation, always as the protector of God's people. Today Catholics also look to him as the patron of police officers and others charged with the vocation to protect. In the time of distress, this prophecy makes clear that God's people will escape destruction, even if their lives are lost in the persecution. Death, the most final time of distress, cannot hold the faithful in the dust of the earth. They shall awake to a splendor known only to the heavens.

SECOND READING: HEBREWS 10:11-14, 18

Once sins have been forgiven, there is no further offering for sin.

Ancient Israel was caught in the never-ending cycle of temple sacrifice. Since the people kept sinning, the sin offerings had to be ongoing. Christians who reflected on the cross understood that the price for sin has been remitted for all time. Jesus assured us that our sins are forgiven. The cycle of bartering with God for forgiveness was ended.

Still, Catholics continue to seek the sacrament of reconciliation. Why, if our sins are already forgiven? The wisdom of the church sees our mortality ever in need of signs to assure us of grace. People who love need signs of love to make the love go deeper. It is not enough to say: she knows I love her; he knows I care. In love, we speak the words and offer the signs of love so that our love is always visible to one another. Likewise, through word and sign, we deepen our understanding of the great forgiveness that Christ embodies.

GOSPEL: MARK 13:24–32
You will know that he is near, even at the door.

Fundamentalist groups are very excited by passages about the time of final tribulation. Though Jesus states plainly that no one can know the day or the hour, he also implies that the wise will be able to discern the signs. Many like to think themselves wise.

The fig tree is the clue to unfolding this metaphor. A farmer or gardener can tell immediately when life is about to come forth, just by knowledge of the plant. In the same way, the practiced Christian can sense ways that lead to life (or sin and death) by reading the signs. Will the sun be darkened and the stars fall down? When God's justice is denied, the darkness of the world has already fallen across human hearts. In the same way, where there is justice, the kingdom has already come.

Questions for Reflection

• How do you deal with times of distress in your life? What sustains you?

• How do you show forgiveness to others? How does receiving forgiveness affect your capacity to love?

• Where do you see the darkening of the sun in your community? Where does God's justice shine most brightly?

Action Response

Do not just talk justice: be justice, which the church defines as giving to God and others what is due them. Give God reverence and praise. Give others respect, compassion, and presence. Be attentive to the opportunities to love.

CHRIST THE KING

The Coming of the Kingdom

FIRST READING: DANIEL 7:13-14

Nations and people of every language serve him.

It is difficult to read this passage of Daniel as Christians and not think of Jesus. Jesus used the title "Son of Man" to refer to himself, and the image of Christ's triumphant reign in the kingdom of God is very like Daniel's description. Yet Daniel did not anticipate a messiah in his use of the term. What he intended was an image of the redeemed people of Israel coming into God's presence in a glorified and worthy form.

When Jesus adopts the term, he points the fulfillment of the prophecy in the direction of his own actions. It is he who receives dominion from the Ancient One. And it is in his kingdom that we find our heaven, our perfect world. We may not be favored with visions in the night, as the writer of Daniel was. But we can trust in the vision of the kingdom as Jesus proclaimed it.

SECOND READING: REVELATION 1:5-8

"I am the Alpha and the Omega!"

In the apocalyptic writing which is the Book of Revelation, we find many expressions that confound us. It is part poetry and song, part mystical numerology and shameless cheerleading. It is the writing of people under persecution, yet it has the arrogant confidence of victory. It communicates the promise of the past, the distress of the present, and hope for the future without pausing for transitions.

Since we are far removed from that time and its presumptions, what is important for us is the cosmic nature that Jesus has assumed in one short generation. The Christian community has made the leap between the Jesus of history to the Christ of faith, as theologians say. In the understanding of the church, he has become the Alpha and the Omega, the one constant throughout all time. As in John's Gospel, he is the word present before creation, and the King of Kings who will come to claim his own at history's end.

By the end of the first century, it was apparent to the church that Jesus was not just a hero, a holy man, a great teacher, or an adopted favorite of

God. In centuries to follow, despite heresies that seek to limit or reduce his stature, Jesus remains the anointed king who is to come and before whom every knee must bend.

GOSPEL: JOHN 18:33–37
"Anyone committed to the truth hears my voice."

Pilate wants to know if Jesus claims to be the king of the Jews. Jesus makes it clear that kingship is his, but he does not call himself the Jewish king. His kingship is broader than over one nation, and what is subject to him is much larger than Pilate's imagination or theology.

We stumble over the identity of Christ the King today. The view of monarchies we can see is not very inspiring. And as Americans, our history has been a conscious departure from the reality of kings and their pseudo-divine rights. But when it comes to Christ, kingship finds its only proper place. The divine right to rule has been given to the son who was entirely faithful to the One who sent him. Sovereignty, complete power over all, is in the possession of the Lord of love. Jesus defines his kingship before Pilate as a commitment to the truth. The borders of his territory are known in our willingness to witness.

Questions for Reflection

• What is your vision of the perfect world? How does it compare to Jesus' proclamation of the kingdom?

• What difference does Jesus' divinity make to your faith?

• Jesus says we hear his voice when we are committed to the truth. In what aspects of your life do you witness to the truth that Jesus teaches?

Action Response

Make the kingdom real for someone this week. Bring comfort to the afflicted, food to the hungry, joy to the sorrowing, good news to the poor. Give someone else a reason to believe that Christ is the king you serve.

Cycle C

Be on Guard!

FIRST READING: JEREMIAH 33:14–16
The Lord is our justice.

Each church year ends with a vision of the Apocalypse, and the new one begins in Advent with the same vision of world-shattering events. Since birth and death both plunge us into territory we cannot anticipate, and rob us of the familiar, it makes sense that time itself begins and ends in chaos.

How strange, then, to find Jeremiah (of all prophets!) in a peaceful interlude. He predicts the coming of safety and security, a time of justice and right. Though he writes to a people doomed by exile, he affirms God's promise to lift them up. The just shoot of David, we understand, will be the descendent of David we anticipate in this season. Jeremiah's prophecy is pronounced six centuries before the birth of Jesus. In our time, we await the day of justice and right when the kingdom of God is established in our midst.

SECOND READING: 1 THESSALONIANS 3:12—4:2
You must learn to make still greater progress.

Paul's first letter to the Christians in Thessalonica is very optimistic. He commends them on many levels, instructs them briefly and blesses them heartily. Yet even in this letter that is, comparatively speaking, a pat on the back for a job well done, Paul exhorts the people to make greater progress in the faith.

We can all take this admonition to heart. Conversion, once a word used to describe the process of converting to the church from a place of unbelief, is now more properly understood as the ongoing work of the Christian. You and I must continue to grow in our fidelity to the Gospel, in our knowledge of God's word, and in the challenge to be people of justice and compassion. No one of us has "arrived" to the fullness of faith. Conversion, a word that means change, is something we have to be humble enough to embrace.

GOSPEL: LUKE 21:25-28, 34-36

"Stand up straight and raise your heads, for your ransom is near."

The terrifying words of coming tribulation seem out of sync in the season of "Deck the Halls" and Christmas shopping. While all the world is preparing for a family holiday, a big feast, a babe in a manger, the church wants us to prepare for the end of the world.

You do not have to be Scrooge to appreciate this liturgical twist. The church calendar, after all, is not "pretend time," when we all act like it is 2,000 years ago and Jesus is coming to be born again. The church calendar reminds us that, in the midst of our daily routines, our fixed cycles of Monday through Sunday, season and plans, God has an eternal plan that is also in motion.

Beyond the cycle of ordinary history is salvation history. Beyond the babe in the manger is the coming of the kingdom. Watch! Be on guard! Look up! This world is passing, gradually, minutely. And much more swiftly, we are passing through it. To be too indulged with worldly desires and cares is to buy stock in a fly-by-night operation. If you would not spend your dollars that way, why spend your life in pursuit of what will all pass away on the great day of which Jesus speaks?

Questions for Reflection

• How do justice and right make everyone "safe and secure," as in Jeremiah's prophecy?

• Name three ways in which you are being called to the change required in ongoing conversion. What one step can you take to begin these changes?

• If today were the great day of the Lord's coming, what would you do to prepare? Are these things you are doing or could be doing now?

Action Response

Choose one of the changes you identified in the reflection questions and begin to prepare the way of the Lord in this season of waiting in joyful hope.

The Straight Path

FIRST READING: BARUCH 5:1–9
Up, Jerusalem! Stand upon the heights.

What price would you be willing to pay for the road to liberation? For the Israelites in exile in Babylon, the price was *tshuvah*, or turning. They had to turn from their service to idols, wealth, injustice, and turn again to the one God. One of the great prophets of the exile was Jeremiah, and his secretary was a man named Baruch. Together these men assisted the people in re-imagining themselves as God's people.

Baruch offers stirring images of hope: a people taking off their misery like clothing to be exchanged for the glad rags of celebration. Peace and justice become their heritage after servitude. Forests lend their shade as a desert people make their way home, and fragrant trees make the journey pleasant.

Who are the prophets among us who help us to re-imagine ourselves as the people of God, and lead us in the great turning of our lives to freedom?

SECOND READING: PHILIPPIANS 1:4–6, 8–11
My prayer is that your love may more and more abound.

People who know that love is at the core of their identity tend to keep loving more. I am not referring to the needy disease that passes for romantic love these days, the can't-live-with-or-without-the-beloved syndrome which our culture holds up as an ideal. Real love, grounded in compassion, is recognizable because it is both just and honest. And folks like the Philippians who find the real love of Christ as their identity, find too that loving makes them rich.

The kind of love the world celebrates makes people feel emotionally bankrupt. They are "the luckiest people in the world," but only until the whole thing falls apart. This neurotic love leads people to become hooked on love, or afraid of it altogether. Real love casts out fear, makes us stronger and more tender people. We "value the things that really matter," and by doing so enable the kingdom to come a little closer. People who walk in love act as though the kingdom has already come.

GOSPEL: LUKE 3:1-6

The word of God was spoken to John, son of Zechariah, in the desert.

The scene is set on a worldwide stage—at least, so far as the Roman empire was concerned. Mark and Matthew were less concerned with placing the story of Jesus beyond its consequences for Israel, but Luke, a Greek convert, insists that the story took place under the shadow of Caesar, Pilate, the tetrarchs, and the Jewish authorities. Though Galilee may be a geographical hole in the wall, this story is for the world at large.

We are beginning the year of Luke this season, and we will begin seeing the story of salvation through Luke's eyes. The word of God comes to John, who emerges from the desert to proclaim the word and fulfill Isaiah's prophecy about the herald. The herald has come to bring a message of salvation for all of humanity. The path being cleared will lead to every door. Anyone willing to walk in the way of the Lord is invited to come on the journey. What an open welcome! Gone are the ancient barriers of them and us. In this season of fresh starts, all are invited to leave the rough and winding ways behind.

Questions for Reflection

• From what do you need to be made free? What will liberation cost you?

• Who shows you what the real love of Christ is? Has the love of the world ever made you poorer?

• As pilgrims on the way of the Lord, we encounter many different kinds of people who share our journey. How do you react to the "unlikely" people you meet along your path?

Action Response

This year of Luke is a great time to encourage ecumenical or interfaith cooperation. Begin or increase the partnership between your parish and local communities of faith. Start small with potlucks or neighborhood projects. Start even smaller. Invite a non-Catholic friend or neighbor to share faith with you over dinner.

Messengers of Joy

FIRST READING: ZEPHANIAH 3:14–18

Your God will sing joyfully because of you, as one sings at festivals.

Imagine God singing joyfully over you! It's hard to think of God getting excited about us. Our lives are mostly small, anonymous; we are each granted "fifteen minutes of fame," as Andy Warhol once said, and that is not always good. Why would God even notice us? Unless our misery becomes too deep and our wails very loud, there is not much in our lives to draw divine attention.

Zephaniah writes at a time before the great exile, when the nation was about as dissolute as it was going to get. In chapter 1 of his book, he declares forcefully that "the day of the Lord," a very dark day indeed, is coming. But in this final passage, he proclaims the joy that will follow, the restoration of the people to the happiness God always wants for us.

The prophets always declare the best of times in the midst of the worst of times. Our joy has its roots in God's delight in us, and that is a given, even in the darkest hours.

SECOND READING: PHILIPPIANS 4:4–7

The Lord is near. Dismiss all anxiety from your minds.

The Lord is near. That is the message of Advent, that God has chosen to become like us and share our food and our fate. God left glory behind and chose the womb. It is an amazing thought.

We often think of God as far away, above and beyond our experiences. Through the person of Jesus, the early Christians understood that God was near, had walked their roads, and was returning soon. More than that, through the Spirit present in their assembly, they knew that God was in their midst. Paul says anxiety has no place in a relationship this tender. Anxiety should be replaced by offering our needs to God in prayer, with gratitude. We are not trying to win the favor of a distant deity. We are in relationship with the One who is as near as our next breath.

So we who are worried about many things can relax. And beyond that, we can rejoice. God's peace stands guard over our hearts and minds, and no human concern can take that peace away.

GOSPEL: LUKE 3:10–18
John preached the good news to the people.

You get a sense of how hungry people are for a prophet when you read John's advice to the crowds. He says very simple, obvious things. Share with the needy. Do not cheat. Do not throw your weight around. And people are ready to call him "messiah."

In our time, people are still aching to be saved by some great leader. Dozens of contemporary gurus offer their books, seminars, and communes to people looking for salvation from themselves and the world that disappoints. The new gurus say simple things: do not eat too much junk, be nice, go for a walk in the woods, and do not worry, the aliens will save us. And many are ready and eager to follow. Unlike the new gurus, however, John the Baptist was not interested in being proclaimed the fearless leader. He pointed immediately to the one who was to come, and humbled himself. What a strange thing to do with power, to lay it down.

John was, of course, anticipating a real messiah who would do the same. We call this good news, the way of surrendering power in order to be lifted up. We have a goal beyond good rules for living, as we follow this leader. Not mere good advice, but redemption from all that kills.

Questions for Reflection

• When have you known real joy? What makes joy possible in your life?

• What do you worry about? How does anxiety affect your relationship with God?

• Who are the present leaders that attract others to follow? What is their message? How would you explain to their disciples what Jesus offers?

Action Response

Become a messenger of joy. Turn your anxieties into fervent prayer, and leave them with God. Reflect on your faith, and write down what you really believe. Practice witnessing to your faith with your words and your confidence. Joy is a sure sign of the presence of God's Spirit.

Littleness

FIRST READING: MICAH 5:1–4

His greatness shall reach to the ends of the earth; he shall be peace.

The great King David came from the humble town of Bethlehem. He was also the youngest of his brothers: a dreamy, poetically inclined boy who nonetheless slew a giant and went on to possess a nation. Never underestimate the power of the small!

When the prophet Micah writes, he envisions a new ruler rising up in David's place, to assume the majesty lost to former times. The new king would be like David, of humble origins, of no worldly account. Like David, the one who would come would rely on God's strength and not human powers. What most peculiarly characterizes this new king is that, though his greatness extends to all the earth, he is the embodiment of peace.

Throughout recorded history, most worldwide rulers are portrayed as the embodiment of war. How else do you get to rule the world? Awaiting a great ruler who would shepherd by means of peace is a strange idea. At least it was until the coming of Jesus.

SECOND READING: HEBREWS 10:5–10

"I have come to do your will, O God."

Why are we reading about the sacrifice of Jesus now, days away from Christmas? The focus of this passage is not really on sacrifice so much as the necessity of the Incarnation. The superficial sacrifices of the Temple had only served to harden the hearts of the people. What would really delight God is a people surrendered in spirit, and that dimension was missing. God became flesh in order to surrender human will. And with that surrender, necessarily, came the risk to the body that led to the crucifixion.

Jesus surrendered his will, relinquishing the safety of his flesh. This is the meaning of incarnation, the vulnerability of the human body to all that assails us, space and time and the will of others. The covenant of will is sealed in a covenant of flesh and blood, which we call to life again in every Eucharist. When we eat this bread and drink this cup, we are pledging to lay down our will in the same way.

GOSPEL: LUKE 1:39–45

"But who am I that the mother of my Lord should come to me?"

The teenage girl runs to the elderly woman's house—two people entirely dismissed by society as irrelevant. Two babies in two wombs, both absurd in their conception, lives not protected by human laws, deemed worthless. Who cares what happens to these four, in their invisible world of poverty and powerlessness?

God cares. The world, groaning under the labor of its age-old sin, cares. The kingdom, in the pangs of its entry into time, depends on them, these two women, these two yet-to-be-born children. How can this be, that salvation history ends up in the hands of a teenager, an old lady, and a couple of babies? If Paul can speak of the absurdity of the cross, from which redemption springs, we can also speak of the absurdity of Christmas, a story in which all the wrong people end up holding a treasure in their hands. And yet, though we may be tempted to dismiss them as the wrong people to entrust with salvation, they prove to be the very people for the task.

Blessed were these women, and blessed the fruit of their womb. Happy, holy Christmas.

Questions for Reflection

• Who are the small ambassadors of peace in your life? In our world? How can you join their number?

• In what ways do you experience the call to lay down your will?

• What is your attitude toward adolescents, the elderly, the unborn, the poor? What does it mean that salvation came to the world first through them?

Action Response

Respect littleness. Make this a season to honor children, the elderly, the poor. Make a commitment to the life of the womb. Represent the powerless in the places where you wield power. Experience the joy of Christmas!

Our Place in the Story

FIRST READING: ISAIAH 62:1-5

As a bridegroom rejoices in his bride, so shall your God rejoice in you.

The happiness of a newly married couple is what the prophet claims as the relationship between God and us. We will know the joyful hope of a fresh start. We will have the powerful pledge of a sealed commitment. We will experience the supportive presence of our families, friends, and communities around us. We will look forward to a lifetime of learning about love and union and fidelity. And new life will spring from the bond we share.

What do married couples say to one another at the end of that first exhausting day together as husband and wife? After the crowds are gone and the ceremonies are now film in someone's camera? "We made it!" "Well, here we go." "Scared? Me too." "Alone, at last." Think of these expressions as exchanges between you and the One who loves you best of all. This is the companionship the prophets enjoyed with God, and the kind that is available for any one of us.

SECOND READING: ACTS OF THE APOSTLES 13:16-17, 22-25

"I have found David son of Jesse to be a man after my own heart."

God's plan is wonderfully specific. God settles on a tribe: Israel. God chooses a particular lineage: that of Jesse and his son, David. God waits for a special moment in time, and calls a herald from the womb: John. And then salvation comes to all the world.

God's plan to save us through Jesus is unrepeatable, but God has other plans that are just as specific. God chooses a certain nation: ours. The Lord has the divine eye on a certain bloodline: your ancestors. God waits for just the right moment, and calls a messenger into being: you. And it is now your task to announce that you are by no means the savior of the world, but that you know who he is and you can point him out should anyone want to know.

John was a unique person in the history of salvation, but in a certain sense we are all called to repeat his performance as herald of good news. We do not have to don the hair shirt and eat locusts, thank goodness, but we do have to point to the Lord in the way we live our lives.

GOSPEL: MATTHEW 1:1–25

"The virgin shall be with child and give birth to a son."

It didn't start with Mary, though the buck certainly stopped with her in a significant way. The family record of Jesus in Matthew's account goes all the way back to the time of Abraham. Abraham was the first to look up at a sky gorgeous with stars and see the promise of God imprinted there. He and Sarah told the story to Isaac, and he to his children, and they to theirs. And over many generations there were many offers from God to advance the relationship, through Ruth's fidelity to David's grand repentances; through kings and prophets and sinners and fools, all the way to a simple carpenter and an adolescent girl, both asked to participate in something neither could understand or explain.

And so we end up with manger scenes that are rather sparsely inhabited by a couple, a baby, a shepherd, and lots of animals, plus a trinity of kings off to the side. A more complete crèche would include the hundreds, perhaps thousands, who influenced the course of salvation history as we know it. Including you and me.

Questions for Reflection

• What sort of intimate time do you share with God? What do you say to each other? How does the relationship grow in these encounters? How are you changed?

• How do the decisions you make for your life act as a signpost to point the way to Jesus for others?

• Imagine yourself at the scene of the Christmas story. What gift do you have to offer?

Action Response

In the midst of celebration with family and friends, find a moment to acknowledge the source of the celebration, God-with-us. Make God's presence a reality for someone this Christmas with your love, who might otherwise miss the good news.

The Care That Is Due

FIRST READING: SIRACH 3:2–6, 12–14
Kindness to a father will not be forgotten.

We all have a shorthand definition for justice, which boils down to fairness. "An eye for an eye" was the Hebrew equivalent of the concept. We can think of it as giving karma where karma is due. That is roughly the human side of justice. But the Hebrew word for justice does not mean fairness at all. It has been translated as meaning "right relationship with all," a more complex situation. It means the opposite of "everybody gets the same treatment."

We have responsibilities toward all of the relationships in our lives. Parents and children have very special responsibilities toward one another, and we live in a society which does not seem to support those commitments. Honoring parents (or children) who do not return the honor is difficult, if not impossible by human means. But God makes all things possible. We can honor our families even when they fail us. And those who do not fail shine a light of witness into a world that sorely needs it.

SECOND READING: COLOSSIANS 3:12–21
Over all these virtues put on love, which binds the rest together.

Like Sirach, Paul has got the concept right, though we may quibble about the details. The tools for discerning right relationship are many: mercy, kindness, humility, meekness, and patience. Imagine what kinds of relationships we might have if we all approached one another in that spirit!

In the end, figuring out how to treat one another according to divine justice is not rocket science. Love is the overarching virtue, and forgiveness closes all wounds. If we live in Christ's peace and lead grateful lives, we will not be confused when we approach each other in a new situation. Wisdom will be made perfect in us, and we will find, in speech and action, the word of Christ dwelling in us.

Paul mentions gratitude three times in this brief passage. Being "dedicated to thankfulness" is a countercultural idea, since we live in an era of whining, criticism, and cynicism. What if we began again from the perspective of gratitude, started small, and worked our way up to full-blown praise?

GOSPEL: LUKE 2:41–52

His mother kept all these things in memory.

Scholars find no less than five themes of Luke present in this short story: The central place of Jerusalem and the Temple to the divine mission. The early foreshadowing of the cross in the "three days" that Jesus is hidden. Jesus' imperative to do the will of the Father. The motif of the journey it takes for all of us to find Jesus. And the role of Mary as first and best disciple.

Mary's example is especially important on this feast. She worries, she searches, she scolds, and she does not understand what is given to her by way of explanation. She behaves like a mother, like a real person. But then she does one thing more: she remembers. She employs the Christian disciple's sacred obligation to keep in holy memory what comes to us from God.

Holy memory is Eucharist, is the telling of stories from Scripture, is theological reflection on the events of our lives and finding a place for them within the context of faith. We do not have to understand everything right away—even Mary was not given perfect understanding. But we can ponder these things in our heart, and keep on searching until holy memory reveals what is now hidden from us.

Questions for Reflection

• How do you (or how can you) honor your family relationships? How does society hinder you, and how does your faith help you in these relationships?

• Measure your relationships according to Paul's criteria of mercy, kindness, humility. Pay particular attention to the way these virtues do or do not appear in your family dynamics.

• What memories do you count as sacred to your story? How has reflecting on them helped you to grow deeper in faith?

Action Response

As this year comes to a close, dedicate yourself to thankfulness. Begin fostering a grateful heart by praying often, thanking God for the people, the events, and the gifts of each experience. Your prayer does not have to be a formal affair, but a brief closing of the eyes, a breathed blessing.

Radiant at What You See

FIRST READING: ISAIAH 60:1–6
Your heart shall throb and overflow.

Think of Jerusalem as more than a place. Think of Jerusalem as an encounter with God, an epiphany. An epiphany is a manifestation of the divine. Jerusalem was the center of epiphany for the Jewish people because David built the Temple there, and the encounter with God happened there in a unique way because of it. Since the destiny of the nation was bound to its relationship to God, Jerusalem and the people were wed in a close-knit union.

The early church began to speak about the new Jerusalem, a city not made by human hands, the ultimate epiphany. The Lamb would be its light, and all the faithful would find rest there. This became the future hope of believers, the immediate destination of martyrs.

We can think of Jerusalem as any place, event, or relationship in which we encounter God in a life-shaking way. When our hearts throb and overflow with the radiance we see, we know we are in Jerusalem.

SECOND READING: EPHESIANS 3:2–3, 5–6
In Christ Jesus, the Gentiles are now co-heirs with the Jews.

Talk about epiphanies! When Paul, a strict Pharisee, encounters Christ, his whole worldview is thrown for a loop. Raised and trained to see his own people as the chosen ones of God—and all others as beneath God's concern—he suddenly is granted the knowledge of "God's secret plan": the Gentiles are God's people too! This knowledge could have shattered a weaker person, but Paul rises to the challenge. Not only does he change his attitude, but he takes upon himself practically singlehandedly the mission to the Gentiles. If they are God's people, they ought to at least be given the good news about it.

Paul's epiphany is the ultimate challenge to fundamentalism of any kind, the religious notion of insiders and outsiders, the I'm-saved-and-you're-not crowd. If Jerusalem is for everybody, metaphorically speaking, then we have an obligation to bring the good news even to the folks we would most like to keep out of our shiny city of God.

GOSPEL: MATTHEW 2:1–12

The star which they observed at its rising went ahead of them.

Epiphany gets its name right here, in the story of the three astrologers from the East. They saw a sign in the heavens, correctly understood it and chose to follow it, no matter the personal cost. These three are fearless pilgrims, walking in the tiny light of a star, traveling by faith. They are called wise because they search the heavens and their dreams for direction from a source they cannot name. And in their zeal, they find the One they are looking for.

The astrologers were the first Gentile followers of Jesus. Without the benefit of Scripture or the stories of salvation, without religion and its rituals, they made their way into the presence of Christ. Many have since followed in their winding footsteps, through many places and years, searching for the light that they do not entirely understand but are willing to risk everything for. Mainstream religion tends to scorn them, banish them to the New Age, ridicule their search. But some of them will find their way to the light, with or without our encouragement.

Questions for Reflection

• Have you ever been "in Jerusalem," a place or time of vivid encounter with God? Describe the encounter. How can you return there?

• What sudden or gradual epiphanies have changed the way you understand your religion? Did you embrace the changes, or did you/do you fight them?

• Do you know anyone who is searching for the light of truth, even though the path they choose is foreign to you? How do you respond to these searchers?

Action Response

Locate the doorway to the new Jerusalem in your life—in those who gather in worship, in a place, or a circumstance—and work to keep that door wide open. Commit yourself to being open to the sacred, and give encouragement to those who are struggling to find their way to the light.

God's Favorites

I set you as a covenant of the people.

Moses was a chosen one. Then came David, and later all of Israel. Being a chosen one may not have been all it was cracked up to be. You had the advantage of God's favor, but that did not mean it would be easy. In fact, being chosen by God usually meant that life was about to get a whole lot more complicated than you ever dreamed.

When Isaiah describes the chosen servant of the Lord, it all sounds great in the beginning. He will bring forth justice to the nations, in the manner of a king. He will offer wise teaching, like a prophet or priest. He will be gentle, powerful, and ultimately victorious. The operative word here, of course, is "ultimately." Between God's favor and victory lies the great abyss of the cross.

Down through the centuries, many would fall in love with God's will and surrender themselves to it. They would become saints, some by way of martyrdom. They would seem to us greatly favored by God, if you could overlook the great trials they endured to get that way. We like to admire them, even dedicate churches to them. But we are less eager to follow in the way of God's favor.

He healed all who were in the grip of the devil.

Peter finds himself in front of an odd audience: a houseful of Gentiles! Never in his Jewish life did he imagine that one day he would be bringing "the good news of peace" to the enemy, a Roman soldier and his family. The recognition of this dawning reality comes to him even while he is speaking to them: God is showing no partiality.

Peter begins to understand now why Jesus showed his power to anyone he met, chasing the demons out of Jews and Gentiles alike. Jesus did not play favorites; or rather, Jesus' favorite was always the one who stood before him in need. The sinful one, the sick one, the one with a burning question: all of these were God's favorites. In this new light, Peter knows that Cornelius and his household are ready to become the friends of God and to receive the Spirit he brings.

GOSPEL: LUKE 3:15–16, 21–22
"You are my beloved Son. On you my favor rests."

The people were convinced that John was God's chosen one, the one they had been waiting for. Okay, so he bruised a few reeds, and did a lot of shouting in the streets. So maybe prophecy is not everything. He was one impressive messenger!

Jesus came more meekly, asking for John's baptism. Afterwards, he prayed fervently, just another believer in the crowd, it seemed. Until the sky opens, Spirit pours down, and a celestial voice speaks, that is. Then it is time to reevaluate who is who.

We are often tempted to define the favored ones of God by their special clothes, fancy job descriptions, and impressive witness, like John the Baptist had. But often the favored ones come quietly into our midst, poured out in prayer, and we do not even see them. A voice from heaven indicating who's who would go a long way to dispel the confusion. But in the absence of that, we can look for the ones who imitate Jesus.

Questions for Reflection

• Name three persons in history who seem to be among God's favored ones. What do they have in common? What do you have in common with them?

• Could you be among God's favorites? How has God made that clear to you lately?

• What are the signs of God's favor? Who bears those signs in your community?

Action Response

Imagine that while you are in prayer, a voice speaks to you the words of favor that were spoken to Jesus. Try to live out the rest of this week with that awareness in the back of your mind: you are the beloved of God, chosen and favored.

From Out of the Desert

FIRST READING: DEUTERONOMY 26:4–10
"My father was a wandering Aramean."

The creed of the wandering Aramean teaches us something about the holy power of memory. The people who recited this prayer were not literally the children of wandering Arameans. Many of them were generations removed from the events to which they gave witness. Most of us do not stand in direct blood relationship to the people of the Bible. But it is the spiritual relationship we have to these events that is important. In professing a creed, we take the history of salvation and make it our own. We invite the remote events to become immediate for us, in all of their original power.

This you-are-there approach to the ancient story incites two responses from the people: one is to share their bounty with others, and the other is to celebrate. If we felt the same close relationship to the story of salvation that the Bible figures did, we would be warmed by the same fire, dancing with the same joy.

SECOND READING: ROMANS 10:8–13
All have the same Lord, rich in mercy to all who call.

Think of the letter to the Romans as the "Cliff Notes" for Paul's epistles. In here you get the highlights of a lifetime of reflection on the meaning of Jesus for human history. This is Paul at his theological maturity. If before he was busy stamping out the small fires of heresy that cropped up in the mission fields, now he is the manufacturer of what will become orthodoxy for the church for centuries to come.

Paul will also become the most misrepresented figure in the Bible. "Confession of the lips" to the claim that "Jesus is Lord" will be mistaken for a minimalist approach to salvation: you are what you speak. He is not denying the need for a living and enacted faith. But he is protesting the idea that law, or circumcision, or any outward human act generates salvation. Salvation comes from God, and disciples know that making Jesus our Lord will save us. It does not get us off the hook just to say it. Saying it is merely the preface to living it.

GOSPEL: LUKE 4:1–13

"Prostrate yourself in homage before me, and it shall all be yours."

The temptation story is a private moment in the otherwise very public life of Jesus. Away from the crowds, without the support of a friend, he has gone into the desert for one of the great spiritual struggles of his life. He will not battle for the life of his mission this way again until the final hour in Gethsemane. At both ends of his ministry, he has to lay down his will and take up that of his Father. Even for Jesus, it is never easy.

The desert is the appropriate meeting ground for the devil. The scarcity of water, the fear of wild creatures, the absence of mercy from the unremitting sun combine to make the desert a desperate place for humans: life meets death here. That is why it becomes a powerful lenten symbol for us, caught in the mystery of death meeting life in the cross and resurrection. Just as Jesus wrestles to clarify his mission and surrender his will, we use this season to wrestle down our egos and examine again our commitment to the mission of the church. Do we want to be the people of God, or do our allegiances really lie elsewhere?

Questions for Reflection

• Does your faith move you to want to celebrate? What contributes to that feeling, or what detracts from it?

• Give three pieces of evidence to prove that Jesus is Lord of your life.

• What are the issues you are struggling with as you approach the lenten desert? How will your lenten practices help you to meet these challenges?

Action Response

Make the Gospel personal to you. Tell what the life and message of Jesus has done for you. Tack it up where you can review it often during Lent.

Glimpses of Glory

FIRST READING: GENESIS 15:5–12, 17–18
A deep, terrifying darkness enveloped Abram.

Maybe no one has ever seen the face of God and lived, but often God showed the divine signature. Smoke and fire became two of God's trademarks. We see them again in the burning bush of Moses, the cloud of glory that hung around the Israelites by day in the desert, as well as the pillar of fire that stayed with them at night. We see them at Mount Sinai at the giving of the Commandments, and a similar manifestation at the Transfiguration of Jesus. The ethereal presence of these elements awakens within us a call to mystery, a presence which is and is not tangible.

So Abram first encounters the Lord. Maybe the smoking furnace made him choke, and the flames of the fire scorched his skin as they came uncomfortably close. He knew that God was powerful, mysterious, and not a little dangerous. For now, it was enough to know that this Great Mystery was entering into a bargain with him, and he was the one who stood to gain everything from it.

SECOND READING: PHILIPPIANS 3:17—4:1
Their god is their belly and their glory is in their shame.

We have a choice: we can imitate the way of discipleship or the ways of the world. We can accept Jesus as our Lord and glory in the love and courage shown at the cross. Or we can settle for making gods of ourselves and finding glory in our own accomplishments.

It all comes down to what we want: to save ourselves, or to be saved by the power of the cross. Most of us, when we are honest about it, prefer to save ourselves. It requires no great act of faith, just dogged work at looking out for Number One. We spend a good deal of our lives in pursuit of self-preservation and shoring up our resources, health, appearance, image. And it seems to make no impact on us that we are all going to die anyway. In terms of our mortality—terms we never quite accept—the cross does seem to offer a more viable salvation.

GOSPEL: LUKE 9:28–36

They saw his glory and likewise saw the two standing with him.

What a wake-up call! It was a typical day in the Gospel of Luke. Jesus was stepping aside to pray, which was part of his routine. His three best friends went with him and, as they often did, went promptly to sleep. (They were not exactly prayer warriors, and they had just climbed a mountain. And they used any break in the action to catch up on their sleep.)

Meanwhile Transfiguration is happening. Wow, and they almost slept right through it! They wake in time to see Jesus shining like a minor sun, and the greatest saints of the Hebrew tradition talking about the ultimate fulfillment of God's ancient promises. Another five minutes of snoring and the whole event might have passed them by.

This is a metaphor for our lives. The world is being transfigured by God's holy grace every moment, and we sleep through most of it. We have got a million reasons why we are not more attentive: family concerns, economic burdens, pressure at work, health issues. Our lives preoccupy us and put us to sleep, while glory shines out and reveals God's presence in our midst.

Questions for Reflection

• When have you had a "near occasion of God" in your life? What did you learn of God?

• How much time do you spend worshiping the "god of the belly" that Paul writes about? How much time do you serve the Lord?

• Where and when are you most awake to God's presence in your life?

Action Response

Turn the tables on the "god of the belly." Just say "no" to service of the self once a day, and use that occasion to serve God in prayer or to be at the service of the needs of others.

Mindful of Our Posture

FIRST READING: EXODUS 3:1–8, 13–15

"I must go over to look at this remarkable sight."

That bush is burning somewhere in your life. Off in a corner, at a distance, some remarkable encounter with God's angel is waiting for you to notice. This isn't a New Age idea, but as old as the Hebrew Scriptures. And you have plenty of biblical responses to choose from.

You can laugh at it, like Sarah, or give it hospitality, like Abraham. You can wrestle it (Jacob), accompany it (Tobias in the Book of Tobit), accept its help (Hagar in Genesis), follow it (Peter in Acts). You can doubt it like Zechariah or surrender to it like Mary. But whatever you decide to do with a manifestation of God's presence, you first have to acknowledge it. The reason we do not have more angel stories is because most of us walk right by. If a bush is burning somewhere in our lives, we do not take the time to go and look.

SECOND READING: 1 CORINTHIANS 10:1–6, 10–12

Let anyone who thinks he is standing upright watch out lest he fall!

So maybe the whole matter of discipleship comes down to the question of posture. Not the posture of our bodies, but of our spirits. When Moses had his remarkable conversion at the bush, he became attentive to God's voice ever after. He had his ear to the ground, his eyes on the sky, his heart open to God's will. Moses is the central figure in the entire Hebrew story because his spiritual posture was close to perfect.

But those who followed Moses were bent double. They walked among the same miracles as Moses for forty years, and never seemed to get it. They never fully bought the idea that God was on their side. They had crooked hearts, tottering faith, wavering loyalty. And so we who everyday can enjoy the miracles of sacraments cannot afford to be too complacent. If we are not in line with the mysteries we share, we may be closer to a fall than we think.

"Cut it down. Why should it clutter up the ground?"

If you have a little plot of ground, so much as a flower pot to call your own, you can sympathize with the vineyard owner. With a little bit of earth in which to encourage things to grow, there is no room for the barren vine, the fruitless tree. Tear it up; plant something that will bloom!

But in Luke's merciful gospel, we always get a second chance. Unlike the fig tree stories elsewhere that end in Jesus cursing the tree and withering it, Luke forms a parable in which a compassionate gardener speaks for the tree. "Let me give it the extra care it may be lacking. Let me give it every chance to come around."

Lent is the season of extra care our hearts may need to soften up and receive the seed of the Gospel. We take this time to allow the Gardener to loosen our roots, water us generously, and fertilize us vigorously in the hopes that any barren ground within us will begin at last to respond.

Questions for Reflection

• Where have you encountered a "burning bush," a sign of God's presence and call, in your life? Where might the bush be burning now?

• Gauge your spiritual posture along the lines of prayer, moral living, generosity, faith, hope, justice, love. How straight do you stand?

• What extra care does your heart need to come alive this season?

Action Response

Time to weed the garden! Get rid of some old habit that clutters up your life and robs you of time and energy. Use that rediscovered plot of ground to plant something fruitful.

Signing On with the New Creation

FIRST READING: JOSHUA 5:9, 10–12

They ate of the produce of the land, and the manna ceased.

You couldn't really say they had lost anything in the deal. For too many years they had lived in the desert, not much to eat, worried about the water supply. The miracle food, like manna in the morning and quails on request, kept them alive through hard times.

But now they had reached a land that was flowing with milk and honey, so to speak, and they could eat of the (only slightly less miraculous) food of the land. The miracle deliveries ceased. Could anyone object?

Sometimes we do object, anyway. We grow used to God's special blessings and are confused or dismayed when they end, perhaps when we no longer need them. Sometimes in order to go forward, something of the past has to be withdrawn. As bewildering or upsetting as that may be, the new thing cannot be possessed until the old way has been relinquished.

SECOND READING: 2 CORINTHIANS 5:17–21

God has entrusted the message of reconciliation to us.

Paul is suggesting here that the entire enterprise of salvation can be boiled down to one word: reconciliation. This one word sums up the life of Jesus, the cross and resurrection, the mission of the church and, incidentally, our role as disciples. The reason we are baptized into this story is to be ambassadors of forgiveness.

Just imagine yourself as "the very holiness of God." What would you look like? Not some pious plaster image, but the face of love, the touch of tenderness, the strength of compassion, the vigor of service, the unstoppable force of forgiveness. When humans divide, you would unite. Where there is bitter silence, you would bring communication. Where there is hostility, you would be peace. Where there is fear, you would be a friend.

And when you become these things and act in these ways, the old you would pass away and the new creation of God's promise would break through like the dawn.

GOSPEL: LUKE 15:1–3, 11–32
"This man welcomes sinners and eats with them."

A man of my acquaintance was disappointed to learn that I am a Christian. "But why?" he demanded of me. "Christianity is a religion for losers!"

I laughed at his unsuspecting insight. "Yes, it is," I admitted. "But the difference between us is, you think that is an insult, and I think that is the good news." Losers, like the prodigal son, are grateful for the invention of Christianity. But he is not the only one. The sick, the blind, the lame, the crazy—all have a lot to be thankful for. So do the dead. So do the poor, those who mourn, those who are persecuted. Outsiders, women, the despised...when you begin to count them up, a lot of people fall into the category of those who have lost something and long for forgiveness, comfort, or justice.

The prodigal son was not the only loser in the story. The father had lost his son, which was a crushing blow. And what the elder son suffered from was perhaps the most devastating loss of all: the ability to feel compassion for his own brother. The Christian story promises to redress all these losses, whether from sin, suffering, or spiritual sickness. All we have to do is come to the feast.

Questions for Reflection

• When has an apparent blessing been withdrawn in your life? What were you offered in its place?

• How has the spirit of reconciliation affected your life? How and why do you offer it to others?

• What have you gained by being a person of faith?

Action Response

Prayerfully consider where you might be called to be an ambassador for Christ right now. Is there a place where reconciliation is needed in your life, relationships, community?

Something Old, Something New

FIRST READING: ISAIAH 43:16–21
I put water in the desert, and rivers in the wasteland.

The story of salvation is as old as the story of the human race. It can be told briefly: we sin, God saves. The story works out so well for us, in fact, that it becomes a kind of comforting bedtime tale.

Which is what Isaiah's prophecy is protesting against. When we treat the story of salvation as a very nice tale with a happy ending, we make God static, and God means to be dynamic. Yes, it is true that our God is the One who parted the Red Sea and performed all those miracles so long ago. But new life is springing forth in every moment, and we can encounter God just as powerfully and much more personally today than in the old stories. God is acting, right now, in your life. Do you perceive it?

SECOND READING: PHILIPPIANS 3:8–14
I wish to know Christ.

Law can be a friend. It establishes the boundaries of acceptable behavior, and makes the law-abider safe and the law-breaker liable. Religious law gives us that same rewarding certainty. We know what to do to be just in the eyes of the law, if not the eyes of God.

Paul's move away from the comfort of the law is daring. He had been guaranteed safety by his knowledge and observance of the law, and was considered "justified" by his life as a strict Pharisee. But he threw it all away in favor of faith in Jesus. Faith means you have nothing to show for it, no evidence, no proof, just the conviction deeply lived. Paul took a leap of faith, and it was a leap into freedom. And he hit the ground running, as we all must, keeping his eyes fixed on Jesus all the way to the end.

GOSPEL: JOHN 8:1–11
"What do you have to say about the case?"

You know one thing for sure: they did not drag the woman to Jesus out of respect for his great learning. The leaders wanted him to come down for or against the law, either way trapping him by his response. If Jesus chose the law, the memory of that horrific stoning would stay with his disciples forever. And if he chose against the law, people would say he was soft on sin.

Of course Jesus finds a third way to answer. Instead of dismissing her sin, he universalizes the reality of sin by daring the sinless one to strike first. What if someone had picked up a stone? A neighbor might call out his secret fault. Or Jesus, who well knew the human heart, might publicly remind the crowd of that one's indiscretions against the law. Rather than saying sin is unimportant, he made it too important for mere humans to arbitrate. And Jesus took that testimony all the way to the cross.

Questions for Reflection

• Have you ever been saved from anything? What does it mean for you to say "God saves"?

• What do you have faith in? Do you put your faith in Jesus? If so, why and how?

• Over whom do you stand in judgment? What would it take to put that stone down?

Action Response

Spend the week in active awareness of the new things God is doing in the world around you. Participate in the signs of new life you discover. Celebrate and be grateful.

Do Not Weep for Me

FIRST READING: ISAIAH 50:4–7
And I have not rebelled, have not turned back.

What is disgrace? It is defined as a loss of honor or a fall from grace. It feels like shame, burns with humiliation. Without a hand laid on you, your life seems in ruins. Disgrace is an intangible thing in many ways, imposed from the outside but pressing almost unbearably against the heart.

God's faithful servant described by the prophet is treated disgracefully, yet he is not disgraced. Beaten, spat upon, struck in the face, he turns a stony look toward the forces around him. He suffers their insults without receiving them internally. He rejects the opinion of the crowd in favor of God's opinion. They may take his life, but they cannot destroy what he is.

The key to the servant's stamina is not simply endurance but attention. Each morning he listens for God's word and then turns himself into a proclamation. The word becomes flesh. It is a familiar story, the story of our faith. When we turn our attention away from the world's opinion, and care only for God's view of us, we too cannot be harmed in any way that matters.

SECOND READING: PHILIPPIANS 2:6–11
Jesus Christ is Lord!

Paul makes it sound simple: have an attitude like Christ's. What is that, exactly? Ungrasping of any greatness, content with "human estate," empty of self and filled with humility, obedient to God no matter what. Not quite so simple after all. But that is discipleship in a nutshell.

The opposite of a Christ-like attitude is an Adam-like one. The old Adam, as Paul would say, grasped at equality with God, not content to be human. The Adam attitude is full of self-importance, more hubris than humility, disobeying the Creator in favor of a mere creature. Because of this, the human became mortal, which has its root in the word for death.

But look at the fate of the new Adam! Because Jesus received his humanity with grace, he is lifted up to the highest place. Jesus embodies his most repeated teaching, that the last will be first. Still we cling to our Adam attitude, struggling to get to the front of the line.

GOSPEL: LUKE 22:14—23:56
"Do not weep for me, but for yourselves and your children."

Do you remember some of the older prayers for the Stations of the Cross? Great attention was paid to every drop of blood, every injured muscle in Jesus' body. As a form of meditation, the Way of the Cross is a wonderful practice and has much to teach us. But it is not meant to be a time of weeping for Jesus.

When Jesus meets the women of Jerusalem (Luke 23:28, or the Eighth Station), he tells them this plainly. The Passion is not just a sad, sad story: it is a great story! It is about the unique intersection of God's love and human courage in history. It is about the length God is willing to go to bring us back when we turn away. The Passion is a thrilling story of steadfastness, forgiveness, and reconciliation. It is also a serious story about the cause and effect of sin, and should give our hearts pause.

Jesus stops to tell the women that the real tragedy is human sin and the destruction it wreaks. In that sense, we can walk the Way of the Cross through our own neighborhoods and contemplate enough tragedy to make us weep.

Questions for Reflection

• When have you known disgrace? Would you be willing to face disgrace for your faith?

• In what areas of your life are you most clinging to control, the sure sign of "grasping equality with God"? How can you begin to put on an attitude like Christ's?

• If you were to make a "Way of the Cross" through your neighborhood or city, where would the stops be?

Action Response

Find some time during Holy Week to make the Way of the Cross through your hometown, pausing at the signs of sin in our world. Consider one way you can testify against the witness of sin.

Seeing Is Believing

FIRST READING: ACTS OF THE APOSTLES 10:34, 37–43

"God anointed him with the Holy Spirit and power."

Jesus might have been the world's greatest teacher, but no one would have paid him much attention if not for the miracles. He showed the Spirit's wisdom, but he also unleashed the power. He healed folks in the grip of the devil, as Peter put it to the Gentiles that day. And when Jesus himself was descended into hell, God raised him up again.

Peter believed because of what he saw. We tend to be a little hard on Thomas for not believing without hard evidence, but in fact the chosen witnesses that Peter mentions all had the advantage of seeing the risen Lord with their own eyes. Peter refers to them as witnesses three times in these verses: those who *saw* something. And seeing is believing.

The Gentiles who hear Peter speak do not have the advantage of seeing what he saw. Nor do we, yet we receive the same invitation to faith. What we *do* see is how Christians love one another—and perhaps, at times, how they do not. Which is the same thing the world sees when it looks at us. The only witness to Christ that lives in this world is the Spirit at work in people of faith. When people see us, will they believe?

SECOND READING: COLOSSIANS 3:1–4

Your life is hidden now with Christ.

"Do not handle! Do not taste! Do not touch!" These are the fearful prohibitions of religious folk at Colossae mentioned in 2:21. They focus on the darkness of the world rather than the light of Christ. Paul encourages them to set their hearts on higher things. Being raised up with Christ means enjoying the company of virtues like faith, hope, and love. Worrying about ritual impurity makes our freedom in Christ seem like a kind of bondage to the threat of sin. That is not the intent of the Gospel.

But religious people are often prey to fear, shame, and guilt, and lose sight of the goodness of the good news. Paul is blunt: hey, haven't we died to all of that? Haven't we shared in the death of Christ so as to share in his glory? Yet so often religion is presented as the avenue of getting in touch with our inner evil. As Jesus might say, "Get behind me, Satan!" The road ahead of us is love, which casts out every reason to fear.

GOSPEL: JOHN 20:1–9
"The Lord has been taken from the tomb!"

It was a morning of extreme urgency. Mary Magdalene ventured out and found the open, empty crypt. The angels, the Gardener-Lord, will come later in the morning. Mary sees only the empty tomb, and rushes to tell the others. She uses the words "has been taken," implying the tomb has been robbed.

Peter hits the ground running, along with another disciple. The other disciple gets there first and looks in. Since Mary got there "while it was still dark," she did not see what he sees: wrappings on the ground. Only Peter goes into the tomb and sees the rest of the story, the neatly rolled head covering in its own place. And seeing this, he believes.

What do we believe? John wants us to consider this before the story goes any further. What does it mean that the tomb is open, the body gone, the wrappings there? Would robbers bother the tomb of a penniless man? Would the Romans gain from removing the body? Or the Judean leaders, who wanted the body to stay put? Who would unwrap a body and steal it away? And who would pause to fold up the head cloth and put it down?

For two thousand years Christians have been calling this event resurrection. It is not just the meaning of Easter, but the reason there are Christians at all. What do you see when you look into the empty tomb?

Questions for Reflection

• What are the miracles in your life? How do they reflect the resurrected Christ for others?

• Were you taught to think about religion in terms of shame or love? How do you think about your faith now?

• Name the experience of the empty tomb for yourself and explain what it means to your life.

Action Response

Bring new life to someone as an expression of Easter faith. Call or visit someone who is isolated. Share food and company. Be a source of joy to those who meet you. Give someone a reason to shout Alleluia!

Probing the Wounds

FIRST READING: ACTS OF THE APOSTLES 5:12–16

Many signs and wonders occurred among the people.

If Peter had time to think about it at all, he must have been amazed. Not so long ago, he followed Jesus from town to town, watching miracles flow from his teacher like water. And now, the crowds followed him around Jerusalem, hoping his shadow would fall over them with a blessing. The thing is, the healings did spring forth wherever he went, carrying the Spirit of God burning like a lamp in his heart. All of the apostles were endowed with this gift of signs and wonders. It was a holy time to be a Christian.

It is still a holy time to follow Jesus. We are the church, commissioned to carry the Spirit of God through the world in our very being. We bring light wherever we go, we bring the truth of human and divine reconciliation. We are the sign of cooperation between the human and the holy forces at work in the world. The crowds are still looking for signs and wonders. Can they look to us, and will we allow the Holy Spirit to spring forth from us?

SECOND READING: REVELATION 1:9–11, 12–13, 17–19

"I am the First and the Last and the One who lives."

Folks were sent to the island of Patmos for being disruptive of the social order. Patmos was a pile of rocks off the coast of Greece, not a nice place to be marooned. From there, John shared the community's distress, not to mention their endurance and hope in the reign of God. Deprived of the community Eucharist, he fell into a vision on the Lord's day and received Christ, not in the bread but in glory.

The comfort of this vision was not for John alone but also for the community of faith. That means it is for us, too, though we tend to avoid apocalyptic literature because it is so obscure. We need someone to translate: lampstands are churches (no light under a bushel!), seven is for completeness, the church universal. The sound of a trumpet always means judgment day. The fellow like a Son of Man is a reference to an earlier vision in the Book of Daniel (7:13, 10:5). It is clear to us that Daniel's Son of Man is Jesus, the one who was dead and now lives.

After creation as we know it gets torn to pieces in twenty chapters of Revelation, the central message of the book remains as it is stated here. There is nothing to fear. No tribulation will outlast or overpower the new creation that lies in wait. The one who holds the keys to death also holds the key to eternal life.

GOSPEL: JOHN 20:19–31
"As the Father has sent me, so I send you."

The wounds of Jesus left a deep impression on Thomas. When he thought of his Teacher in those days after the crucifixion, he saw those nails penetrating his limbs again, and that spear lacerating his chest. He had pledged to go up to Jerusalem to die with Jesus (11:16), but instead he watched his hopes pierced on the cross. It is no wonder he responded to his friends' assertion with such vehemence. The brutal image would not leave him.

The final confrontation with the glorified Christ was also, for Thomas, an encounter with the wounded Christ. He had to look at the One who suffered while he did nothing. He was invited to touch the wounds and put his faith, if not in words, then in those wounds. That made Thomas a believer pretty quickly.

What does it take to make a believer out of us? Words, wounds, memories, glory? We may take different routes to faith, but the crucial thing is to get there. May we contemplate what brings us to faith, and count as precious what sustains us there.

Questions for Reflection

• How do you free the Spirit of holiness to work in your life? Where are the Spirit's signs most evident in your life?

• When you receive Christ on the Lord's day, what does it mean to you?

• What made a believer out of you? What sustains your faith today?

Action Response

Support the faith of those around you. Speak with your children, parents, friends, neighbors about what you believe. Pray together; pray for others. Respect the faith of those whose beliefs are different from yours. What is not against us is for us.

You Know That I Love You

FIRST READING: ACTS OF THE APOSTLES 5:27–32, 40–41
"You have filled Jerusalem with your teaching!"

When the high priest accused the disciples of disobeying Temple orders, Peter and the apostles volley back with stinging words of reproach and testimony. Clearly, they are not going to stop preaching the message of Jesus.

The deleted passage tells us the Sanhedrin was ready to put them to death for this. But then a teacher among them spoke, Gamaliel, who has a reputation outside of the Bible for being a wise rabbi. He points out that what is from mortals generally falls apart, but what is from God is unstoppable. And he counsels them to let the men go. "If it comes from God, you will not be able to destroy it; you may even find yourselves fighting against God" (5:39).

The apostles are released after a flogging, but they are so full of joy to have suffered for the name of Jesus that even the beating was sweet. This may sound ludicrous, but consider that only weeks earlier, Jesus had been killed before their eyes. Finally they have the courage to suffer for his sake. They went right back out there, teaching in the name of Jesus.

SECOND READING: REVELATION 5:11–14
Everything in the universe cried aloud.

John's vision is the kind of harmony the world has not known since sin divided us one from another, and silenced the great song of praise on the earth. Jesus once warned that if mortals ceased their hosannas, the rocks and stones would take up the chant. The testimony to glory happens all around us, yet our senses are dull and we do not hear it.

John's senses are awakened in his vision, and so he has "audition" as well: he not only sees what lies beyond the veil but also hears it. This is the literal meaning of revelation, the lifting of the veil between the seen and unseen. He has access to the sound of the Great Amen, the song of harmony between heaven and earth. We join our voices with the angels in every Mass, when we sing our hosannas and our Great Amen. As the word suggests, our Amen is the "I agree!" or the "Me too!" that we offer in a chorus we will not hear for ourselves until the veil is lifted at last.

GOSPEL: JOHN 21:1–19
They knew it was the Lord.

All of this talk about "knowing" it was Jesus leads us to believe that his glorified body was significantly different than the one before his death. Mary who loved him had not recognized him near the tomb. His appearance had undergone a substantial change.

What they recognized, of course, were the signs of Jesus. Where there were no fish, suddenly there is abundance. Where they faced no breakfast after a thankless night at sea, suddenly there is a warm fire and bread and fish. He distributes the food to them and they know this stranger is the Lord.

Peter is asked to profess his love, three times. He is distressed to have to repeat it, but in fact we must repeat our love over and over if it is to be credible. His threefold profession erases his triple denial, and he is asked to be a leader and a follower both. This is the essence of Christian leadership: to profess love often, and to remember in the exercise of authority that we are followers, too. Only then are we fit to tend the lambs.

Questions for Reflection

• Have you ever found yourself fighting against God? Who prevailed?
• What have you seen or heard that helps you to lift the veil between you and glory?
• Name those who both lead and follow with love, in your community or in our times. What do they teach us?

Action Response

Contemplate the signs of Spring for the song of glory which they sing unnoticed. Join your prayer to theirs and remember that prayer is not only asking, but praising.

No Snatching from God's Hand

FIRST READING: ACTS OF THE APOSTLES 13:14, 43–52

"I have made you a light to the nations."

The story of exclusion is nothing new. The Jewish community of the first century was pleased to hear Paul and Barnabas and consider the revelation they had to offer. Until, of course, they went to the Gentiles with the same Gospel. Then some of the synagogue crowd wanted no part of it. It was as if they were throwing pearls before swine!

Religious folks often want to keep clear of those whom they have identified as sinners. They want to make sure their sacraments are not soiled, their holy places are kept free from contamination. If the priest chooses the company of the sinner over the purity of their tables, watch out! Such a priest will find himself, like Paul and Barnabas, on the other side of welcome.

And so Jews have shunned Gentiles, and Christians Jews, and Catholics Protestants, and vice versa, down through the centuries. We forget the "light to the nations" clause. The Gospel is not the property of any group. The good news does not play favorites.

SECOND READING: REVELATION 7:9, 14–17

"God will wipe every tear from their eyes."

Who might we find in the uncountable crowd of John's vision? These are the ones who washed their robes in the blood of the Lamb. Martyrs, certainly, would be there. They obviously survived "the great period of trial." And those who did not give up hope during desperate times, but continued to attend to the sick and suffering, the poor and the abandoned.

We might see nurses, doctors, wartime chaplains, social workers. We might see parents who cared for their children through crisis, spouses who remained faithful during the hard times. Children who cared for aging parents despite the cost would be there. Friends who stayed constant during public humiliation and failure. Priests and religious who stayed true to the message of the Gospel in an age when such fidelity is seen as absurd.

The reason this crowd is uncountable is because there is room for all of us there, if we remain steadfast during the period of great trial. Such a time comes to every life. On the other side of the trial, God stands ready to wipe away every tear.

GOSPEL: JOHN 10:27–30
"No one shall snatch my sheep out of my hand."

This is what is known as blessed assurance. Jesus describes the one he knows as Father as "greater than all." And he is one with the Father, so what is true for him is also true for the Father. When Jesus says his sheep do not get snatched from his hand, that means they are as good as with God. This is our sheep insurance, offered at the basic cost of discipleship.

That is the hard part, naturally. Hearing the voice of Jesus in every situation is not too difficult; but following is where the action is. And that is often where we are not. After awhile we stop listening to Jesus because it is too painful when we choose to ignore him. And once we stop listening, we are in danger of being really lost. Calling "Lord, Lord," Jesus pointed out, is not the same as being a follower. The sheep know the sound of the shepherd's voice, and they come when he calls. And there is no snatching a sheep so close to the shepherd's hand.

Questions for Reflection

- Which group gets shunned in your community? How can you bring the Gospel witness to them? *Homeless Go out amongst them*
- How do you remain steadfast in times of trial? *Prayer for God's strength & Guidance*
- Where do you hear the voice of Jesus in your life? How do you respond? *To help with the Homeless — feed & clothe them & with God word*

Action Response

Spend some time, at least a quarter of an hour, in silent contemplation. Choose a spot that encourages you to pray, before the tabernacle or in some quiet place. Ask the Shepherd to speak to your heart. Follow the call as you understand it.

The Old World Is Passing

FIRST READING: ACTS OF THE APOSTLES 14:21–27

They related all that God had helped them accomplish.

You know the joke that starts with the good news, and ends with the bad news canceling it out? Well, the early Christian preachers told it in reverse. Paul and Barnabas are clear to their communities that discipleship involves many trials—the bad news—before we enter the reign of God at last. Of course, God's reign is so fantastic that the trials will seem like a bad dream by comparison. So all were encouraged to persevere in the faith.

The elders in the community were the people charged to keep telling the Christian gospel of bad news/good news, and they had to get it in the right proportions. It would be dreadful for any community to end up with leaders who only told the bad news and unfair to the community who only heard about the good news. So the disciples fasted and prayed and chose their leaders under the guidance of the Spirit.

The question of balanced leadership is still vital in the church today. Perhaps we ought to engage in more prayer and fasting for the sake of our leaders.

SECOND READING: REVELATION 21:1–5

"See, I make all things new!"

What would a holy city be like? We often think of cities as the playground of the devil. Greed makes its nasty living there, and poverty struggles against loss of heart. The dividing lines between haves and have-nots are keenly felt. Opportunity abounds, but it is not for everyone, and not all of it is good. Our cities are far from holy.

The holy city is the place where God dwells among us. The pain and sin of our cities have no place there. There is no division, nothing to mourn, and no death. Do we want to live in such a place? No competition, no one getting ahead of the rest, no prejudice, no in-crowd? Many of us are not ready to live in this new Jerusalem: we stand to lose too much.

Now is the time, John boldly suggests, to lose it all. Lose whatever keeps you from attaining that holy city right now. You surely can't take it with you, but in fact the wealth and attitudes of our unholy cities prevent us from entering the city of God altogether.

GOSPEL: JOHN 13:31–33, 34–35
"Now is the Son of Man glorified."

In the ironic way of the kingdom, things are not what they appear to be. Humiliation is about to become majesty. The king will be treated like a criminal, put to death in the manner fit for slaves of the empire. Death is going to be transcended in resurrection. Everything will be gathered with its opposite as heaven and earth are reconciled on the cross.

In the face of all that is about to come, Jesus issues a new commandment: "Love one another." Most commandments tell us precisely what to do, or not to do. "Love one another" is not so explicit. It does not establish guidelines or set protocol. It calls us into a kind of relationship. It makes us responsible for one another.

In that sense, the love command calls us into community. We are commanded to do one thing only, to care for one another as Jesus cares for us. And if we do that one thing, it will be the only thing we need to do.

Questions for Reflection

• Does your community have leaders who balance the good news and bad news of faith? How do they do this, or not?

• What disqualifies you from entering the holy city of God right now? How can you prepare yourself for this place?

• Make a list of ten ways you can be obedient to the love command before sundown today. Hang onto the list and see how many of them you can put in practice.

Action Response

Get ready for the new Jerusalem! Live as a citizen of the holy city right now, even if that makes you seem like a Martian to your family and friends. Denounce prejudice. Repair division. Be generous in the face of poverty. Deny the impulse for greed. Be compassion and consolation to those around you.

Peace

FIRST READING: ACTS OF THE APOSTLES 15:1–2, 22–29
"Unless you are circumcised...you cannot be saved."

The first council of the church in Jerusalem was fraught with controversy. People were worried sick about "the changes" Paul and Barnabas were proposing for the faithful. Since the original followers of Jesus were observant Jews, it was understood that putting your faith in the good news of Jesus meant entering the Jewish covenant. But Paul was teaching, essentially, that you could be a follower of Jesus without "becoming Jewish." Many disagreed with him virulently.

So the missionary apostles returned to headquarters in Jerusalem to decide the question once and for all. And the word came down to free the Gentile Christians from the burden of Mosaic law with the exception of four minor rules. In Paul's version of the council, even these four regulations are dispensed with (see Galatians 2:10).

We, the heirs of Gentile Christianity, owe a lot to that first council. What is most useful for us is the role the Holy Spirit played in the decision. The question was not handled democratically but "pneumatically," through the discerning power of the Spirit. Discernment should not be a lost art in the church. The Spirit is still with us.

SECOND READING: REVELATION 21:10–14, 22–23
The glory of God gave light to the city.

We see the holy city at last through the evangelist's eyes. Its foundation is laid in twelve courses of stone with the apostles' names etched into them. The city is a perfect cube, symbolizing completeness. It is made of precious materials and its light is the glory of God itself. There is no house of worship because God is there. The veil between us and the sacred is lifted.

For now, though, we need our churches. We need sacred times and places, ritual actions and sacraments, holy food and life-giving water. We need places to gather and prayers to say. We need to be confronted with God in story, song, and symbol. Otherwise it will be too easy to forget the light of the Lamb that we cannot see, and the beauty of a city we can only imagine.

GOSPEL: JOHN 14:23–29

We will come and make our dwelling place with you always.

Christ's farewell gift to those whom he loves is peace. But what is this peace?

Jesus distinguishes between his gift of peace and what the world offers under the same name. Although he encourages his followers not to feel distress or fear, he is not peddling mere peace of mind. Jesus promises that the one who is true to his word out of love will know the indwelling presence of God. When we shake hands at the sign of peace during Mass, are we blessing each other with the hope that a holy peace may enliven us and penetrate the world through us? Are we inviting God's peace to dwell in us so that "it is no longer I who live, but Christ who lives in me"?

Maybe we are not ready for this peace yet. Maybe there is still a war going on; that is, whether or not we want the Spirit of Christ to take up residence within us.

Questions for Reflection

• What role does the Holy Spirit play in your life?

• How does the church help reveal the light of God's glory to you in this day and age?

• What do you intend to offer to your neighbor at the sign of peace at Mass?

Action Response

Pray for the unleashing of the power of the Holy Spirit in your life. Ask for the kind of faith the apostles had. Be prepared to make room in your life for change!

ASCENSION

Sending Down the Promise

FIRST READING: ACTS OF THE APOSTLES 1:1–11
In the time after his suffering he showed them in many convincing ways that he was alive.

We have all known seasons of suffering. Sometimes they are brought about by the loss of someone we love, or an illness or injury. Sometimes we become depressed based on factors we cannot control: the destructive choices of a spouse or child, the state of the economy and its effect on our lives. Whatever the source of our suffering, it is the greatest blessing when the cloud lifts and life is restored to us, in one way or another.

And we go about like Jesus, making very convincing signs of new life within us. We plant flowers this Spring, after the long winter of sorrow. We take off the clothing of mourning and put on a fresh shirt, get a haircut. We gather with friends whom we have put off visiting when we were beset with sadness. We reach out to offer our help, after so long being on the receiving end of sympathy. When new life comes to us, it is unmistakable and uplifting to everyone around us. It is an ascension of body and spirit. It is the fulfillment of God's promise.

SECOND READING: EPHESIANS 1:17–23
May you know the immeasurable scope of God's power in us who believe.

Have you ever been zapped by God? In the middle of your humble way, your usual routine, you are called into some event of biblical proportions, clearly called out of business as usual and into a deeper commitment to faith than you had planned on.

This is one of the things Paul is talking about when he says (with some irony?), "May you know the power of God working in you as I do!" Being zapped by God can be fun, once you get used to it. It is unsettling by design; it is supposed to unseat you and draw you to the next place. It can also be upsetting, surprising, amazing, and terrifying, depending on your personality and how fiercely you cling to life on your own terms. If you have not experienced it yet, you will: just keep your eyes open and one hand in God's hand. God reserves the right to use anyone who volunteered for this mission through baptism.

GOSPEL: LUKE 24:46–53
"See, I send down upon you the promise of my Father."

Jesus tells his disciples: stay right here! God has ordered you a new suit. God is going to clothe you with power from on high. Me, I would run for the hills, most likely. How long would it take to ride a donkey from Jerusalem back to Galilee? After all, look where all that power got Jesus. Raised from the dead, sure; but before that, it looked pretty bad. Being clothed with power, make no mistake, also means being charged with a commission to wield it.

But the disciples remain in Jerusalem in the now-famous upper room, perhaps because they were never really a very imaginative bunch. Or perhaps it is because they had no place left to go, fearful of returning to their homes and families with all the uproar in the streets since the crucifixion. And Jesus is true to his word, sending down God's promise like wind and fire. The passion of language will overtake them, and they will be transformed beyond recognition. But that is another story. For the purposes of this feast, it is enough to reflect on the promise of the power to come. Are you ready to welcome the power?

Questions for Reflection

• Describe an experience of ascension in your life, from pain to being lifted up in hope. What contributed to your experience?

• Consider an occasion when you have known the power of God moving through your life. How did you respond?

• The power of God's Spirit resides within you. What do you do with it?

Action Response

Surrender to the irresistible power of God's Spirit. Do not wait to be zapped—volunteer for God's mission and ask God to show you the circumstance or relationship in your life that needs to be lifted up.

Spirit and Bride Say, "Come!"

FIRST READING: ACTS OF THE APOSTLES 7:55–60

"Lord Jesus, receive my spirit."

The martyrdom of Stephen is modeled directly on the death of Jesus. This is not a surprise, since Luke wrote Acts to show the reflection of Jesus' ministry in the work of the church. Stephen cries out to Jesus as Jesus cried out to his Father, "Receive my spirit," and "Do not hold this sin against them." His stoning, the first death of a disciple, is the paradigm for how followers should face the end, with courage and compassion.

Right before the crowds rush upon him, the veil is lifted for Stephen as it was for John on Patmos. He sees God's glory, the sight that Abraham and Moses and rare prophets were privileged to see. Though Stephen's eyes are fixed on glory, the onlookers cover their ears as if they hear blasphemy. Holiness is often mistaken for profanity by those whose hearts are closed to God's word. They will not accept the One who comes at an hour and in a situation that defies their religious expectations.

SECOND READING: REVELATION 22:12–14, 16–17, 20

Amen! Come, Lord Jesus!

We hear a lot about the millennium these days. Polls show that a remarkable number of people think the end of the world is near, or that Jesus might be headed this way very soon.

But the coming of Jesus is an event that is happening all the time. Theologians call this idea "realized eschatology," since the proper term for the end of the world is the *eschaton* (ES-kah-ton). A realized eschaton isn't just an interesting theory: scholars take their cue from Jesus' words that the kingdom of God is at hand—readily available!

So how real is our eschatology? Do we live as citizens of the reign of God, or of the world, or do we have dual citizenship as we frantically serve both masters? Do we acknowledge or deny the presence of Jesus in the world, who promised, "Lo, I am with you always, to the end of time"? We do not need a millennium to get us close to the edge of eternity. Eternity is available and Jesus is ready whenever we are.

GOSPEL: JOHN 17:20–26
"I living in them, you living in me...."

It is passages like this that make people run in the other direction from John's Gospel. The synoptic Gospels—the other three "same-sounding" ones—are accessible because they tell stories in easily recognizable forms. But the discourses in John are long, mystical, and strange-sounding. They echo the sound of ancient mystery religions popular twenty centuries ago.

It is wonderful to think that, on the night before he died, Jesus prayed for you and me. The unity in the prayer connects all the dots—Jesus' relationship to the One he knows as Father, Jesus' ties to his disciples, and our union with one another. "That all might be one, as you and I are one." It is an ambitious prayer.

Perhaps Jesus took the time to knit us together in a final prayer because he knew how fragile is our communion, and how easily fragmented our unity. The love between two people can quickly turn to hate—how much more endangered is the union which binds across cultures and centuries?

Questions for Reflection

• Where do you least expect God to be? What would you do if you found the Holy One there?

• List your allegiances: to God's reign, to the world and to its demands for your attention. How might the proportions need to change?

• Connect the dots in your life, to family, friends, community, church. What relationships are broken and in need of mending? Which relationships need to change?

Action Response

Strive for unity in all of your relationships at home, work, or in the greater community. Refrain from using divisive language. Exclude no one. Speak up against prejudice. Ask for forgiveness often and be prepared to give yours.

Speaking the Fire

FIRST READING: ACTS 2:1–11

They made bold proclamation as the Spirit prompted them.

The story of Pentecost is like the Tower of Babel told in reverse. Instead of having a confusion of language in which those present could not understand one another, we have confusion because those present *can* understand one another!

The story of Babel tells how sin caused humans to be divided against each other, to the point of losing the ability to communicate. When the Spirit of holiness descends, the reconciliation of heaven and earth is shown to mend the breach in language. Where there was frustrated relationship, now there is understanding.

As grade school children, many of us were taught to pray to the Holy Spirit for wisdom. We also memorized the seven gifts of the Spirit in order to prepare for confirmation. But we forget about the gifts of wisdom and understanding when we most need them, in our frustration with present relationships. When communication is vital, the time to entreat the Spirit has arrived.

SECOND READING: 1 CORINTHIANS 12:3–7, 12–13

All of us have been given to drink of the one Spirit.

A child once fretted how the Holy Spirit could be both a dove and a parakeet. "Whoever said the Spirit was a parakeet?" his mother asked. "Well," said the child, "it is a bird with a gift for language; and didn't Jesus say God would send a parakeet?"

This joke is not funny unless you know John 14:26. Paraclete is the Greek term for advocate; and Jesus promises this Spirit will teach us everything. Saint Paul furthers the catechism on the Spirit here by spelling out its many gifts (12:8–10; for the traditional list, see Isaiah 11:2–3) and fruits (Galatians 5:22). Its greatest gift would seem to be the unity of the members of Christ.

Since we are baptized into one Spirit, the things which set us apart—race, gender, circumstance—should not keep us apart. Unity is the fundamental lesson the Spirit seeks to teach us. To the extent we have not learned it, we are not living up to the call of the Spirit within us.

GOSPEL: JOHN 20:19–23
"As the Father has sent me, so I send you."

The word "apostle" means "one who is sent." In that sense, we are all baptized into the mission of being apostles. Our reception of the Spirit is the same commissioning the disciples received in the upper room. So what are we waiting for?

Maybe we are afraid, like the early disciples who huddled in that room. Maybe we are skeptical, like Thomas. Maybe we are waiting for an appearance, a sign, further instructions, a personal invitation.

Well, here it is! This is Pentecost, the feast day of being church. This day marks the beginning of the partnership between humanity and the indwelling Spirit. Ask God to awaken within you the power of the Spirit and to release the gifts that are uniquely yours. Make this prayer with as much passion as you dare. And stand back—such prayers are answered with more fire than you may intend.

Questions for Reflection

• In which relationships do you find communication most difficult? Have you ever called upon the Holy Spirit for guidance in speech?

• Where is the call of the Spirit to unity being most urgently felt in your community?

• Read Galatians 5:22–23. Which of the fruits of the Spirit are present within you? Which are you in most need of receiving?

Action Response

Pray, pray, pray. Gather with family or friends and pray for an outpouring of the Spirit in your home, parish, community. Ask for the courage to be sent, as the apostles were, to speak the message of the Gospel fearlessly in your life.

God at Play

FIRST READING: PROVERBS 8:22–31

"I was God's delight, playing before the Holy One all the while."

Wisdom is a lovely figure in the Hebrew Scriptures. She appears in Proverbs, Sirach, and of course the book of Wisdom itself, portrayed as an elegant hostess, an unfailing guide, the proper companion for the friends of God. Wisdom is God's firstborn, a participant in the creation of all things, and continues to accompany those who seek her as they make their way through the world.

Who or what is Wisdom, now identified as one of seven gifts of the Holy Spirit? Sirach speaks of Wisdom as God outright, or an attribute of God's divine personality. Paul picks up on that when he later identifies Jesus as the Wisdom of God. He contrasts the Wisdom of God against the touted wisdom of Greek philosophy. Do you want the partial wisdom of fallible mortals, or God's own Wisdom in Christ?

John's Gospel begins with the poetic image of the Word-with-God before the start of the world. This Word, "through whom all things were made," becomes part of the creation he helped to fashion. The claims of Wisdom in today's passage seem very much like the Word John proclaims.

The play of Wisdom is holy play, from which all good things come. We are invited to become the companions of Wisdom and make our lives like those of children: creative, playful, full of beauty.

SECOND READING: ROMANS 5:1–5

This hope will not leave us disappointed.

It is easy to boast about the good things that come our way, but Paul says Christians should even boast of their afflictions! Is this some kind of weird spirituality or what?

Many of us remember a certain kind of popular devotion that seemed focused on suffering. But suffering itself has never been the point of our faith. Suffering comes into every life, and what we do with it defines us and deepens our faith. As Paul says, we are strengthened by trial, and virtues are honed in us, and hope has a chance to flower.

Suffering that leads to new life, like that of Jesus on the cross, is redemptive suffering, "bought back" from being a tool of destruction and recreated as a tool in God's hands. If we allow our afflictions to be redeemed in this way, we too can boast that they are part of the blessings we receive from God.

GOSPEL: JOHN 16:12–15
"The Spirit of truth will guide you to all truth."

The solemnity of the Holy Trinity has been called an "idea feast." We are celebrating a doctrine, and not a moment in salvation history, so it may seem a little odd.

The doctrine of the Trinity emerged in opposition to heresies of the fourth and fifth centuries. It has been celebrated by the church for at least a thousand years. The reason the feast persists is because it is something of a wonder to think of God in this way: Creator, Redeemer, Sanctifier. To say that all things come from a divine being is a claim most religions are willing to make. But Christianity goes farther than that. Much farther.

We say Jesus is Lord, the Wisdom of God, the Word of God made flesh. That is a big claim, to say God would and did become one of us. Then we go one step beyond and say God is still with us, right here in our assembly, dwelling in my being and yours. That is an even *bigger* claim, considering who I am, at least. (I can't speak for you.) I suspect we will keep on celebrating this mystery a while longer.

Questions for Reflection

• Where in your life are you creative? Playful? Appreciative of beauty?

• Have you ever experienced or seen affliction turned into grace? What assists you in permitting that transformation to happen?

• What difference does the reality of the Trinity make to your life as a Christian?

Action Response

Make a commitment to play before the Lord with Wisdom. Do something creative. Take time to walk in beauty. Find a friend and engage in some healthy, relaxing play.

Took, Blessed, Broke, Gave

FIRST READING: GENESIS 14:18–20
"Blessed be God Most High."

Melchizedek is a curious character. He is not a priest in the sense we normally imply, not a cultic priest from the Levite line of Aaron. He is called a king here, of Salem, which in later generations will be known as Jerusalem. Yet he is also called a priest, and Psalm 110 will sing forever about his order of priestliness, and Jesus will be called a priest according to Melchizedek in the Letter to the Hebrews. Why? The king does bring out bread and wine, and we immediately hear Eucharist in that. But here it is meant as simple hospitality to a returning hero of combat. Melchizedek does not bless the bread, he blesses Abram.

And that is where his priesthood lies, in his ability to bestow a blessing in the name of the Most High. Melchizedek seems to be God-appointed, not a priest by heritage but by special commission from the Most High. That is why Jesus is later compared to him and not to Aaron, the first great priest of the Hebrews whose line would later serve in the Temple. Jesus is not born a Levite either, but of the boisterous tribe of Judah. His authority to bestow a blessing is from God alone.

As we all share in the priesthood of the baptized, it is good to consider what true priestliness is. We may not all be called to bless the bread and wine, but we can ask for God's blessing on our children, our communities, our projects, and our daily bread.

SECOND READING: 1 CORINTHIANS 11:23–26
"This is my body, which is for you."

The feast we celebrate, formerly known as Corpus Christi, originated in the thirteenth century. A French nun, Juliana of Mont-Cornillon, had "revelations" which led to a universal acknowledgment of the feast from Rome within a generation. She wanted to draw attention to the marvel of our Eucharist, and this she succeeded in doing.

Until recent times, this feast was celebrated with a eucharistic procession. But for Catholics, every day is an opportunity to receive the Eucharist or to contemplate before the tabernacle the mystery of God's perfect union with us. This feast serves to underline what is before us all the time.

In this passage, which the church will come to know as the Institution Narrative, Paul recites the story of how our Eucharist began. How we would gather if Jesus had not instituted this ritual for remembering is hard to say. But having it, we come to know God as our food, the staff of life and the cup of our gladness.

GOSPEL: LUKE 9:11–17
They all ate until they had enough.

Took, blessed, broke, gave. Those are the four actions Jesus repeats both here and at the Last Supper. They spell out the activity of our Eucharist, as well as our call to be food for a hungry world.

Took and broke are both aggressive, even violent words. They remind us that Jesus was taken, and broken; what we commemorate at our table is not a gentle story. Blessed and gave are both words of generosity. They remind us that our dinner is a celebration, a party where gifts are given and each member is honored. There is cause for rejoicing here.

Curious, though, how the blessing comes after the taking; how the sharing follows the breaking. The violence is mixed in with the gladness, and sorrow penetrates the celebration. Unless the bread is broken, you cannot have the sharing. In the same way, we come to understand that until we are willing to be taken, we cannot know the fullness of the blessing that awaits us. And unless we are prepared to be broken, we cannot give ourselves entirely to the mission that is ours.

Questions for Reflection

- How do you exercise your priestly responsibility of blessing?
- What does the Eucharist teach you?
- Where has your faith "taken" you? How have you been blessed? Where is your brokenness? What do you give?

Action Response

We live in a culture of cursing: episodes of "road rage" as we drive, impatience with the foibles of others, sarcasm and a critical eye for everyone who gets in our way. Start today to exercise the power of blessing. Bless and do not curse everyone you meet.

Saving the Best for Last

FIRST READING: ISAIAH 62:1–5

The Lord delights in you, and makes your land espoused.

There is no shutting up a true prophet. Oh, you can kill them, and many of the prophets were put to death by angry rulers. But the message goes on and on, often with more force and impact after their death. The fierce love of Jerusalem and the people who were entwined with its destiny kept the prophets crying out, though all the king's men were raised up against them.

A land once forsaken and desolate receives the new name, "My Delight." To anyone who has known abandonment, how good that sounds! A fallen people will be raised up and known as the delight of God. The prophet's message of hope rings out through the season of desolation, promising vindication as bright as the dawn. Each of us are called to bear this new name into the world.

SECOND READING: 1 CORINTHIANS 12:4–11

To each person the Spirit is given for the common good.

No use being humble about it: I make great lemon squares. And from time to time it is given to me to share a word from the Scriptures which helps people. I have brought both of these gifts to the service of the church many times in my life as a Catholic. Sometimes people like my lemon squares better than my commentary. I am happy to be of service either way.

Paul assures us that the church needs the gifts of each of its members in order to accomplish its ministry in the world. Some will be given wisdom, some will be models of fidelity, some will heal and others will proclaim God's Word. Some will bring hospitality into cold places, others will provide a meal where there is hunger. Some will comfort the sad and the frightened. Some will raise what is dead in our hearts to new life. Whatever gift we are given, it belongs to the Body of Christ.

GOSPEL: JOHN 2:1–12
"People usually serve the choice wine first."

The steward at the wedding knew how things were done. You serve the good wine while people are sober enough to care about vintages. And as the celebration goes on—wedding parties could last for days back then—you gradually serve up some all-but-undrinkable beverages. Who would notice on the third day what they were drinking?

He is the first one in John's gospel to greet the paradox of the kingdom: the last will be first, the first last, and the choice wine comes up when you least expect it. You know not the day nor the hour for anything, so be alert at all times and do not be surprised by the surprises. The steward, more interested in serving the guests than pondering this event, hurries off to do his job. But the disciples come to have faith in Jesus after this display of authority over the elements of water and wine. We too find our faith strengthened in the water and the wine. We know the choice wine is saved for the last meal, the only one we need in the kingdom.

Questions for Reflection

• How might you be called to be a prophet of God's delight in your family or community?

• What gifts do you have to place at the common good of the church?

• What are the lessons that you learn in sharing the Eucharist? Why is communion so important to Catholics?

Action Response

Offer some of your choice wine to those who could most use it. Share companionship—the real human and holy communion of presence—with someone who suffers loneliness without community. Invite them home to dinner, go for a walk, maybe even bring them to church. Give someone the gift of being present to them fully.

Getting the Message

FIRST READING: NEHEMIAH 8:2–4, 5–6, 8–10
Ezra read out of the book from daybreak till midday.

It was, admittedly, a long haul. The men, women, and children old enough to understand listened to the reading of the law for at least six hours. The law of Moses had been ignored before the exile, and the restored community was anxious to get it right this time. They were willing to subject themselves to this pitiless "cram session" to get the message straight. As they realized how far short from the terms of the law they had fallen, the crowds began to weep without restraint.

Ezra realizes the people are hearing all of this as bad news, so he is quick to change the mood. He tells them to throw a party! Reconciliation to the will of God is not a sad story. It is not about how bad we have been, but how much God wants to bring us back. It explains why the sacrament we called confession has changed so much: not a time to beat our breasts alone in the dark, but a communal celebration of God's great forgiveness and love. The hour of reconciliation is a holy hour, a happy hour. Rejoicing in the Lord is our strength!

SECOND READING: 1 CORINTHIANS 12:12–30
You, then, are the body of Christ.

The present-day church worries about dissension, but it is a story as old as the church itself. The body of Christ has always been part medley, part mob scene. It is a wonder we get anywhere, and no surprise that church history moves very slowly.

The answer to dissent within the church is as old as Paul's advice to Corinth. Everybody does not have to be the same, think the same, do the same. But there has to be unity and a common goal. There has to be respect for the differing parts. There has to be honor for the lesser parts from the greater parts. The so-called greater parts are charged to make a special effort to see to the needs of the lesser members. The most presentable part is not going anywhere without the least presentable part. History proves that out.

Some factions on both sides of the debate would like catholicity to mean uniformity. Yet we need to let prophets be prophets, and administrators be administrators. But oh, it is hard not to be Corinthians, and want to whip everybody into line.

GOSPEL: LUKE 1:1–4; 4:14–21
"Today this Scripture passage is fulfilled in your hearing."

Jesus surrounds himself with no air of mystery in Luke's story. He chooses the prophecy about the servant of the Lord quite deliberately to explain who he is. He is the anointed one, the Messiah. He comes with good news for the poor, the sick, the captive. He comes to bring jubilee, the year of favor in which all debts are revoked and people can begin fresh and free. He is liberation from the ancient debt of sin.

Any questions?

Well, as we know, Nazareth is not exactly pleased to have this Scripture fulfilled in their hearing. After all, they know Jesus, son of Mary and Joseph, a local boy who now thinks he is the answer to all their prayers. If he had come down from the city, perhaps, some big name from Jerusalem, they might have been more receptive. A position with the Sanhedrin or some credentials might have seen him further. But he is nobody, really. He is one of them.

Questions for Reflection

• How have you experienced the changes in the sacrament of forgiveness? Is this a sacrament you celebrate, fear, or avoid?

• Is there dissension about the ways of the church in your family? Parish? How do you resolve the differences?

• Imagine that this year has been declared a year of jubilee, and you can begin again, fresh and free. How will this freedom change your life?

Action Response

Jesus has consecrated all of time as an eternal season of jubilee in which the debt of sin is canceled and we are free. Celebrate your freedom in the sacrament of reconciliation. Forgive those who have trespassed against you. Ask for forgiveness from those you have wronged. Be free.

FOURTH SUNDAY OF ORDINARY TIME

Wearing God's Protection

FIRST READING: JEREMIAH 1:4–5, 17–19

Before you were born I dedicated you.

Jeremiah was born into troubled times. The world around the fertile cres-
cent was being delivered from Assyria to Babylonia, and Egypt alone among
the nations was able to resist the powers of change. Israel itself was already
two nations, Judah in the south and Israel in the north. The people of God
were torn between surrendering to Babylon or joining the resistance in
Egypt. The kings of the promised land could not hold out against the forces
of history, and new cultures with their own gods swept over the people with
tantalizing power.

In other words, it was a lot like our own times. Our global consciousness
makes us vulnerable to the movements of history like never before. We are a
divided people, torn by politics, race, means, and need. We are carried off by
the gods of capitalism and media, not to mention the oldest idol of all, the
craven self. We need help. And prophecy offers its ancient medicine: become
the consecrated people you were born to be. Become a pillar of iron against
changing fortunes, circumstances, and values. Stand up for God's word, and
history cannot crush you, nor will any event of life prevail over you.

SECOND READING: 1 CORINTHIANS 12:31—13:13

Love never fails.

The community at Corinth was impressed by the razzle-dazzle gifts of the
Spirit, as anyone might be. They sought to speak in tongues, to heal, to see
miracles. But Paul points them to the most miraculous gift of all: the power
of love. Because we today have downsized love to mean merely romance,
the word no longer inspires much awe. Yet in Paul's poetry, it becomes mag-
nificent, mesmerizing.

All else is failure, Paul assures us. All else is loss, rubbish, a waste of the
gift of time. We can grace the world with our eloquence, wisdom, and power.
We can perform great sacrifices and do good deeds. But our love alone is
what will be counted. We must be careful stewards of our hearts.

What does love look like? Paul does not define it, but rather describes it.

Love is not a whispery romantic thing, but a strong, Amazonian approach to living. It does not exist in itself but comes into being with others. God, who is love, desired a world in which love could reach its fulfillment in relationship. This one passage of Paul's is spiritual direction enough for a lifetime.

GOSPEL: LUKE 4:21–30
Jesus went straight through their midst and walked away.

At first the people were in seventh heaven. A great prophet was in their midst, and he was one of their own! It made them proud. But then Jesus accused them of vanity, and reminded them that prophets often had to take their gifts outside the community to be heard. Though true, these words enraged his listeners. In their anger, they turned murderous, as people who feel shamed often do. They would have killed him that very day if they had gotten their hands on him.

The funny thing is, they do not get their hands on him. The crowd rises up in the synagogue and runs him out of town, intending to force him off a cliff. Yet they are not able to do it, and Jesus just parts the crowd like the Red Sea and walks away. In Luke's view, Jesus wore God's protection like a shield. He never had to relinquish his life, and so his final surrender to the cross is all the more amazing. He let God choose the day and the hour; until then, he was obedient to God's power alone.

Questions for Reflection

• What are the names of the gods that claim your attention? How do you resist them?

• Choose one sentence from Paul's litany on love that describes your efforts to love. Which sentence describes how you need to grow in love?

• When do you allow the voice of the mob to tamper with your obedience to God's will?

Action Response

Practice walking through the mob as Jesus did. When popular opinion demands that you think or act a certain way, disregard the group mentality and "just say no." Rediscover the freedom of being a citizen of another kingdom!

FIFTH SUNDAY OF ORDINARY TIME

We Pause for Self-Knowledge

FIRST READING: ISAIAH 6:1–2, 3–8
"Holy, holy, holy is the Lord of hosts!"

What is holiness? We think of it as moral perfection, even caricaturing it as the slightly snobbish person wearing a halo. Isaiah was the prophet consecrated to the pursuit of holiness, and he did not imply that image at all. God is holy. To Isaiah, how God differs from us is the measure of holiness. How we grow more alike to God, then, is the measure of God's holiness taking up residence within our lives.

The story of the call of Isaiah to prophecy begins with his vision of the Holy One in full divine authority. We could call this story the Washing of the Lips. Like the story from the Last Supper, the washing of the part implied the cleansing of the whole. Isaiah, unlike Peter, understood this at once. To have clean lips was to be made entirely clean. And so he leaps at the chance to be the prophet of God: "Here I am, send me!"

Most of us fall in the same camp as Moses, Jeremiah, and Zechariah when it comes to responding to God's call in our lives. We have many reasons why God should find someone else: we are too slow of speech, too young, too old. What we really mean is, we do not want to be that holy. We do not want that coal pressed to our lips. Life could never be the same after that.

SECOND READING: 1 CORINTHIANS 15:1–11
I am the least of the apostles.

Paul is often accused of having a runaway ego. He sets himself up for teasing, and he got his share, if we read his defensiveness accurately. But he had his humble moments too. Like a bumper sticker which reads "I Brake for Self-Knowledge," Paul is the first to acknowledge his failures.

Yes, he was among the most ferocious persecutors of the early church. At one time he made it his mission in life to kill Christians and stamp out the virus of their gospel. And then, of course, he became "infected" with it himself. And no one pursued its spreading as zealously as he did, before or since. Paul had an experience of the divine so powerful, he knew himself a sinner in the midst of it and sought holiness ever after.

So Paul joins the prestigious list of those who have seen the Lord. How many of us would find ourselves on that list?

GOSPEL: LUKE 5:1–11
"Leave me, Lord, I am a sinful man."

It was Peter's turn to "find himself," in the grand scheme of things. He had been a fisherman for as long as he could remember. He and his partners James and John had grown up by that lake, had been friends, and had lived in relative obscurity during that time. Then, unexpectedly, Jesus gets into his boat, and the rest is history: salvation history!

When Jesus gets into our boat, obscurity is no longer a possibility. Think about it: Peter, James, and John became *Peter, James,* and *John*! Three guys who fish became the privileged three friends of Jesus. A handful of frustrated fishermen became the most successful fellows on the lake. And not just because of that one day's catch.

Peter's response is the now-familiar pause of self-recognition: he is a sinner, not worthy of this honor. But Jesus tells him not to fear. It is to sinners that holiness comes, and in whom the Spirit of holiness chooses to dwell. Having ears to hear, these men leave the past behind and go with Jesus immediately.

Questions for Reflection

• What is the main reason you resist the call to holiness in your life?

• When did you most powerfully "see the Lord"? What did you learn about yourself in that encounter?

• Imagine Jesus getting into your boat (your life) today. What about your present life-style would cause you fear or shame? How would you have to change?

Action Response

Begin a deeper surrender to holiness right now. Find the most beautiful thing you can think of and praise God for it. Stand in the presence of this wonder and invite the awe you feel to seek a home in you. Carry the spirit of reverence in you like a perpetual light.

Blessing and Cursing

FIRST READING: JEREMIAH 17:5–8

Blessed is the one whose hope is the Lord.

Forget what you know about blessing and cursing when you read Scripture. We use the terms very loosely in our common experience. When we give someone our blessing, we imply that they go forth with our support. When we curse someone or something, we express our contempt.

Biblical blessing and cursing is different. Though blessing evolves into a liturgical expression of God's generous love, it originally meant simply that God is delighted. In the creation story, as God brings each thing into being, the divine response is to bless it and call it good. In the same way, cursing implies that someone or something is excluded from God's pleasure and abandoned to the effects of sin. In Genesis, God curses the serpent, but not the couple. Though under the constraint of sin, they are not lost.

Jeremiah reminds us of the central truth of religion: God is our refuge. If we depend on what human striving can achieve, we are lost to sin and its ruinous effect. If we are rooted in God, then we will know God's delight.

1 CORINTHIANS 15:12, 16–20

If Christ was not raised, your faith is worthless.

The people of Corinth are Greeks. They assume that life is composed of body (inferior) and spirit (superior), and if there is life after death it is an adventure of the soul freed of the flesh. They are grateful at the chance to dump the body once and for all, so they have edited out the resurrection from the dead. They do not want that. They just want the new improved status of life after death, and they are willing to settle for Jesus as a wisdom teacher.

Paul writes to tell them emphatically that faith in the resurrection of Christ is non-negotiable. The teachings of Jesus are not given simply to make you wise. Salvation from sin is not a gift for the present life, or to improve your spirit life hereafter. The whole point of faith in Christ is to be rescued from the ultimate wage of sin, which is death. If Christ rose from the dead, then we can hope confidently to follow him in resurrection. If Jesus was just another guru, Paul would not be wasting his time.

"Blessed are you who hunger; filled you shall be."

Congratulations, you poor ones!

This phrase has something wrong-sounding about it, but it comes closest to the meaning of the beatitude. Being poor has nothing about it to merit congratulations, and it is surely no blessing to live in need. But the blessing, Jesus proclaims, is not in the poverty but in God's favor. God is pleased with the one who is poor, and not delighted at all about the rich.

So is Jesus saying God is guilty of classism, preferring the economically devastated to the ones who have earned their way to a better life? Will God disapprove of the person who has money to spare?

Luke is not suggesting that God would like you better if you closed your bank account and gave away your house. What he is saying is God delights in being the salvation of the one in need. So if you are in need, God promises every good thing: a place in the kingdom, the great banquet, a time to laugh. But if you have plenty, you too must become the delight of the poor. The curse of a full belly is its potential to forget the hungry one not far away.

Questions for Reflection

• In what part of your life do you know yourself to be blessed? Is there an aspect of your life that seems cursed?

• Who would you assign to the category of "wisdom teacher" in our present day? How does Jesus differ from them?

• How are you poor? How are you rich? How might you give from your wealth?

Action Response

Almsgiving stares us in the face this week. Give a scary amount of money to your favorite service or justice organization if you have it. Volunteer some time to a group that needs you. Be more available to a lonely neighbor, an elderly relative, a child who is crying out for attention.

People of Earth, People of Heaven

FIRST READING: 1 SAMUEL 26:2, 7–9, 12–13, 22–23

"Who can lay hands on the Lord's anointed and remain unpunished?"

I have a five-year-old friend who loves Bible stories. Recently she heard the story of the very messy relationship between Saul, the first king over Israel, and David, the anointed king in hiding. Well, she was not going to put up with Saul's hatred of young, popular David, David's fugitive days, or his pitiful band of 600 men against Saul's 3,000-men-strong army. So she stepped into the story and bartered a truce. Everybody lived in the palace happily thereafter.

Alas, my little friend was not there when she was needed. Nobody brokers the peace between these two men, and eventually Saul dies by falling on his own sword and David gains the kingdom. A crucial detail of the story was David's unwillingness to strike Saul down himself. As God's anointed, he would not murder God's original anointed. As one chosen to rule on earth, he still respected the things of heaven.

Often when people complain about this or that in the church, they fail to distinguish between the things of earth which frustrate them, and the things of heaven which claim their allegiance. We do not have to murder the church to change it. If our way of thinking is "anointed by God," our faithfulness will be rewarded. The chair of authority will in time come our way.

SECOND READING: 1 CORINTHIANS 15:45–49

First came the natural and after that the spiritual.

Adam is described as the man of earth, and we know what that means, being of earth ourselves. Adam is frail, mortal, prone to sin, yet capable of deep yearning for more than the limits of humanity allow. Adam can exercise great gifts and enjoy many pleasures, but only within the uncertain box of time. Health, age, and circumstance whittle Adam away. In the end, whatever Adam loves or does, he is finished.

The man of heaven, the last Adam—Jesus—is a different kind of person as his origin implies. Heaven is vast, endless, eternal. Heaven has no limits, no uncertainty, and no sin, since sin means separation from God. Now, we

300

have no choice about being like the first Adam, as we are born of earth. But we can make the choice to bear the likeness of the one from heaven.

GOSPEL: LUKE 6:27–38

"You will rightly be called children of the Most High."

The teaching of Jesus in Luke has a crazy, uneven sound to it. Luke is the gospel of radical dispossession. While Matthew tells us that Jesus said, "Do not turn away a person who wants to borrow from you" (5:42), Luke has Jesus say, "Give to all who beg from you, and when a person takes what is yours, do not demand it back" (6:30). Now that's radical!

Jesus ups the ante in unbelievable ways throughout this passage. Love and do good for your enemies. Return a blessing for a curse. Pray for people who harm you. Do not strike back when people slap you, but offer them the other cheek. This defies the time-honored rule of reciprocity. Who would accept such a backwards way of living, contrary to the laws of self-protection and self-interest? The answer, of course, is that a disciple of Jesus would.

And why should we do what defies logic and any human sense of fairness? Because that is how God operates, Jesus says, so the children of God can do no less. God is good to the ungrateful and the wicked, which is really not what they deserve. And oh, by the way, the ungrateful and the wicked are you and me. We should be prepared to mete out what we hope to have measured back to us, and that is surely not a strict sense of justice.

Questions for Reflection

• How do you resolve the "messiness" of many stories in the Bible? How do you resolve the messiness of evil in our own day?

• How do you betray your earthly origins? How do you reveal your heavenly likeness?

• Which of Jesus' radical love commands in today's Gospel is most difficult for you to follow?

Action Response

Practice the discipleship of radical dispossession this week. Offer goodness in exchange for evil. Bring a blessing where there is cursing. Defy reciprocity, and learn what it means to be in the likeness of God.

The Heart's Abundance

FIRST READING: SIRACH 27:4–7
The fruit of a tree shows the care it has had.

We have to presume these proverbs had instant recognition within the wisdom circles for whom they were written. Unfortunately, it isn't so with us. Those of us who regularly eat corn that comes out of a can or fruit that comes in a cellophane bag may not get the point of these proverbs at first glance. When a sieve is shaken, do the husks appear? Does a fruit tree require a lot of care? Non-farmers may have to take this on faith.

I can vouch at least for the test of the kiln which the potter must face. In high school art class, my friends and I invented rare images, some extraordinary (my friend Ginny's delicate mask) and some just odd (my turtle ashtray.) But when all these pieces went into the kiln, Ginny's mask exploded and my turtle, embarrassingly enough, survived. The flaw in the mask was undetectable but real. The sturdiness of the turtle was unsuspected but true. So through our words, sooner or later, our true character will emerge.

SECOND READING: 1 CORINTHIANS 15:54–58
You know that your toil is not in vain when it is done in the Lord.

Death is really the door to new life. Wealth and power in this world is really poverty in the next. Paul reminds us that things are not always what they seem to be. The ancient law, which was to guard us from sin, actually helped to perpetuate the cycle of sin by focusing us on individual behaviors rather than the attitudes which spawn them. And so we sin, which leads us to the consequence of death.

And then: the cycle is broken! Thanks be to God, Jesus came to announce the kingdom with its upside-down perspective. Now death is not to be feared. Sin is not the end of the story. The results of our labors in faith cannot be known by the poverty of our harvest, which sometimes is embarrassingly small. To see rightly, we cannot use our eyes, which are trained on the world, but our hearts, which are open to the kingdom. Then we will know that things are surely, thank God, not what they seem.

GOSPEL: LUKE 6:39–45
"Each of you speak from your heart's abundance."

Here are more parables about how the truth will sneak past our best intentions and present itself. If we do not see the way clearly, we cannot pretend to be guides for others. (Parents, teachers, pastors—and people who write Scripture commentary—beware!) In the end, what is within us will make itself known to all.

That is why it is one of our most urgent responsibilities to guard our hearts. We must guard against bitterness, hopelessness, needless anxiety, cynicism, unfocused rage, and unforgiveness. It is our primary duty as Christians to love well. We are mandated to love God and one another, and to work our way up to love of enemy and the really tricky ones. We need hearts that are pliable and love that is growing. We cannot afford to surrender to "heart disease" of any kind, those ways of thinking, living, and remembering that cause us to harden our hearts.

If we take care to allow only goodness into our hearts, we will have goodness to share. We speak what we know. We give who we are.

Questions for Reflection

• What might people learn from a typical conversation with you?

• Look around you with your eyes. Record what you see. Now look with your heart. What more do you see?

• Take a quick tour through the contents of your heart today. What do you find?

Action Response

What do you read, watch on TV, listen to in music, take in from your relationships? Do you take in goodness, or husks that will emerge when you shake the sieve? Spend one day rejecting any influence that is not good for your heart. Consider making this a life-style.

Faith Which Astonishes

FIRST READING: 1 KINGS 8:41–43

All will learn of your great name and your mighty hand.

Solomon's wisdom may have made him a wealthy and powerful king, but it also made him a great man of prayer. His original prayer for wisdom got him into the Bible. This prayer, which actually runs from verses 23–53, is his first public prayer in the sanctuary of the newly finished Temple. And among all the things he finds to pray about on this most special occasion, he offers a prayer for foreigners. Imagine: a prayer for outsiders!

This was not the way most Israelites prayed. When they prayed about foreigners at all, it was often more like this: break their necks, show them your mighty power, O God! Solomon, however, anticipated a peculiar thing. He expected that outsiders would come to worship God at the Jewish Temple, from all corners of the world. And when they came, Solomon asked that the God of Israel would hear their prayer and answer them. Could Solomon, with his wise eyes, see all the way to the conversion of Gentiles to the Jewish Messiah to come?

SECOND READING: GALATIANS 1:1–2, 6–10

Even if we or an angel from heaven should preach to you another gospel, let a curse be upon him!

Just as Solomon surprised us by expecting faith where no one thought to look for it, Paul is astounded by finding no faith where he had every reason to expect it. He thought he had done a good job of bringing the Galatians to faith in Jesus; but no sooner does he leave the area when the people falter, following after other teachers. "Anathema sit!" (Be accursed!), Paul writes in Greek, cursing them with the words that would be used for excommunication from the church thereafter.

Parents, catechists, and other mentors often find themselves in a position like Paul, seeing those whom they have led in one direction go off independently in another. It is painful and frustrating to experience the loss of possibilities we had imagined for those in our care. But "Anathema sit!" might be going a bit too far. The Shepherd often goes out over the hills in search of lost sheep. We do not want to write them off in the heat of passion, and miss the opportunity to pray them into the Shepherd's arms.

GOSPEL: LUKE 7:1–10
"He deserves this favor from you, because he loves our people."

You will not find these lines in any other Gospel, about the centurion who loved his Jewish constituents so much that he built a synagogue for them (verse 5; for the parallel account, see Matthew 8:5–13). This is a classic Lucan theme, that there are Gentiles out there just hungry for the revelation which comes from the Jews. Here, after all, is the man Solomon once prayed about, the foreigner who reverences the God of the Israelites! Jesus may have helped him even if this were not true, but chances are good that he would not have approached Jesus if this were not true.

The Jewish elders were impressed by the centurion's show of faith, but Jesus was more impressed. The man even showed respect for the Jewish law which forbade a Jew to enter a Gentile's house. He sends word to Jesus not to make himself unclean by coming to his house, but only to speak the word and his servant would be healed. This foreigner knows that the power of God is not limited by space and time. And for his extraordinary faith, he receives the healing he seeks.

Questions for Reflection

• Do you pray for non-Christians, people not of your nation or race, people not at all like you? Could you pray like Solomon, asking God not to smite "foreigners," but to hear their prayer, just like yours?

• Do you curse or bless your enemies? What is the result of your choice?

• Do you believe that God's power to heal is not limited by time and space, but can occur in any place at any hour?

Action Response

Pray to be given the kind of faith the centurion shows in the gospel story, but know that even a mustard seed faith can move a mountain.

God Has Visited

FIRST READING: 1 KINGS 17:17–24

"O Lord, my God, let the life breath return to the body of this child."

During the time of famine which Elijah had predicted, all of Israel suffered. The widow who had taken the prophet into her home survived as a result of her kindness: her jars of flour and oil were bottomless as a special favor from God. But this favor did not prevent her son from taking ill, and eventually succumbing to the sickness. The widow felt betrayed, maybe even singled out for God's punishment. After all, the eye of God was trained on her household, thanks to the prophet.

It is difficult, in the midst of the rage that comes with grief, not to think that God is deliberately harming us. When we ask the heartfelt question, "Why is God doing this?," we hear the default answers we have learned, from religion or from life. We must be in the throes of punishment for sin. We must not be loved. We must be forgotten or betrayed or abandoned.

God restores the son through the prophet in this story, but our losses and our rage are not often easily answered. Would the widow have forgiven God and Elijah if her son had not been restored to her immediately? For those of us who must wait in faith for a future resurrection, clinging to the promise is sometimes very hard.

SECOND READING: GALATIANS 1:11–19

The gospel I proclaimed to you is no mere human invention.

Paul did not follow the usual channels of catechesis, conversion, and further mentoring. God snatched him up from a life of fiercely dedicated orthodoxy as a Pharisee and commissioned him personally for apostleship. He came to know Christ not through evangelization and study but through a direct encounter with the Risen One. This is the source of his great authority.

Because Paul was self-taught, or God-taught, he is a bit unruly and uncontrollable. It is hard to tell a mystic what to do or to get him to answer to the usual authorities. Ask the popes and bishops who had to reckon with Francis of Assisi, Catherine of Siena, Teresa of Avila, or Mother Teresa for that matter, what it is like to try to keep a mystic in line. You have to accept at some point, as Peter and James evidently did, that one mystically appointed is going down a very individualistic path. And while they are at it, they are widening the trail for others to follow.

GOSPEL: LUKE 7:11–17
"God has visited his people."

Naim is nowhere; which is to say, it is five miles south of Nazareth, another nowhere town which happens to be Jesus' hometown. I come from nowhere too, a little coal town that few have ever heard of. No one outside of it has any reason to care about its citizens: retired old miners who suffer from black lung; widows who live in crumbling homes in alleys; children who play on pavements cracked into hundreds of pieces by trees so old they go on to tear up the street. But I believe God sees the citizens of that little town and cares for them, just as Jesus cared for the sorrow of a stranger he saw in a passing funeral procession in Naim.

Naim is nowhere, but no place is "nowhere" to God. God hears every cough of a dying miner, sees every tear of a lonely widow, and can count the cracks in the sidewalks where poor children play. God has visited places like Naim before, and promises to lift every one of them up into paradise.

Questions for Reflection

• What makes it possible for you to wait in joyful hope for an answer to your losses?

• How many others can you name, in the past or our own times, who seem to have been visited by a vision from God which empowers all they do?

• Where would you like God to visit, and what would you like God to do there? How might you go there as an ambassador for God?

Action Response

Take a walk through your neighborhood, mindful of what God sees there. Observe everything: buildings, trees, animals, people. Pray for the neighborhood that you see, in its wealth and its poverty.

Covering a Multitude of Sins

FIRST READING: 2 SAMUEL 12:7–10, 13
"The Lord on his part has forgiven your sin: you shall not die."

He was a murderer and an adulterer, by God's own accusation. Why, then, does David get off the hook? Some folks in the Hebrew Scriptures get struck down in their tracks for touching a sacred object out of turn. Yet David is spared for far worse offenses.

What saves David's life is his great honesty, coupled with his great love. David is the first to admit his guilt, although he does not exactly seek Nathan out to go to confession about it. Nathan has to trick him into implicating himself by telling him a parable about a rich man who steals a poor man's lamb (see verses 1–6). Once he is implicated, David hangs his head and knows what he has done. He has caused great offense to the Lord who has given him everything a man's heart could desire. And he repents it.

The one who loves much is forgiven much, and David has been fervent in his love for God till now. The lesson we might take to heart here is to love lavishly, like holy fools, not knowing when our love might stand as the only character witness in our favor.

SECOND READING: GALATIANS 2:16, 19–21
I will not treat God's gracious gift as pointless.

Paul seeks to make the opposite point to the Galatians than is attested in the other two readings today. God, Paul suggests, has a love which covers a multitude of our sins. God's love, demonstrated by Jesus in his life but especially from the cross, restores the balance of justice and peace that was destroyed by our allegiance to sin. What was torn is made whole, not because we are so good at loving, but because God is.

That is why Paul gets so animated when folks suggest that being good citizens and obeying the law of Moses is going to get them saved. Our obedience and all the love in our hearts is not good enough to save us. No matter how many prayers and good works we rack up in our favor, only God can save us. The choice to be saved is not ours; it is never ours. Salvation is a gift from God. And a gift is not something you take, it can only be given.

"That is why her many sins are forgiven—because of her great love."

Jesus never doubts the rumor that the woman who bathes his feet is a sinner. He says quite freely that she is forgiven her many sins, though he does not bother to list them. Simon, however, was very attached to every one of her sins, enjoying his moral superiority as a Pharisee.

The story Jesus tells Simon reinforces this difference between the one who forgives and the one who delights in the sin of others. Two men owe a certain moneylender different sums. (Here, amazingly, Jesus identifies himself with a moneylender!) Both debts are written off, as if the moneylender does not differentiate their value. To the moneylender, these two debtors are the same: neither one can pay. So they are treated the same, and both sums are written off.

If Simon could have heard it, he would have understood that he, a Pharisee, was being equated in God's eyes with a notorious sinner. His small, hidden sins were the same to God as her flamboyant, high-profile infractions. She may have been wearing the red dress and he the modest prayer shawl. But to God, both of them were in need of forgiveness, and that was what God was offering.

Questions for Reflection

• Where and how do you spend your love?

• What does God's gift of salvation save you from?

• How do you feel about the small-time sinner being equated with the high rollers: grateful or cheated? (This may depend on who you identify with!)

Action Response

Think of your love as currency. Imagine you have a million dollars worth of it, and you have to spend it all today. Go spread it around!

A Question of Identity

FIRST READING: ZECHARIAH 12:10–11
I will pour out…a spirit of grace and petition.

The prophet Zechariah was anticipating a new world order, something like what we talk about today. A world of peace and justice, a world without barriers and suffering. When the new spirit would come upon his people, it would bring with it clear vision. And once they would see clearly, surely they would lament their former ways.

A comparison is made between the mourning in Megiddo and that day of clear vision. In Megiddo the pagans honored a divinity called Hadadrimmon with songs of lamentation. Zechariah predicts that the God of Israel might realistically be honored in the same way should the people come to know their sin. John the evangelist recognizes the potential of this prophecy to speak to the piercing of Jesus on the cross. Centuries of saints and mystics, their eyes opened, have wept before the cross. The gift of tears, as Teresa of Avila called it, comes to those who truly see.

SECOND READING: GALATIANS 3:26–29
Each one of you is a child of God.

Paul writes to the Galatians with great indignation. He has heard that his authority has been undermined by subsequent teachers, and the young community is in disarray. At various points in the letter, Paul curses the new teachers, and calls the Galatians as a whole—in a word—stupid. Trust Paul not to make nice when the Gospel is at stake.

And yet, Paul does not write to the Galatians just to vent. He also provides a thorough reiteration of his basic teaching, including these kindly words: "Each one of you is a child of God." Stupid, maybe; but one of God's own, beloved and provided for. He insists on an end to the divisions among them, no privileged status for Jews over Greeks, no room for men lording it over women, or slaves perceived as less than free citizens. All are surrendered to the same Christ and are therefore one in Christ.

We as a church can learn much from what Paul has to say. Sometimes the teachers among us sway us this way and that, and sometimes our allegiance to the idea of the moment makes us downright foolish in the eyes of faith. We have to stop this kind of behavior. It makes us seem as dense as the Galatians.

"Who do the crowds say that I am?"

Almost everyone believes Jesus existed and did at least some of the things Scripture says he did. But how we talk about who Jesus is and what it means that he did those things is where the lines are drawn between the faithful and the rest of the world.

In this conversation with the disciples, a lot of possible identities for Jesus surface: a reincarnation of John the Baptist, recently put to death for preaching repentance. The return of Elijah, who never really died but was swooped up to heaven by the will of God. Any of a number of prophets long dead. The Messiah of God. The Son of Man. The suffering servant prophesied in Isaiah.

What the crowds say about Jesus is never so important as what we say about him. Is he *my* Lord, or just the Lord of my religion? Is he *my* savior, or a savior hung on a cross on the wall of my parish? Is he *my* teacher, or a great teacher of ancient times? Does he heal *me*, or was his healing just for lucky lepers of the first century? We can argue the theology all day, or for all time. But the only Jesus that matters for us is the one we really believe in.

Questions for Reflection

• Contemplate an image of Jesus on the cross that has meaning for you. What do you see when you reflect on it?

• Do you think there are signs of prejudice or favor in your parish? In your diocese? In the church as a whole? Support your answer.

• Jesus poses the question to you: "Who do *you* say that I am?" No pious talk, just the facts.

Action Response

Engage in a week-long meditation on the cross. Put yourself in front of a different image of Jesus for a few minutes every day and ask the question, "Who is Jesus?" Write down your answers each day. Share what you learn.

The Day of the Challenge

FIRST READING: 1 KINGS 19:16, 19–21
"Please, let me kiss my father and mother goodbye!"

You have to feel some pity for Elisha. There he is out in the field, minding his own business, trailing after twelve yoke of oxen. And then Elijah shows up and flings his cloak over him and strides away. The gesture is grand and dramatic and wordless, and Elisha understands it. He has been chosen to bear the mantle of the great prophet. He passes the first test; he is perceptive.

Can we blame him for what happens next, for wanting a moment to adjust? Vocations, when flung at us, catch us mid-life, off-balance. Perhaps plowing a rocky field is not much of a job, but plowing the nation as God's prophet is another thing entirely. Elijah's response to Elisha's plea may seem insensitive, but remember: the call to be God's prophet is seldom about warm fuzzy relationships. Prophets are wild, undomesticated creatures. They pull God's yoke, and they carry in their bellies a word of fire.

Elisha slays the animals, demonstrating his commitment to plow a new field. He provides food for his family one last time. And then he takes up his new career, in the same spirit of silence as it came to him.

SECOND READING: GALATIANS 5:1, 13–18
It was for liberty that Christ freed us.

The Galatians are having a bad day. The Jewish members of the community are insisting the Greeks be circumcised to share in salvation. Paul has just wished aloud that those insisting on circumcision go all the way and castrate themselves (see 5:12). Ouch. Yes, it gets nasty in Galatia, as the way of the Spirit is opposed by the way of the flesh.

As Paul sees it, adherence to the ancient law means not surrendering fully to the confidence that Jesus really saves. Could more be required than the crucifixion to pay the price of sin? Will a little bloodletting on the part of every male add to the value of the cross? Love is the key, an inward reality, not an outward sign. The vicious division of the community is evidence of their lack of love.

When Paul speaks of freedom from the law, he is aware that some will abuse this idea to the point of licentious behavior. He is quick to remind the Galatians that freedom to love carries its own responsibilities. One who is free to love is not free to do just anything. But one who experiences the freedom to love will not want to do anything else.

GOSPEL: LUKE 9:51–62
"Let the dead bury their dead."

"Let the dead bury their dead" is not a polite thing to say to someone who just wants to provide a simple, human service to his father. A service, it needs to be said, that was required under Jewish law. Burying the dead and honoring one's parents were both mandates, not suggestions.

But time is short, and Jesus is on his way to Jerusalem and his death. The shortcut across Samaria leads to shunning this time, as the Samaritans are not keen on a prophet destined for Jerusalem. The disciples would like to see them punished, but Jesus is not going to dignify that request with anything more than a curt reprimand. There is no time to lose.

To those who want to follow him, Jesus points out that the way he is going holds no glamour. Those who hesitate, Jesus rejects. The only disciples Jesus can use are those who put their hand to God's plow and do not look back. You can only plow a straight line if you keep your focus on what you are doing—like Jesus, who is making a beeline for Jerusalem and the cross.

Questions for Reflection

- What field do you plow? Would you leave it if you were called to go elsewhere?
- Are you free to love? What are the responsibilities that come with love?
- Have you ever put your hand to the plow and not looked back? What did you leave behind, and why did you leave it?

Action Response

Look back for a moment on the line you are plowing with your time, energy, resources, and relationships. Is it straight, or wavy, or going in a circle? Consider how you might plow a straighter line for the kingdom, and make one definite adjustment to your aim this week.

Reason to Celebrate

FIRST READING: ISAIAH 66:10–14

In Jerusalem you shall find your comfort.

Somewhere in our depths, there is a longing to return to a time and place where we are utterly cared for. My sister talks about how she feels going home to visit our parents. Though she is herself the mother of three, going to Mom and Dad's means getting to be the daughter again, if only for a few hours. The grandparents take charge of her children. My mother serves her coffee and a piece of pie. For a few serene hours, she does not have to lift a finger.

Jerusalem became the metaphor for that "home again" feeling in the Hebrew Scriptures. It was the place where God was in charge, and all needs would be provided for. It was the place of rest and comfort, as warm and secure as being an infant in the arms of a loving mother. The image is not intended to be simply abstract ("your heart shall rejoice") but also sensual ("your bodies will flourish like the grass"). For a people carrying a heavy load, what a wonderful thing it is to contemplate laying that burden down.

Sometimes we talk about the heavenly Jerusalem as if we have to die to get there. But every time we lighten the load for someone, we are Jerusalem for them.

SECOND READING: GALATIANS 6:14–18

All that matters is that one is created anew.

Paul is saying that we are all crucified with Christ in our willingness to claim the cross as Christians. We may wear the cross, genuflect before it, sign ourselves with it, and be buried under it. But more than that, we agree to carry the cross like Simon of Cyrene. We shoulder the burden of our sisters and brothers. We witness to our faith even when our words will cost us. We do not walk away when injustice causes the innocent to suffer.

And Paul takes it one step further when he says he is crucified to the world and the world crucified to him. From the moment he became a disciple, the world died to him with all of its empty promises and passing glories. He lived his life in service of the new Jerusalem, not the old. Paul is a tough act to follow, but he issues the invitation.

GOSPEL: LUKE 10:1–12, 17–20
"The reign of God is at hand."

Isaiah celebrates the new Jerusalem. Paul boasts of the cross of Jesus Christ. Here Jesus invites his disciples to celebrate the reign of God, and we know these three things speak to the same reality. It is like receiving three invitations to the same party.

Who were the seventy-two invited to the party? The number is chosen for its symbolic value to represent the whole world (seventy and seventy-two are numbers related to the "family of nations" in Genesis). These seventy-two might have included your average parishioners today: some keen on their faith, some a little conservative in their involvement, some not regular in their attendance. All were sent, they went "everywhere," and Satan fell from the sky like lightning.

Today *we* are the seventy-two, invited to go out there and cause Satan to collapse, witnessing against one evil at a time. God knows there are many to choose from. Find a friend, and get moving!

Questions for Reflection

• Describe a time when someone was "Jerusalem" for you, lightening your burden and offering you comfort.

• How has your faith invited you to die to the world in its goals and values?

• Which two evils do you feel personally addressed to challenge in your family, parish, or greater community? How can you and a friend begin your testimony against them?

Action Response

Actions speak louder than discussion groups. Become an official member of the "seventy-two club" today. With a friend or group of friends, pledge to personally and visibly confront at least one circumstance of evil.

Not Exactly Rocket Science

FIRST READING: DEUTERONOMY 30:10–14
"This commandment is not too mysterious and remote for you."

Had the concept been available, Moses probably would have addressed the crowd by saying, "Come on, folks, this isn't rocket science! I'm not telling you anything you haven't heard before or can't figure out through common sense. This is something already in your mouths and in your hearts. Don't lie, don't steal, don't kill, don't disgrace your spouse, don't forget your parents, and don't forget God." See how easy that is?

Easy to say, anyway. But what is simple counters the human will. And that will, the most powerful aspect of being human, is also what makes us "in God's image." That Godly piece of us keeps trying to set ourselves up like divinities for our own private devotion. We have our own favorite commandment: bow down and serve me! Sad to say, that commandment usually gets more obedience than the other ten combined.

Moses urges the people to surrender heart and soul to God's law. If we would begin by laying down our fiercely independent and self-seeking will, God's law would be second nature to us.

SECOND READING: COLOSSIANS 1:15–20
He is before all else that is.

Paul is declaring what scholars call the pre-existence of Christ. John's Gospel makes the same point when he says, "In the beginning was the Word, and the Word was with God and was God." Using poetic language, John is simply saying, "There was a Christ before there was a Jesus." There was a second person in the Trinity before Jesus, the human, was born in Bethlehem.

Paul also approaches the pre-existence of Christ on the level of poetry. In fact, this passage from Colossians seems to be an early Christian hymn that Paul is quoting, whether or not he composed it. It does not give the details of how Christ became Jesus and entered into time and history. It does not explain how Jesus juggled two job descriptions simultaneously: being the one through whom "everything continues in being" while having fish with his disciples on the lake.

What this poem does tell us is that it pleased God that Jesus should do so. The absolute fullness of divinity rested in him and with it, Jesus chose to lay all privilege down and reconcile the ancient breach with the cross. Poetry preserves the mystery as it reveals the truth.

GOSPEL: LUKE 10:25–37
"And who is my neighbor?"

Trust a lawyer to ask a question like this! "Just exactly who is my neighbor, Lord?" So Jesus tells a story beloved of children in Sunday schools everywhere, the simplest story in the world. As we suspected, the titles and roles of these characters in the story mean nothing in the end. The truth of who they are is revealed in their hearts, and their hearts are revealed in their response to human suffering.

This is crystal clear in our own assemblies, though we pretend it isn't. Standing in the sanctuary does not make you pious, and a show of piety does not make you a friend of God. Nor does being cast as an enemy of God—the non-Catholic, the non-churchgoer, the person who leads a life of suspicious morality—mean you are not a lover of your neighbor and, by extension, of God as well. We humans are sitting in the cheap seats, and we cannot see as God sees from the perspective of eternity. Rather than asking, "Who is my neighbor?" we ought to be asking, "How can I help?"

Questions for Reflection

• In what aspect of your life does God's will and your will collide most frequently?

• How do you approach the matter of mystery in faith? What does it mean to you in your everyday life?

• Tell the story of a time you saw an "enemy of God" do the right thing. How did it challenge you?

Action Response

Let there be no more "enemies of God" in your heart. Practice thinking differently about the types of people you regard as reflexively bad. Avoid slander, sarcasm, and stereotyping of groups. Begin to see in every person a beloved child of the same God.

SIXTEENTH SUNDAY IN ORDINARY TIME

God as Guest

FIRST READING: GENESIS 18:1–10
The Lord appeared to Abraham by the terebinth.

Here is Abraham on a hot day, sitting under a tree near his tent. He reminds me of the older folks in small towns who sit on their porches in the summer and watch the world go by. They speak to friend and stranger alike: "Hot enough for ya?" Abraham is like this, a contented old man who has a herder's wealth, a wife who has stuck with him for a century, everything a man in his world could want. Except an heir.

And then three strangers come by, and Abraham opens his mouth to say, "Hot enough for ya?" But the words die on his lips. In these three, he instinctively recognizes the God he has been following since he left his homeland. How does Abraham know it is God? The Trinity has not been invented yet as a way of representing the nature of God.

However Abraham knows they are from God, he knows what to do when God comes calling. Quickly he offers hospitality, prepares the finest meal he can, and waits on the Lord. Are we as quick to see and respond, and as generous in our response, when God comes calling?

SECOND READING: COLOSSIANS 1:24–28
This is the Christ we proclaim.

The idea that God might become the guest of Abraham may not challenge our faith, but it was a big challenge to many of Paul's peers that God would choose to dwell among the Gentiles. The Gentiles! Pagan, immoral, sexually perverse, ignorant of God's law and no friend to God's people Israel! Why would God be bothered with such people?

The second mystery is, why would Paul? Why would Paul call himself the Apostle to the Gentiles, and find a career in proclaiming the Gospel to them? Why would he go to jail, from which he writes this letter, to save a bunch of sinners? We know the answer: for the same reason Jesus went to the cross. Sinners, after all, are the only people who need saving. And we know who the sinners are, in all humility.

Every person stands in need of being completed by Christ. That is why

Paul spreads his teaching liberally, on foot and by boat across Asia Minor. The passion that motivated Paul made him often an outcast, so that Christ would be a guest throughout the world.

GOSPEL: LUKE 10:38–42
"One thing only is required."

I have often been a guest in Martha's home. I visit with someone whom I have longed to see, and am treated with great kindness and attention to my every need. The best china, the nicest desserts come out, and I never see the bottom of my coffee cup, for it is vigilantly refilled. Yet all the while, enjoying every good thing that comes to me, I am longing for my friend to sit down. After all, I have come to be with her, not her dishes.

I have also been to Mary's house. The moment I come in, she grabs me by the arm and we sit down. We talk, laugh, the hours go by and maybe I am hungry, or I have to cough before a glass of water is offered. The room gets cold and no one closes a window or stirs up the fire. I may be uncomfortable at Mary's house, but we have a darn good visit.

It is best, of course, not to have to choose. Martha's hospitality was welcome and good. Mary might have been more considerate of her sister, sharing the chores *and* the chance to be with Jesus. But if the choice has to be made, presence is always the better part. The relationship will keep without the cookies, but not without heart speaking to heart.

Questions for Reflection

• How do you know when a person or a circumstance in your life is from God?

• Where does Christ the guest find welcome in your life?

• Are you more like Martha or Mary? How do you share presence with those who are important to you?

Action Response

Be a good host to God this week. Be on the lookout for God on the road, or Jesus in the unlikely stranger. Remember that Jesus comes to us, too, in the friend at our door. Welcome God as guest, however the Holy One comes.

Cosmic Negotiations

FIRST READING: GENESIS 18:20–32
"What if there are at least ten there?"

Here Abraham shows off the tremendous bargaining skills which made him a rich man as he haggled from town to town on his lifelong journey. Charming and self-effacing, he is also tenacious in his dickering. And is he ever bold: "Should not the judge of all the world act with justice?" Imagine saying that to God!

But of course, the Bible is filled with such phrases. There is a Yiddish word for throwing the gauntlet down before the Almighty, *chutzpah*, which means "a lotta nerve." You have to be awfully gutsy to confront God with the state of the world and dare the Divine to respond. Job does it, the prophets often do it, the psalms make a habit of it. Jesus hurls *chutzpah* from the cross: "My God, my God, why have you forsaken me?" Such challenges are not made in the absence of faith, but in the absolute conviction that God is listening and God will act.

By comparison, some of our prayers are watery and vague. We do not ask much, maybe because we do not expect much. Weak prayers often betray weak faith.

SECOND READING: COLOSSIANS: 2:12–14
God pardoned all our sins.

Imagine owing a huge sum of money, more than you could ever hope to repay. The one to whom you owe this bond has no love for you and would not hesitate to see you put to death, to serve as a warning to others.

And then, amazingly, a champion of your cause appears. He snatches up your bond and pays for it—with his life. And gradually you come to know that he did this, not just for you, but for everyone who ever owed a debt they could not pay. He took on your chains so that you could all go free. What would you do with the rest of your life?

This is the Christian story, from Paul's perspective. He wants to tell everyone this good news, that his debt and yours was nailed once and for all to the same cross. He too will give his life, out of gratitude for his champion.

The question remains posed to you and me: what are you doing with the rest of your life?

GOSPEL: LUKE 11:1–13
"For whoever asks, receives; whoever seeks, finds."

If there was ever a cosmic negotiation, it is the Lord's prayer. First, we praise God, then we list our petitions: We need food, please. Oh, and forgiveness; and please do not make the temptations harder than we can bear. Amen.

In return, we offer the assertion that we also forgive those who do us wrong, and we are nowhere near as just as God. But Jesus knows we are not as good as our intentions. He adds the little story about the man who will not help his neighbor out of friendship but will capitulate in the end out of exasperation. That is more like us. We forgive those who wrong us because it is often more practical to do so. Even psychology tells us that we have a personal investment in forgiveness: it is the healthy choice, over the gradual descent into mental illness which comes from holding a grudge.

What makes God *God* is that God does not need a reason or motivation to forgive us. God shows mercy because it is the nature of love to be merciful. If we ask, if we seek, if we knock, we will be served. That is a cosmic negotiation worth pursuing.

Questions for Reflection

• What kind of language would you use to plead before God for your community, your cause, your life?

• Were you ever forgiven a great debt, of money or wrongdoing? How did you respond?

• What kinds of things do you ask God for when you pray?

Action Response

Pray for an infusion of God's grace in your life, and the life of your community. Petition for an end to violence, hate, and immorality in our towns and cities. Ask and it shall be given to you: we are promised that from one we can trust.

Christian Economics 101

FIRST READING: ECCLESIASTES 1:2, 2:21–23

Vanity of vanities!

Some of us love our jobs, some of us hate our jobs, and many of us just do our work (whether within the house or outside of it) with numbing indifference. But the one thing we all seek is meaning, a sense of purpose, the feeling that what we do with our days is not irrelevant to the universe. The church has written much about the dignity of human labor, recognizing that we are co-creators with God through the work of our hands. One thing is sure: the despair of no purpose puts us on the road to mental illness.

The writer Qoheleth decries the vanity (literally, "vapors") of earthly work that leads only to earthly gain. The right car, right house, and right friends will, at the end of our lives, go up in smoke as readily as if we had been satisfied with humbler circumstances. Is there a world we can build that will not pass away? Is there a task we can perform that will lead to something lasting? The mission of the church testifies that there is.

SECOND READING: COLOSSIANS 3:1–5, 9–11

Your life is hidden now with Christ in God.

Many things keep us "rooted in earth" and concerned with this world. Love of family, the value of our work, friendships we have formed over the years, our very bodies—all of these factors are real and good and in no way should be seen as unholy. Christianity does not imply that we should become "otherworldly," more concerned with the life hereafter than the life here and now.

Instead, we Christians have a vital investment in what happens to our world. We are stewards of this planet and keepers of one another. To be "intent on things above" means to be mindful of the real powers at work in the world, not the superficial tin gods of commerce and politics. We have to see clearly past the lies of world-speak, which tell us how to dress and who to use to get ahead. We have work to do in the world, but we have to remember whose payroll we ultimately serve.

GOSPEL: LUKE 12:13–21
"Avoid greed in all its forms."

The person in the crowd had a legitimate request of Jesus, so he thought. All he wanted was what was rightfully his by law: his share of the inheritance. But Jesus is not interested in his plight at all. Jesus treats the matter like a useless question.

Money is no useless matter to us. It generates the life we know and want to keep. We go to great lengths to make money, sometimes doing things we do not like or are not particularly proud of. We need money to survive in this culture, and we need it to take care of those who depend on us. And if we splurge once in a while on some unnecessary thing, is that so bad?

Jesus is not intent on laying a guilt trip on you about how you spend your money. He just wants us to be clear that the getting of money is a temporal matter that has a mortality of its own. If the getting of money is what your life is about, what will you do when the life of money is behind you? The time is coming for each of us when a million dollars will simply be so much paper.

Questions for Reflection

• How would you define the purpose of your life? How does what you do with your days accomplish that purpose?

• In what ways do you feel tugged to serve the world? In what ways do you serve the higher realm of God's kingdom?

• Make a list of all the things you spend money on regularly. How many of those things will last longer than your lifetime?

Action Response

Put your treasure in lasting things this week. Give time to someone who asks for it. Give money to someone who cannot pay you back. Give love to those who depend on you.

Keep the Lamps Ready

FIRST READING: WISDOM 18:6–9
That night was known beforehand to our forebearers.

The rescue from Egypt defined the faith of the Israelites in every generation. It was a dynamic event which lives still in the retelling at every Passover meal. God saved the faithful, and led their enemies along their chosen path of destruction. God has done it, and God will continue to do it.

This salvation required full participation on the part of the people. God announced the coming of the angel of death, but the people had to be vigilant for his coming. They had to stand and eat their bread like people about to flee. They had to mark their houses with the blood of the covenant to signify their allegiance. The story does not say if there were some too lazy or preoccupied with business as usual to comply. We only know the fate of the vigilant faithful.

Their story is our story. We stand awake and sober, aware that the angel of death has not ceased his rounds. We share our Eucharist on our feet, men and women on a journey that takes us far into the world and beyond. The night is known to us. We cannot live as those who are deceived.

SECOND READING: HEBREWS 11:1–2, 8–19
God has prepared a city for the faithful.

I like this image of Abraham and Sarah, not receiving the fullness of the promise of God, but seeing it and saluting it from afar. I imagine them shoulder to shoulder, two old people who have learned to love well over more than a century together. They are great friends to one another. They have laughed a lot and cried a lot together. They both learned difficult lessons about trusting in God's word. And in the end, they trusted God enough to leave the future in divine hands. They salute the promise to come, and take their bow from salvation history.

What they only saw from afar, we have in our possession: the fulfillment of God's promise in Jesus Christ. Sometimes, though, it seems as though we are looking at it backwards from an equally far distance in time. Jesus may seem twenty centuries behind us, as obscured by time and place as if he were a fairy tale. We salute the cross as a great achievement of the past, but it may have no present significance for us. It takes faith to see the power of the cross winning victories in the world right now. It takes faith to let the Spirit Jesus promised work in us to achieve those victories.

GOSPEL: LUKE 12:32–48
"Let your lamps be burning ready."

Peter wants assurances. He is not quite the blockhead he is often painted: his question reveals his suspicion that Jesus is speaking very directly to his disciples and not issuing a general press release. This business about getting a purse fat with the wealth of Godly things and surrendering your worldly treasure is an intermediate-level demand of the kingdom. Being a good steward of the master's household is only required of those who actually are handed the keys.

Do you hear the keys jingling in your pocket? As Catholics, we are handed a great many gifts and inherent responsibilities. As Americans, we are also well endowed. We are being personally addressed by this story of the steward who is entrusted with much. We can never say we did not know what was expected of us. The light of our lives should be burning night and day, illuminating the way for others.

Questions for Reflection

• How do you participate in the saving power of God?

• What keeps Jesus from being merely a great hero of the past in your life?

• Which keys has God entrusted to your possession? What doors might they unlock for others?

Action Response

Consider something you have that someone else might need: knowledge, a skill, your company, some material goods. Be a good steward and share what you have.

The Time of Division

FIRST READING: JEREMIAH 38:4–6, 8–10

"Jeremiah ought to be put to death."

King Zedekiah is a ruler with no backbone. One faction wants to kill the prophet, so he agrees to their plan. The next faction wants to save the prophet, so he gives them leave to do so. It isn't that Zedekiah is not clear on what is right: he knows that Jeremiah is from God, but he also knows that Jeremiah's truths make the kingdom uneasy. When the people start to take sharply opposed positions, it is time for a king to watch his back.

The divisions in Zedekiah's kingdom can be found everywhere that God's truth is being spoken. God's truth is aimed right between the eyes of the world's power and authority, and those who have a lot have much to protect. The powerful are not going to relinquish what they have without a fight. Prophets, in times of division, have to watch their backs too.

SECOND READING: HEBREWS 12:1–4

Let us keep our eyes fixed on Jesus.

Jesus is our greatest example of what to do with the opposition of (fellow) sinners: nothing. Nothing, that is, except what we would do if the truth were not opposed. We should continue to be faithful. We should continue to speak the truth and live out of it. If there is a cross awaiting us at some point down the road, that should come as no surprise. Trying to avoid it would be like trying to sidestep a train.

Jeremiah ends up in the cistern because he kept right on saying what people did not want to hear. He persevered with the truth. Jesus remained faithful to the truth and was brought to the cross. Neither one, thanks be to God, remained there. For when we are faithful, God proves twice as faithful. As the letter to the Hebrews puts it, a cloud of witnesses have stood before us, testifying to this same truth. It is our privilege to enter their company.

GOSPEL: LUKE 12:49–53

"I have come to light a fire on the earth."

He was announced at birth as the Prince of Peace. But that never meant Jesus was going to be harmless. A lover of children, the friendless, and the poor: yes. A mascot of gentle platitudes: no way. Jesus came to bring real peace into the world, but that peace came at a price. It meant we would have to relinquish our participation in some very popular fictions that have kept the world going for a long time. It meant that we would have to make room for the truth.

Truth is hard on families, on communities, and on nations. When a family stops pretending that Mom's drinking is not really a problem, there is going to be trouble. When a community acknowledges that it has racial inequalities in its midst, expect a blow-up. When a nation admits that its economy is based on the oppression of certain groups, no one is going to be comfortable for a long time. Truth leads to division before a lasting peace can be achieved. What passes for peace before that, of course, is only the sound of a chorus of denial.

Questions for Reflection

• Who speaks the truth in your family? In your community? On the global scene?

• When you find the truth opposed in conversation, policy, or the example of someone's life, how do you respond?

• What are the uncomfortable truths emerging in your community? How do you face them as a follower of Jesus?

Action Response

Try spending one day as a truth speaker. Do not be silent when others are creative with the truth. Tell no white lies. Be real with people. Find out what happens when you start standing up for the truth.

TWENTY-FIRST SUNDAY IN ORDINARY TIME

The Narrow Door

FIRST READING: ISAIAH 66:18–21

I come to gather nations of every language.

The prophecy of Isaiah is full of surprises. Though the people of God maintain an exclusive identity in much of the Hebrew story, often in Isaiah we find an open invitation to the nations to come and enjoy God's blessings. But here, the invitation even has scholars amazed: the prophet says that God is going to welcome outsiders into the priesthood itself!

How could Isaiah have foreseen a thing that was beyond the vision or even the wishes of his contemporaries? Gentile priests of the Lord? What an idea! As shocking as that idea was in his time, the idea of a wider priesthood causes as much alarm today. We still like the comfort of our categories, insiders and outsiders clearly defined. If you start letting the outsiders in, what kind of world do you have? How can you make sense of such a new creation? Better to relegate prophecy to the past, and not let it speak a living word to us.

SECOND READING: HEBREWS 12:5–7, 11–13

Make straight the paths you walk on.

When I was thirteen, a young boy in our town died while disobeying a rule that all of us ignored regularly. He had been trespassing on the grounds of the local cement company and diving into huge vats of sand after hours. It was great fun; none of us realized how easily it could lead to suffocation. After his death, we all faced long talks in the parlor with our parents, and new rules restricting our freedom. The town's children felt mutually on parole. All of the extra discipline was to save us, not to punish us. But you could not tell that to the children.

Discipline is the part of religion that nobody likes to talk about, but it is also part of the story. At the moment any mention of discipline is out of fashion. But just as forgiveness and celebration are part of our faith, so is the need to temper human freedom with limits. We can set them for ourselves, or society may set them for us. But if we do not accept the limits that are binding on us, they will be enforced by powers larger than we are. A mortal creature expressing itself like a divine one is going to encounter a brick wall sooner or later.

GOSPEL: LUKE 13:22–30
"Try to come in through the narrow door."

Recently I saw a painting called, "The Narrow Gate to Heaven and the Wide Gate to Hell." The narrow gate had only two people attempting entrance. They each had an open prayer book and seemed to be praying their way through. Near this entrance was a man peddling crosses with a name printed clearly on each. "Pick up your cross" was never simpler than this. Meanwhile a crowd milled around the other gate. Men on horses and leaping dogs added to the liveliness of the scene. It was clearly a more attractive entrance, if you could overlook the skeletons that were dancing among them.

Looking at a painting like this, I am always impatient to find a third gate somewhere. No, I do not want to dance with skeletons, but I also do not want to imitate the dour piety of portrait saints. I think it is possible to dance with the saints, dance with your cross, dance through the narrow gate all the way to the reign of God. Why should the devil have all the fun? If religious folk looked livelier, perhaps more people would try the narrow door.

Questions for Reflection

• Of all the nations and peoples that prophecy claims will appear before God, who will you be most surprised to see there?

• What kinds of disciplines do you strive for in your life?

• Who are the dancing saints in your life? How do you continue the dance?

Action Response

Create a kindly discipline in your life. Plan to take better care of your body: quit smoking, eat healthy meals, drink less, sleep more. Take unnecessary walks. Waste less time worrying. Spend more time in silence. Love more. Refrain from bitterness.

Feasting with Beggars

FIRST READING: SIRACH 3:17–18, 20, 28–29

Humble yourself the more, the greater you are.

I know a rather wealthy woman who lives in a great house on a hill. Not many people know this, but at night she drives around in a van and gives out sandwiches and hot chocolate to people spending the night in doorways. One man wept as she arrived at his corner. "Today is my birthday," he kept saying over and over, "and you came."

There is something very powerful about the sight of a strong person helping a weaker one. When Jimmy Carter goes to some destitute corner of the world and sits down with a poor woman, or some celebrity becomes an activist for the voiceless, we are amazed at the sight. We also find ourselves, on some level, doubting their sincerity. The great so seldom take an interest in the powerless, it is hard to credit it when they do. Yet this is the kingdom paradigm: the greater we are, the more we should make ourselves immediately available to those in need. The good that comes into our lives is not for ourselves alone.

SECOND READING: HEBREWS 12:18–19, 22–24

You have not drawn near to an untouchable mountain and a blazing fire.

When Moses encountered the Lord on Mount Sinai, the people began to wonder if Moses really saw and heard all he claimed to. What made him so favored, after all? So the Lord revealed the divine presence to the people in the raging power of the natural elements. And the people begged Moses to keep his encounters with God to himself from now on.

The image of ascending God's holy mountain is much kinder in Hebrews. The heavenly Jerusalem has more order, less terror. The danger of encountering God and maybe dying of the privilege is past. Jesus has mediated the chasm between God and us, and now there is a bridge we can cross to arrive in the divine presence safely. The bridge is called forgiveness. It means, despite who we are and where we have been and all we have done, there is a place prepared for us in God's assembly.

GOSPEL: LUKE 14:1, 7–14

"When you have a reception, invite beggars and the crippled, the lame and the blind."

On a street downtown stands a building which houses an organization called the Center for Independent Living. It is a place where newly disabled people learn how to navigate again after the loss of sight or mobility. I wonder if they feel welcome in our assemblies, or if our churches are even physically accessible to them.

I was in a parish where the pastor finally tore out three rows of pews near the front so wheelchair-restricted Catholics would not have to park out by the doors like unwelcome guests. I have heard of another parish that welcomes the local home for mentally retarded adults at their liturgies. There is a lot of extra noise and excitement at these Masses, and it defies everyone's need for order in worship. Somehow, I don't think God is offended. Meanwhile, there is the parish that unfortunately stopped serving coffee and donuts after Mass because "the homeless kept coming in and eating them!" We are all learning what it means to say that God sets the table and invites everyone to come forward. These are not painless lessons.

Questions for Reflection

• When have you seen the strong help the weak? How do you lend your strength to others?

• Which God seems more real to you, the God of the untouchable mountain, or the one Jesus calls Father?

• Are any groups of people marginalized in your parish? Are any groups absent altogether from your parish? How might they be welcomed in?

Action Response

Welcome someone in who is often left out. Invite that person to your next barbecue, picnic, or even to sit with the usual gang at lunch. Invite someone unchurched to your parish. Invite the newcomer into the community.

The Big Picture

FIRST READING: WISDOM 9:13–18

The deliberations of mortals are timid, and unsure are our plans.

I often find myself trying to outguess God, applying my own motives in Divine territory. Why, for instance, would God "want" or "permit" my best friend to come down with tinnitus? Why did my sister die at the age of forty-two? Why did the rains come so relentlessly to California last winter, and wash people's houses into the sea?

I want God to answer for these events, but I never stop to consider the questions God might be asking of me: why do you sin and sin, regardless of the graces and blessings I shower upon your life? Why do you refuse to share when you have more than you need? Why do you pass up the suffering sister or brother who asks for your help? Why do you not come to me in prayer, when you believe I am always here for you?

Sometimes I get so busy minding God's business that I forget to account for my own. The big picture is not accessible to me from the vantage point of mortality, but I can see pretty clearly my own piece of the puzzle. I need to spend less time second-guessing the grand plan and more time seeking the wisdom to make straight my own path.

SECOND READING: PHILEMON 9–10, 12–17

My prayer is that your love may more and more abound.

The story behind the letter is curious. Evidently Paul has encountered a runaway slave in prison, one who was "useless" to his master in former times. But Paul renames him Onesimus, which means "useful," and teaches him the Gospel of Jesus. Onesimus is now a brother in Christ, and though his status in the world has not changed, in the kingdom he is now family.

Why didn't Paul insist that Philemon free this man, take a stand against the institution of slavery? Paul says only that he would like to have Onesimus on the mission trail with him as a fellow servant of the Gospel. But he does not force Philemon's hand. Instead he sends the slave back to his master, and asks Philemon to receive him "as you would welcome me."

It is like so many stories in the Gospel in which we hear of someone encountering Jesus. They are taught or cured and then they walk off the pages of Scripture for good. What happens to them? Does their meeting with Jesus make a difference in their lives, or are they swallowed up into the same old circumstances? It is a question we might ask of ourselves. Has knowing Jesus made us truly free, or do we serve the same old master?

GOSPEL: LUKE 14:25–33
"You began to build what you could not finish."

On the other side of town stands a blue house elevated on mammoth jacks. Evidently someone decided to undertake a huge project: to move this house to another location, or to rebuild the foundation for greater structural support. Underneath the house, however, tall weeds have grown, and small bushes are becoming trees. That house has sat on those jacks for a long time.

Every time I walk down that street, I find myself smiling in sympathy. Somebody ran out of money, or momentum. That happens to me, too. I have projects piled here and there in my house, and promises I did not keep piled up in the recesses of my heart. In the same way it is easy for us to get baptized, or to take communion, and not follow through on the obligations we have assumed with those actions. Often, our Christianity sits up on jacks, while minor injustices grow into major ones all around us. Our discipleship cannot be just another project we mean to get to, later. If that house sits up there too long, it is all going to come tumbling down.

Questions for Reflection

- What are the questions you find yourself asking God? What questions might God put to you?
- How would your life be different if you were not a Christian?
- What aspects of your life remain "unfinished business"? How can you begin to tie up these loose ends?

Action Response

Begin this week to work on the big picture. Repair a broken friendship. Clean out a closet; clear out the clutter of unnecessary activities. Decide what is important and focus your energy on building the kingdom.

Lost and Found

FIRST READING: EXODUS 32:7–11, 13–14
"I see how stiff-necked this people is."

We often talk about God's plan as if there were only one. Actually, it appears that God has a huge desk covered with blueprint after blueprint. Technically speaking, all of them are God's plans. And if Plan A does not work, Plan B is launched almost at once.

We get this sense from God's heated conversation with Moses. While the Ten Commandments are being issued on the mountain, the people are breaking most of them below. Plan A had been to deliver these folks from slavery in Egypt, but now God is willing to move on to Plan B, raising up a new nation out of Moses. God, the most creative being in the universe, always has another idea.

This is important to keep in mind during those times when we fall away from what we perceive to be God's plan for our lives. Any departure we take, in sin or confusion, can always be countered by God's actions to draw us back into the weave. Nothing is lost that cannot be found. They do not call God the Creator for nothing.

SECOND READING: 1 TIMOTHY 1:12–17
Christ Jesus came into the world to save sinners.

Paul's writings can border on hyperbole, but I do not think he goes over the top when he calls himself the worst of sinners. After all, he is not talking about spending his nights in barrooms. Once he was a persecutor of Christians, zealous enough about his religious beliefs to put people to death who disagreed with him. Killing in the name of God is a special kind of evil.

Sometimes we hear debates about whether or not people can change very much; if nature or nurture makes us who we are in some irrevocable sense. We each have many possibilities, grave sinner or remarkable saint. If we think we have gone too far from grace and cannot make our way back, all we have to do is throw ourselves on the mercy of Jesus, as Paul did.

If we know someone who has gone very far and is afraid they are lost, we can assure them with confidence that God can meet them right where they are. Nowhere on the spectrum of sin are we beyond the transformation that can make our lives whole again. Jesus died for sin so that we don't have to.

"Rejoice with me because I have found my lost sheep."

A lamb. A coin. A son. The losses suffered are very different, but the outcome of each story is the same. Rejoice with me! the shepherd cries. Rejoice! says the woman to her neighbors. Let us eat and celebrate! the father declares. There is cause for rejoicing here. What was lost is found.

When the assembly gathers on Sundays, we call it a celebration because we find joy in the reality that each of us has been found through the death and resurrection of Jesus. Humanity spent centuries wandering in the night like lost children; many people still do. Cut off from our Maker and one another, we are adrift from the meaning of our existence and purpose. Many people eat, drink, and are as merry as they can be, knowing that death awaits.

We who are reconciled to God and one another in Christ have life in abundance. We have love to share, good news to report. We have power to put at the disposal of the powerless, and much, much joy to celebrate. In every hour we find opportunities to bring mercy to those who are still wandering in the dark. If you can recall just one occasion when someone was Christ for you, then you know what it can mean to hold out that hope for others.

Questions for Reflection

• When have you made radical departures from the path of grace? How did God draw you back?

• Are there people you know who seem far from grace? What can you do to invite them to return?

• Who has been Christ for you? When and how have you been Christ for someone else?

Action Response

Participate in the religious education of children. Support your local parochial school, volunteer to train as a catechist in your parish, buy a children's Bible for children you love. Above all, give a good example to children, that they might grow in grace and faith.

The Right Kind of Friends

FIRST READING: AMOS 8:4–7

Hear this, you who destroy the poor of the land!

Amos was a shepherd in the south who felt compelled by God to preach against the vices of the wealthy northern kingdom. You can imagine how the northern city dwellers responded to this country boy showing up with his out-of-town accent and unfamiliar dress. Likely he had a poor hearing for his message, which inflamed his speech all the more.

Amos denounces the people region by region; he is both methodical and thorough in blasting just about everyone. We can compare him to someone coming out of the backwoods and pointing a finger at the evil rampant in all directions, "And you New Yorkers, and you evil Californians, and you, citizens of the Beltway...." The prophecies of Amos are about condemnation and destruction. There isn't much room for repentance, which is why the school of Amos has few adherents today.

But of course, Amos was right in what he had to say. The rich continue to trample on the poor, and God cannot be deceived by superficial pieties. The Lord still hears the cry of the poor.

SECOND READING: 1 TIMOTHY 2:1–8

I urge that prayers be offered for those in authority.

Liturgists have a pattern they follow in writing the General Intercessions used at Mass. First we pray for the church, and then for world leaders. Then we pray for the needs of the local community and finally for ourselves. Praying for leaders is very important. Our civil and religious leaders greatly shape the reality out of which the rest of us live.

Being a leader does not mean you have a keen grasp of the "vision thing" or any special skill or virtue in decision making. Circumstances draft some of us to be leaders when we might have preferred a role out of the limelight. You learn as you go, and you make mistakes, some of which affect the lives of others. Because the stakes are higher for leaders than for the rest of us, our leaders need all the prayers they can get. And those of us who are not leaders—at least, not at the moment—have an obligation to pray for those who are.

It is easy to grouse about the pastor, the boss, the president, or the pope, and lay all the blame for our problems at their doors. Substitute that impulse with a quick prayer. Both you and the particular leader may change more than you expect.

GOSPEL: LUKE 16:1–13
"Make friends through your use of worldly goods."

Most of the parables seem like child's play. At least, their meaning is apparent to children, though harder for adults to put into practice. But the story of the devious steward leaves many people scratching their heads. What is Jesus saying here? Is he congratulating a cheat for being good at what he does? The point of the story is that the steward knows how to make the kinds of friends he will need to survive beyond his present situation. He uses material goods to plot his course toward salvation.

Jesus regrets that we religious folks are not as adept at using this world's goods for our spiritual survival. We don't know how to make friends with the people who will really count in our favor in the end. After all, the last will be first and the first will be last. We who find ourselves at the front of the line, therefore, better make lots of friends at the back of the line.

The only sensible use of our power and resources is for the sake of the poor. If we neglect them, when the center of authority pivots from the world to the kingdom, we may find ourselves on the bottom with no friends in high places to speak for us.

Questions for Reflection

• What is the relationship between judgment and repentance?

• Under whose authority do you find yourself? Over whom do you have authority?

• Who is on the "bottom" of your local community? Will they have reason to speak for you in the world to come?

Action Response

Make a commitment to pray for those who have authority over you. Ask for the prayers of those who are under your authority, especially children, who are eager pray-ers.

Don't Get Too Comfortable

FIRST READING: AMOS 6:1, 4–7
Woe to the complacent in Zion!

Amos is a conservative, but not a party pooper. It is not revelry per se that he objects to: it is the indifference of the rich to the suffering of the poor. Which they—by the way—are responsible for.

Jesus never condemns the rich outright for being rich, but he does make a serious point about camels having a better chance struggling through a needle's eye than the rich do in being virtuous. Wealth blinds us to the suffering of others and even makes us deaf to the ways in which our acquisitions come at others' expense. Think of the shocked silence that comes over people in this country every time we learn that a ten dollar sweater is made by underpaid workers. If we are honest, we admit that it is not that we did not know; we just did not want to know.

Being wealthy means we can look past the janitors, receptionists, retail clerks and waitresses who serve us and not ask or care if they have health insurance, if they are paid a fair wage for their work. Wealth makes us blind, deaf, and, in some cases, callous. And if we stretch out on our couches and begin to think this is the way it should be, then woe to us, indeed.

SECOND READING: 1 TIMOTHY 6:11–16
Seek after integrity, piety, faith, love, and a gentle spirit.

As young people we learned how much the company we keep can shape our own values. Those who find their values shaped in the likeness of Christ seek out Christ-minded people to companion them on the way of faith.

In the letter to Timothy we get a useful description of what Christ-minded people look like. Integrity tops the list: people who present themselves without affectation and mean what they say. After that come the traditional religious values of piety, faith, love, and steadfastness. The end of the line is a gentle spirit, which is a hard thing to maintain in an aggressive world like ours.

Gentleness is not respected; it is even mocked, from the playground on out. But part of the "good fight" of faith is fought with the peculiar sword of gentleness. It slices through belligerence and testifies against violence. It is the only thing, in fact, that does.

GOSPEL: LUKE 16:19–31
"Let Lazarus be a warning to my brothers."

What does it take, to make a rich person care about the fate of a poor person? I can only speak for myself, being wealthy in the sense of having more education and more access to the good life than most of the world's people. Sometimes it takes guilt to get me to care, one of those tragic pictures of war-torn countries and suffering children. Sometimes it takes moral outrage, when I hear what government has done in my name. At times my faith will motivate me to do justice or act charitably, in a thoughtfully impersonal sense. But most of the time, a personal encounter with a suffering person will have the greatest impact on me.

My heart is hardened in all the usual ways. I have learned not to care about most of what I see and hear in the news. Like many in this country, I am affected by compassion fatigue: the awareness of global suffering has led to the instinctive shutting down of natural concern. But Jesus will never ask us how we felt about poverty, only what we did about it. So whatever it takes to motivate you—guilt, anger, faith, experience—employ it for the sake of the kingdom. The only thing we cannot afford to feel is indifference.

Questions for Reflection

- Are you willing to support establishments that treat their workers fairly over other businesses where you can save money?
- Measure yourself against the qualities mentioned in Timothy. Where do you need work?
- What motivates you to show your concern for the poor and others who are in need?

Action Response

Read your local diocesan paper or newsletter to find out how Catholics in your area are helping to relieve the burden of poverty locally. Consider ways that you, your family, or your parish can contribute to the effort.

If Only We Had Faith!

FIRST READING: HABBAKUK 1:2–3, 2:2–4
If the vision delays, wait for it.

The prophet Habbakuk adds a useful dimension to the polite dialogue of theology: direct challenge to God for not taking better care of the people who call for help! Pierre Wolff wrote a book some years back with the same theme, titled *May I Hate God?* The question is relevant today, as Catholics struggle with the matter of loyal dissent, and how one can both honestly and faithfully express conflict within communion.

In the prophecies of Habbakuk, God's response to dissent is to reaffirm the vision of justice and to invoke the patience that the faithful know well. Faith, by definition, means acting from within the darkness, counting on the light to be revealed. If we are waiting for the vision to arrive in order to place our trust in it, we will be disappointed. Faith is only necessary when our hope is yet unseen.

SECOND READING: 2 TIMOTHY 1:6–8, 13–14
The Spirit God has given to us is no cowardly spirit.

Oh, to be "strong, loving and wise!" This composite description of life in the Spirit sounds nearly like the fruits of the great American fable of Oz. And just as in that myth from our heartland, we learn that the Spirit dwells within us, and supplies all we need.

This is important for Timothy and his community to hear, as they are beset with the usual attacks, false teachings, and self-proclaimed gurus of truth that deny in part or in whole the gospel that Paul preached. The deposit of faith is in need of no Wizard of Oz to dispense it, no tricks or mantras to make it work. The Gospel is ours, and the Spirit makes it live in us.

GOSPEL: LUKE 17:5-10
Increase our faith!

More is better. At least, that is what we are taught to believe, and it is no wonder that the disciples, seeing all that faith has accomplished in Jesus, would ask for more of that. But Jesus splits that desire wide open like an axe through wood. Getting to be first on the spiritual charts defeats the whole notion of growth in faith. It is not about what we can do: it is all about what God can do in us.

Jesus says that the servant, after doing everything ably and well for the Master, has only done what a servant is called to do. Christian discipleship is not the business of earning gold stars or meriting God's grace. If we are invited to the Lord's table, it is through God's graciousness and not our righteousness that we will be seated.

Questions for Reflection

• What circumstances in life have compelled you to challenge God? How can expressing ourselves openly in prayer deepen our trust in God?

• The Spirit of God is no cowardly spirit, the writer of Timothy maintains. Has the Spirit ever led you to act more bravely than you thought possible?

• Jesus teaches that the smallest amount of faith can do miraculous things. What has faith led you to accomplish recently? What is faith calling you to achieve in the future?

Action Response

Make a list of the gifts of the Holy Spirit that are active in your life (review 1 Corinthians 12:3-10 and Isaiah 11:2-3 for suggestions). How does God work through you to manifest these gifts? Pray to become a more effective vessel of God's grace.

Acknowledging the Source

FIRST READING: 2 KINGS 5:14–17

Now I know that there is no other God in all the earth.

Acknowledging a debt to others or expressing gratitude: both of these take a certain surrender of time and ego. Naaman the leper came a long way for a healing from Elisha, and nearly went home without it, because of an unwillingness to let go of ego. But once the surrender was made, he was healed, and he was not about to make the same mistake twice. With the humility of a child, he took the time to return, acknowledging God and the prophet in God's service.

Most of us are quick to approach God with intercessions, yet slow with prayers of praise or thanksgiving. It is true that gratitude is an admission of our mortality, limitation, and need, and it does bounce the old ego. This is precisely why a grateful heart does us so much good!

SECOND READING: 2 TIMOTHY 2:8–13

There is no chaining the word of God!

The life of an evangelist is one long announcement of the Gospel, which, although intended as good news for the world, is not always so good for the evangelist. Paul winds up imprisoned for his zeal, branded as a rabble rouser when all he was doing is acknowledging his source. Not stopping to catch a breath, he continues to preach in chains: if we have died with Christ, we shall also live with Christ.

Paul amazes me, the way street preachers always amaze me, shouting at the top of their lungs what a weary world scarcely wants to hear. Whatever you think of the method, you have to wonder at the courage and conviction which propels it. And since we are all called to evangelize, the question must be faced: do I display the courage and passion in my witness that these folks do?

GOSPEL: LUKE 17:11-19
One came back praising God in a loud voice.

What must be said, first of all, is that all ten lepers were remarkable people. They came to Jesus for healing, exhibiting two of the spiritual gifts: faith and hope. And when Jesus told them to report to a priest, they revealed a third gift, obedience, hastening off to do what he had commanded.

In the Books of the Law, a cleansed leper had to be officially inspected by a priest in order to be pronounced clean. Without touching them, Jesus ordered them to act as though the healing had already taken place. And these remarkable ten were prepared to claim the healing even before they could see it.

But one of the ten was even more exemplary than the rest: the one who returned to give thanks. It was to that one alone that Jesus imparted something better than a healing: the assurance of salvation.

Questions for Reflection

• How many occasions have you had today to be thankful? How often did you stop to acknowledge the source?

• How do you fulfill the baptismal call to evangelize? To whom do you witness your faith? To which people or groups are you most reluctant to witness?

• In both the story of Naaman and the leper tale from Luke, the one who was grateful was a foreigner. Why was this detail included in these stories? What impact does it have on us today?

Action Response

Invent a variety of characters for the ten lepers in the gospel story. Let nine of them tell their reasons/excuses for not returning to thank Jesus, and the Samaritan share why returning was necessary. What does this each you about your own impediments to thanksgiving?

To Be Earnest in Prayer

FIRST READING: EXODUS 17:8–13
Moses' hands remained steady until sunset.

Moses raised his hands in prayer, holding the staff of God, emblem of the Lord's protection since the delivery from Egypt. And, with a little help from his friends, he kept his hands raised till sunset, when the battle was won.

That's some kind of praying! Yet I must admit, I have known some champion pray-ers in my time: rosary sayers, novena keepers, Charismatic speakers-in-tongues, meditators, contemplators, candle-lighters, and breviary-chanters. Paul's injunction to pray unceasingly is something they've taken at face value, and the world must be encircled with their entreaties like Saturn with its rings.

I am not, myself, a champion pray-er. But like Moses, I have learned to keep my hands up there, with a little support from my friends.

SECOND READING: 2 TIMOTHY 3:14—4:2
I charge you to stay with this task.

This time, the injunction is not to pray unceasingly but to preach and teach relentlessly. We all know folks who are forever preachy, but that is certainly not what is implied here. The urgency in this pastoral letter comes from the conviction of the early church that Jesus was to return shortly and the judgment of the world was at hand. If you had a chance to rescue another person—or a handful of people—or a world, wouldn't it make sense to exert yourself to the limit for such a cause?

At the close of the movie *Schindler's List*, the man who saved hundreds of Jews from the Nazi death camps laments the opportunities he missed to redeem even more. Anyone who has suffered through apocalyptic times understands the passion that compels the writer of Timothy to stay with the task despite the cost or inconvenience. If we believed that people of all times and seasons are equally urgent in their need of the Gospel, would our zeal match our conviction?

GOSPEL: LUKE 18:1–8

Will the Son of Man find any faith on the earth?

Luke loves a good widow story. A woman whose husband had died was as vulnerable and powerless as a child. And since Luke's theme is the justice of Jesus, widows are as plentiful as injustices in his stories.

In this ironic parable, the so-called poor helpless widow overpowers the omnipotent crooked judge, not by physical or legal resources, but by sheer persistence. The judge in the end is afraid that the widow might even strike at him(!), which must have made Jesus' audience laugh. If even a malevolent mortal could be cowed into rendering justice, how much more must a good God be counted on to supply it? God's fidelity to justice must be answered with our persistence to seek it.

Questions for Reflection

• There are many ways to pray, publicly and liturgically, privately, with words or in silence. How does prayer fit into your faith experience? What avenues of prayer are most powerful for you?

• The call to preach and teach seemed delegated to those in formal religious life for generations, but no longer. How do you answer that call in your circumstances?

• Find other widow stories in Luke's Gospel. What do these widow stories have in common? What do they teach us?

Action Response

Have you ever had a prayer partner? Consider inviting someone close to you to help support you in prayer. Meet regularly, share intercessions, or sit together in contemplation.

Lifting Up the Lowly

FIRST READING: SIRACH 35:12–14, 16–18

The prayer of the lowly pierces the clouds.

A preacher friend of mine often says, "In the reign of God, if you are not poor, you better be a friend of the poor." Despite Ben Sira's protestation that God has no favorites, it is pretty clear throughout the Scriptures that God has an eye for the least, the weakest, and the despised of the earth. Pope John Paul II has called this "the preferential option for the poor," and insists that the church has a mandate to opt for the poor in its discernment as well.

If the Lord is responsive to the cry of the poor, and if we will be judged according to our relationship to God's little ones and their need for justice, then we had better give the poor a reason to put in a good word for us.

SECOND READING: 2 TIMOTHY 4:6–8, 16–18

The Lord will continue to rescue me.

Southern Catholic writer Flannery O'Connor declared that the task of every Christian is to prepare one's own death in Christ. In death as in life, we are to witness with courage and integrity to our faith in the Gospel. Paul's acceptance of his imminent martyrdom contains the seed of what all Christian death should reflect: surrender, confidence, forgiveness.

Like Paul, we have nothing in this world we need to cling to, so we can be poured out willingly. Our confidence is in the God who saves us and rewards our faith. Our forgiveness of those who have wronged us flows naturally from the forgiveness Jesus extended from the Cross, which Paul imitates gladly from prison. With not so much as our indignation to hold us bound, we can pass freely from this world to the next.

GOSPEL: LUKE 18:9–14
O God, be merciful to me, a sinner.

Pomposity is always laughable. The Pharisee in the parable makes his prayer absurd with an exaggerated sense of his own virtue. We can imagine the crowd around Jesus chuckling at the comic rendering of this well-known pious attitude. Perhaps even a Pharisee or two was able to laugh at himself, although self-important people seldom have a sense of humor.

Contrast this with the reaction of the tax collectors who may have been in the crowd. Matthew, one of the Twelve, was beaming as he looked out over the people and saw old colleagues of his, startled at finding themselves on the kind end of a lesson for a change! Could there actually be a land where showy virtues would be dismissed and sinners would have a chance? Heaven is such a place.

Questions for Reflection

•Who are the poor in your community? Don't limit your answer to only those with material deficiencies. Are you one of these poor? How can you befriend them?

•Are you prepared to die? What can a Christian do to "prepare one's own death in Christ?"

•Do you think of yourself as righteous or as a sinner? What might the spiritual benefits be in praying the tax collector's prayer?

Action Response

How can you contribute to the divine plan to lift up the lowly? Is there a timid person in your midst who needs an invitation to speak? Has someone in your community been excluded who could use a welcome? Are the poor being served?

Nothing Will Be Lost

FIRST READING: WISDOM 11:22—12:1

You love all things that are.

In the middle of a section on divine retribution comes this passage reaffirming God's essential nature as "lover of souls" and source of mercy. Anyone who suffers from a neurotic dose of guilt should post these verses on the refrigerator! Wisdom tells us, first of all, that what happens here on earth is small theater, a crumb fallen from the scale during measuring. And at the same time, not a thing remains in existence without God's purposeful willing of it. What is vital is that God is aware of all, loves all, and has mercy on all, because everything belongs to God.

The world teaches us to focus on the crumb that falls from the scale, to read our fate in what is lost: through crime, the economy, world events. It is countercultural to direct our gaze on the lover of souls, and to believe that nothing will be lost.

SECOND READING: 2 THESSALONIANS 1:11—2:2

Do not be so easily agitated.

The community at Thessalonica has been thrown into disarray. Evidently someone has prophesied that the day of the Lord, "that great and terrible day," has arrived. Has Jesus returned? Is the world about to end? Confusion seizes the group, as some panic, others are skeptical, all are afflicted with unrest. This is not an antique fear. Every age has seen its fringe group rallying for Armageddon, claiming their messiahs, prophesying doomsday. Millennialism, the bizarre fear of round numbers, will surge up again in just a few years.

Paul's pastoral response is still a valid one. Do not be deceived by false prophecy. Do not be swept up by the spirit of the moment. The day of the Lord will be unmistakable, so don't surrender to paranoia and terror. One last thing: if Jesus is the Lord we are following, his return is supposed to be good news.

GOSPEL: LUKE 19:1–10
Today salvation has come to this house.

According to Luke, it started out very simply for Zacchaeus. He was trying to see what Jesus was like, that's all. He was not pledging discipleship, was not making professions of faith, when he climbed that tree. And when Jesus looked up and spoke to him, he really saw what Jesus was like: this teacher invited himself to stay at his house! And Jesus called him by name, so he must have known exactly in whose house he would be a guest. Everyone on the street that day knew too. The murmur was audible: "Gone to a sinner's house."

Zacchaeus was transformed by the realization that a man like Jesus would choose to reside with him. It would change the way he did business, and it would change his entire way of relating to others, even if others did not change in relation to him. That is the way it always is. Jesus comes to a sinner's house and offers him—and us—the opportunity Zacchaeus had, to be saved or to stay lost.

Questions for Reflection

• Consider how much time each day you spend being exposed to the bad news: in the newspapers, TV, radio, gossip. How much time do you spend with the good news? How would life change for you if you turned your gaze to the "lover of souls?"

• Have you ever encountered a false teacher? How do you discern the truth of a teaching?

• Jesus has invited himself to your house tonight. What will he find there? What can he save that was lost?

Action Response

Make a commitment to spend ten minutes a day with the Scriptures for one week. Choose your passages from the Gospels and read only as much as you can savor for one day. Let this good news interact with the overexposure to bad news.

Becoming Like Angels

FIRST READING: 2 MACCABEES 7:1–2, 9–14

The King of the world will raise us up.

The Books of the Maccabees concern the politics of Palestine in the second century B.C., focusing on the attempt to suppress Judaism by foreign powers. The books are fairly obscure among the Scriptures; my friends used to joke that, if you were having trouble finding something in the Bible, it was probably in one of the Books of the Maccabees.

The first book of the Maccabees is concerned with the here and now, while the second explores the theology of the afterlife. The Pharisees who would question Jesus in the next generation developed their understanding of resurrection through stories like the one we read today. The unshakable faith of the Jewish martyrs demonstrates the confidence that divine justice demanded an afterlife where the wrongs of human society would be set right. Unjust suffering must be answered by restoration and retribution. The lives of the seven brothers and their mother were not irretrievably lost, nor are ours.

SECOND READING: 2 THESSALONIANS 2:16—3:5

May the Lord rule your hearts.

The Thessalonians, unravelled by false prophecies of the end times, have been soothed by Paul's review of his teachings. In this passage, he asks for their help in prayer, to keep such confusion away from those who spread the Gospel.

We should pray to be delivered from confusion in our times! The more I read how Christianity is bandied about by politicians who claim to be shaping policy with Christian values, the more I resent the manipulation of that identity. As Paul reminds us, there will always be those who use the name of Christ in self-serving ways. But we are guarded and strengthened by the Lord who rules our hearts with love and constancy.

GOSPEL: LUKE 20:27–38
Children of the resurrection are children of God.

The Sadducees bring a bad parody of the Maccabees story to Jesus. Instead of seven martyred brothers keeping faith with God's law, they tell of seven brothers faithful to Levirate law by marrying the same woman. If the resurrection is for real, they ask, who gets the woman?

Jesus brushes off this ludicrous question as a product of the children of this age. Levirate law, even marriage itself, is a temporal issue. Jesus knows that the heart of the inquiry is the plausibility of the resurrection, which he affirms by appealing to Moses, the giver of the law, an authority the Sadducees respect.

People destined to become like the angels are not to be bound by legalism and human controls. In the resurrection, nobody "gets the woman," because women and men will know the freedom of being children of God.

Questions for Reflection

•How does the afterlife address human injustice? Is it enough to await justice in the world to come?

•What kind of confusion and evil are at work in our society? How can we as Christians address it?

•What do you believe about the resurrection? What does it mean to become like the angels?

Action Response

Often in charitable solicitations, the higher level donors are called "angels." Think of a context at home or in your community where you are being called to be an angel, to give a bit more of your presence, help or protection. Practice being like an angel this week.

How to Behave in the Endtimes

FIRST READING: MALACHI 3:19–20

Lo, the day is coming.

Malachi is the last of the twelve minor prophets, so called because their prophecies are short enough to fit all on one scroll together. Though his writings were at the end of the scroll, Malachi was important enough to be quoted by Jesus to clarify the role of John the Baptist (see Malachi 3:1 and Matthew 11:10) as the messenger of preparation for judgment.

And the day of judgment is coming, Malachi insists. Those who fear God will come out ahead of those who surrender to a skeptical and uncommitted age. So how does one prepare for the judgment? My Pentecostal friends in college would make us laugh by staging a "rapture drill," referring to the belief that the Second Coming of Christ would include a snatching up to the heavens of those who were saved before the destruction of the earth. During this drill, my friends would stand with their arms raised, waiting to be "snatched up." The point of the humor was, of course, that one cannot prepare for such an unearthly event, that the real test of readiness is the way we live in relationship to God and others every day.

SECOND READING: 2 THESSALONIANS 3:7–12

You know how you ought to imitate us.

News of impending destruction affects people differently. Some will flee, some urgently work up a defense, some surrender, and some eat, drink, and be merry. In Thessalonica, some of those who believed that the endtimes were near quit their jobs and decided to kick back, not seeing any point to their old routines. Idleness and disorderly conduct threatened the Christian community and its mission.

Paul writes to assure them that the Second Coming of Christ is not an excuse to opt out of human responsibility. On the contrary, the anticipated return of Christ is all the more reason to work tirelessly and purposefully for the church's mission, to proclaim the Gospel by word and example. If we all had one more night on this dear planet, we could not do better than to use it as laborers in the field, awaiting God's harvest.

GOSPEL: LUKE 21:5–19
I will give you words.

The disciples are always interested in the big picture. So Jesus talks about the destruction of the Temple in Jerusalem, as well as wars, famine, false prophecies and omens in the sky. All of this will come to pass around you, Jesus assures them. But the only thing you will have any control over is your own testimony. Take care to speak the word that is given to you.

Every generation has seen horror enough to qualify as apocalyptic. Yet we still attempt to set our cosmic watches by current events, to outguess the day that is coming like a thief in the night. The only useful piece of apocalyptic advice is Jesus' injunction to speak the wisdom that is given to us by God. When the time is at hand, those of us who have been fed by the word of God will have a word at our disposal to speak. The rest of us might well be speechless.

Questions for Reflection

• Imagine that you have gotten advance notice that the end of the world is tomorrow. What would you have to do to get ready for the "sun of justice?"

• Paul reminds us that we are all to work tirelessly to proclaim the good news of Jesus. In what ways have you proclaimed the good news in your words, actions, or relationships this week?

• You have been called before a tribunal to give witness to what you really believe. What do you have to say about God? Jesus? The church? The life of discipleship?

Action Response

Consider your response to the first question today. Choose one thing that you would do if prompted by the imminent end of the world, and do it—even if the world does not end tomorrow. Be that much more prepared for the endtimes!

CHRIST THE KING

Our Sovereign Lord

FIRST READING: 2 SAMUEL 5:1–3

You shall shepherd my people Israel.

The divine right of kings is something that we who are governed by a president cannot quite appreciate. We elect our leaders, criticize them continually and then eject them from office without feeling the least bit ruthless. But the relationship of a people to their king is different. The belief that God has spoken first in the selection makes the ascendancy of a king a sacred event.

When the tribes of Israel meet David in Hebron, it is after political struggles and battles that took the lives of the former king and his son, both dear to David. It is a bittersweet meeting, and an opportunity to begin healing divisions. The people recognize their oneness with David, bone and flesh. And they acknowledge that God has chosen him to shepherd them.

The anointing of this most famous king of the Jews stands in sharp contrast to the kingship we celebrate on this last week of our church year. The one whom the gospels call Shepherd and King is bone and flesh with us, and one with God.

SECOND READING: COLOSSIANS 1:12–20

He is before all else that is.

The Hymn to the Primacy of Christ is an exalted celebration of the place of Christ in salvation history. First before creation, first in the resurrection, all was brought into being and is sustained through the great reconciler of earth and heaven.

This is what sovereignty is, what it means for us to say "Jesus is Lord." No power can match the fullness of God that resides in Christ, no creature with the confidence of children in the arms of a tender mother, knowing we are safe, protected, home where we belong. No demon within us or enemy from without can overcome us. Death itself loses its definition. The reign of God belongs to Christ, and we are called into it from every darkness into a communion of light.

GOSPEL: LUKE 23:35–43
"This is the King of the Jews."

Our first reading reminded us what a temporal king is; the hymn from Colossians tells us how the glorified Christ reigns. But in the Gospel, we come to understand in brutally practical terms what it costs to be the sovereign Lord of all. It is somewhat poetic and antiseptic theology to say, "Christ reconciled everything in his person." It is messier, more poignant to realize that the reconciliation came at the point of a nail piercing skin and bone, while followers looked on silently, leaders jeered, and criminals blasphemed.

They called him King of the Jews, and they intended it to be an absurd title. How could this pitiful sight think of himself as the Son of David! He did not bear any sign of God's favor, battered and humiliated as he was. Yet there was one person who saw past the matted hair and blood-stained face to "the image of the invisible God." The good thief, as generations would call him, was rewarded for his clear vision with paradise itself.

On this last Sunday of the year, we are asked to contemplate the face of a King, so that we will recognize sovereignty when we see it.

Questions for Reflection

• In our country, we have taken great pains to separate earthly and divine authority. How has this worked for and against us?

• No power is greater than Jesus Christ. How does this challenge us in our struggle with sin and its effect in our lives?

• Where do you see the face of Christ the King in the world? How can you best serve this King?

Action Response

Make a list of the things that hold some power (sovereignty) over your life (e.g., financial concerns, the need to please, greed, a lack of forgiveness). Pray over this list, and ask for the grace in Jesus' name to be freed from bondage to any power other than our sovereign Lord.

Solemnities
& Feasts

IMMACULATE CONCEPTION

Nothing is Impossible

FIRST READING: GENESIS 3:9–15, 20
"Because you have done this, you shall be banned."

Debates about the literal historical reliability of the Genesis stories seem to miss the point. Fact is, it's more true than history. We all dream of a wonderland where we can lay down our burdens and fears. We all know that something is terribly wrong with our world, and ourselves; that something is missing which we need to be whole.

We miss "the garden," whether we call it childhood, or heaven, or the vacation that never ends. We catch glimpses of it when we are in the arms of love, or on that fantasy tropical vacation, or maybe when we topple into bed after a full and satisfying day. We see it in the trusting eyes of children who have not yet been betrayed.

We believe in the garden, although we have only seen it on the horizon. We believe in our finer selves even though they may rarely surface. We long for a time when we fail ourselves and those we love no more. And on that day when sin troubles our hearts no longer, we hope to step into the garden of God's making.

SECOND READING: EPHESIANS 1:3–6, 11–12
God chose us in Christ to be holy, and blameless, and full of love.

How good it is to be chosen! Those of us who were the last to sit in the bleachers during gym class, when teams were selected, know this. The terror of exclusion haunts us from our earliest memories. We want in; we want to belong.

Paul assures us that we have been "in" since before the world began. God has always had us in mind, and salvation has always been a done deal. There is a certain economy to God's plan, theologians tell us. God would not create a world only to lose it to the grip of sin, destruction, and death. The primary Hebrew experience of God is that God saves. The fundamental teaching about Christ is that Jesus saves. God will gather up the fragments of our broken world so that nothing may be wasted. There is no garbage in all of creation.

We belong. We belong to God. We are chosen for holiness, born for love, and God's Spirit will not rest until we find our true nature at last.

GOSPEL: LUKE 1:26–38
"Nothing is impossible with God."

"Immaculate conception" is a highly technical term, relating to a doctrine about sin that seems a great distance from our own experience. We are not immaculately conceived; nor is much about our world so pure and perfect as that. Is this then a time to celebrate someone else's victory over sin?

Mary was good—we have to take God's word on that. The angel goes to her house because she found favor with God in a unique way. God was with her, and she was chosen to embody the miraculous.

Later centuries would spin around her a cocoon of doctrines to preserve the singularity of her experience as Mother of God. Her birth-giving was virginal, her own conception in Ann's womb was immaculate. Her body, touched by holiness, would not know decay in the end. Mary's story is wrapped in the miraculous, and her body becomes the Ark of the Covenant, the tabernacle of Holy Presence. Mary's body itself becomes one of the greatest symbols of Christianity. It is one mortal place where the victory over sin and death has already been achieved.

That is why we celebrate this solemnity as a feast of Mary and a feast for ourselves. The holy action begun in Mary's life, from the first moment, continues to live and move and have being in us. Our world and our own hearts may not be pure, but we too are touched by holiness and called to be tabernacles of Holy Presence. And what we carry within, we will become.

Questions for Reflection

• What does paradise mean for you? How do you have to change to receive it?

• How do you show that you belong to God? How do you show others that they belong?

• How can you be the bearer of holy things to others?

Action Response

Strive for a deeper purity in your life. Absorb less junk food, junk news, junk entertainment. Feed yourself what is healthy and lasting. Care for the tabernacle that carries God's presence to others.

To Treasure and Reflect

FIRST READING: NUMBERS 6:22–27
"The Lord look upon you kindly and give you peace!"

The expression "to let one's face shine upon you" is a Hebrew idiom for smiling. God smiles at us, and with good reason. God loves us. And when we look at those who are dearest to us in the world, can we keep from smiling?

The idea of God's love is pretty abstract, just like the idea of your love is or mine. Love has to be shown, in word and deed, with presents and presence, with help and forgiveness. The priestly blessing that Aaron gives is a way of presenting God's love to the people. God will sustain you, so the blessing goes, and smile upon you, and be generous in giving you what you need to live in peace.

Many people do not believe in God's love because they have never felt themselves blessed. They do not come to our churches because they have never seen the smile of God shine over their lives with love. Maybe they have never seen God's smile of love because they are waiting for you or me to show it to them. Maybe the blessing they are waiting for has to come from our hands.

SECOND READING: GALATIANS 4:4–7
You are no longer a slave but a son and heir!

Before my sister was to be married, she asked me to give her what she really needed for a wedding present: my indentured servitude for the week before the wedding! Have you ever been in the vicinity of a full-blown bride-to-be? If not, take my advice: buy her a blender and don't cut any deals.

The moment of freedom for any servant is precious. Even if it is that golden moment on Friday afternoon when you are off the clock and your time is your own, you have tasted the joy and release of freedom. When the burden is lifted from our shoulders, we feel as if for the first time the true weight of the load and the wonder of its surrender.

The coming of Jesus into our world—and more personally, into our hearts—brings that same lovely sense of relief. We do not have to carry the weight of our sins anymore. The clock has stopped ticking, and death has no sting. No longer slaves to the past, we can look forward with joy to the future. Children of the promise, we can sit down and relax. We are heirs to every good thing, because Jesus has come to be brother to us.

GOSPEL: LUKE 2:16–21
Mary treasured all these things and reflected on them in her heart.

Mary had a lot to treasure in her heart. There was Gabriel's visit to her, and her visit to Elizabeth. There was the conception of a child that would be called Son of the Most High. Then there was the birth of her child in a strange city, under hard conditions, but with a good man at her side to help and protect her and the baby. And then the shepherds showed up.

These people smelled of animals and long periods of time without a bath. They were wild and unsocialized people who lived in the wilderness to care for their animals. When they stumbled into her presence on that eventful (and likely exhausting) night, they told wild stories. An angel, a proclamation, a Messiah, a heavenly host! None of it would have made any sense, except that Mary knew about angels and proclamations already.

The one with the good voice sang the first Christmas carol, imitating the angel: "Glory to God in the highest...." Mary decided it was time to start treasuring, as these events were not likely to be repeated in her lifetime, or anyone's. Did she guess that we would continue to reflect on them until the end of time?

Questions for Reflection

• How is God smiling upon your life right now? Count your blessings and thank God.

• When have you experienced the freedom of surrendering a heavy load? How does your faith lighten your load at this time?

• What memories do you treasure and reflect upon? What lessons do they teach you?

Action Response

Bless the new year, and be a blessing for those around you. Treasure the good and holy things in your past, and reflect on how you can share your treasure with a needy world.

A Sign that Will Be Opposed

FIRST READING: MALACHI 3:1–4

There will come to the temple the Lord whom you seek.

The times of Malachi were not the best of times. Although a remnant of Israel had returned from a generation of exile in Babylon, they did not exactly return as a grateful, loyal people. The period of relief at being set free was followed by business as usual. The priests returned to cheating the temple sacrifice. The people traded in the wives of their youth for the foreign women of Canaan. And still they had the gall to ask: why does the Lord not come to the Temple? Why does the Lord not answer our petitions?

The writer of this prophecy—who remains anonymous to escape reprisals (Malachi means only "my messenger")—predicts an unexpected answer to the people's prayer. There will indeed be a manifestation of God in the Temple. The day of the Lord's coming is not far off. But the answer to their false prayer will be fire and judgment, the separation of the faithful people of Israel from those who broke faith.

SECOND READING: HEBREWS 2:14–18

Since the children are of blood and flesh, Jesus likewise had a full share in these.

Robbing the devil: that's quite the opposite of giving the devil his due. The writer of Hebrews claims that robbing the devil is the job description of Jesus. Contrast that with the claim in Malachi 3:8 that the sins of the people are essentially robbing God of justice.

The corrupt priests of the first reading are challenged by the image of the faithful high priest of God. The day of the Lord foretold his arrival, and the Holy Spirit claims the Temple of our lives.

But a day in the Bible is never a twenty-four-hour day. The historical day of Jesus must be met with the day, any day, when we allow the Holy Spirit to be released in us. Jesus, who once lived in flesh and blood, seeks yet to be incarnate in our day through us. We have been rescued from death, but temptation still looms as the phantom that can swallow the new creation of each hour. Today can be the day when Jesus robs the devil one more time.

GOSPEL: LUKE 2:22-40
"This child is destined to be the downfall and the rise of many."

Joseph and Mary have come for the ritual purification after the birth of a son. Were they surprised at what they heard? They know that Jesus is God's glory, the Son of the Most High as Gabriel revealed. But Simeon's prophecy takes their understanding beyond wonder. Jesus is to be the light to the foreign world of the Gentiles. He will make and break many of his own people. Mary herself will suffer as this life unfolds, as she watches her son become a sign opposed by a world that does not want this revelation.

How do you turn and take such a baby home again? How do you retrace your steps and return to obscurity, becoming a holy family in the shadow of unmarked years? Obedience—the root meaning of which is to listen—must have been challenged by listening to such grave and ominous words. Joseph, who is not mentioned in this prophecy, must have felt the shortness of his years. Mary must have felt apprehension for the sorrow to come. But they shoulder their responsibility and take this tiny new life home. The sign of opposition that would become the cross was salvation prepared in the sight of all the peoples. That was enough for them to know.

Questions for Reflection

• The Book of Malachi was intended to be a frightening prophecy. Who are our modern Malachis? Is their message effective?

• Consider a day that has been for you a day of the Lord when evil was robbed of its power in your life. What prevents today from being such a day?

• Are you an obedient listener? To what authority(ies) do you listen? What prompts you to disobey?

Action Response

Consider a sign of God's power that is opposed by the world, e.g., the struggle for equality and justice, forgiveness of enemies, fidelity in marriage or to one's commitments. Ally yourself to such a sign and become yourself a living sign that will be opposed.

Return to Me

FIRST READING: JOEL 2:12–18

Even now, says the Lord, return to me with your whole heart.

I wonder at the idea of a national day of repentance. The prophet Joel envisions it so clearly: drop what you are doing and return to God. Right now. Never mind if you just got married or just got ordained; gave birth to a baby or are contemplating your own death. Whatever you are doing, it is not as important as this. Turn your heart. Right now.

It reminds me of the saying from William James about the three things required to change your life: 1) start immediately; 2) do it flamboyantly; 3) no exceptions. In a sense, this is what the season of Lent is for, starting with the flamboyant sign of Ash Wednesday. Here we are, a nation of Catholics, advertising mortality to a world obsessed with youth and in denial of aging, sickness, and death. We spend the day with dirty faces, telling everyone at work and in the supermarket and in our neighborhoods that we know, for a fact, that this world is passing and so are we. Ash Wednesday is the feast of "no kidding."

On this feast of no kidding, we have to be clear-eyed, honest, and sincere in our desire to reform our lives.

SECOND READING: 2 CORINTHIANS 5:20—6:2

In Christ, we might become the very holiness of God.

The urgency of this day is brought forward in Paul's appeal: *Now* is the time! *Now* is salvation! We want to wait for a convenient time, perhaps when the cost of reconciliation with God has depreciated. Right now we have families to organize, businesses to run, problems to solve. This is not a good time for religion to intrude on us. Perhaps later on, when my child isn't sick, when the money isn't so tight...?

What we often fail to realize is that what God is holding out to us with both hands is not bad news, another burden to carry, another expense to be paid out. It's grace! It's forgiveness! It's salvation! And we could use a little of those things right now. Joining hand and heart to God, which is what reconciliation means, is something that could help us while the child is still sick, while the money is tight. When we are drowning, it would be foolish to say, "I don't have time to be saved right now; I've got my hands full just drowning!" In this hour, we most need to stretch out our hand.

GOSPEL: MATTHEW 6:1–6, 16–18
"Your Father who sees what is hidden will repay you."

In grammar school I had a friend named Melanie. Now Melanie was religious. She was always slipping away from us during recess to go into the church and pray. She whipped through one novena after another the whole year 'round, and excused herself even during television to keep her hourly dates with God. Melanie was a saint. I wanted to be like her.

Maybe Melanie will someday be up for canonization. But I have known other folks that I would campaign for too: Bernadette, a mother of nine children under the age of ten, who manages to keep every one of them clean, fed, and well loved. John, who cares for the elderly with respectful attention. My brother David, who lives with his diabetes and its rigors and limitations without fanfare. Teresa, who has lived a horrible life of deprivations and losses and still believes in tenderness. These hidden saints do not have a lot of pious stuff hanging out of their portfolios. They would not look like much to a Vatican commission seeking certifiable miracles. But the One who sees in secret sees them, and I bet they will make the communion of saints.

Questions for Reflection

• What needs to change in your life? How can you begin, even in small ways, to make the changes?

• What would you most like to be saved from in your present experience? What would you like to be saved for?

• Who are the saints around you? What do they do to look like "the very holiness of God"?

Action Response

There is still time to settle on a lenten discipline, if you have not already done so. Think of one way you feel moved to better your heart, and decide on one way you can begin to plant the seed of love.

Keep Holy the Memory

FIRST READING: EXODUS 12:1–8, 11–14
"It is the Passover of the Lord."

The story of Passover is a dark passage from slavery to freedom, leaving a trail of blood and weeping in its wake. The angel of death, unlike other celestial visitors, is no gentle spirit. The streets of Egypt, like the shores of the Red Sea, would be strewn with the dead before Israel walked free.

Other kinds of oppression require other kinds of deaths. When truth is suppressed, many lies must die for truth to be set free. Our cultural lies about who is beautiful, who is valuable, who must be put to death. Our moral fictions about who is categorically good and who is bad must be exposed. If we do not murder the lies about what will satisfy the human heart, then those lies will smother the search for real love and real hope.

Tonight we keep in holy memory the night of Israel's great liberation. At the same time, we acknowledge the sober reality that the cost of freedom is often very high.

SECOND READING: 1 CORINTHIANS 11:23–26
"This cup is the new covenant in my blood."

When it comes to redeeming a world from the grip of sin, God did not get off easy. If there was a way to wave a wand and make salvation available, Jesus did not choose it: he did not look for the quick fix for a broken world. Jesus wanted to show us the way to freedom by walking the road himself.

The deliberateness of the choice is what stuns us. Jesus sat calmly at supper that night with his friends, celebrating a feast day. Master of his own table, he performed the role of head of household in the breaking and sharing of the bread. In the familiar ritual action, he saw a foreshadowing of his self-offering, and told his disciples—as he had so often before—what was to come. And he asked them to remember, when the events of this hour were past, what he had said and done that night.

We still do. Sometimes with as little understanding as those who first shared the meal, we come to the table and eat the bread, drink the wine. We do it because Jesus told us to, and we know this is the way we will come to understand what he did and why he did it. We may celebrate this supper a hundred times, or thousands of times, in our lifetime. If just one of those times leads us to understanding what we do, it will be enough.

GOSPEL: JOHN 13:1–15
Jesus realized that the hour had come.

The Transfiguration on Mount Tabor was an amazing event, but just as startling to the disciples was this transformation of Jesus at the last supper. He went from Lord to servant in a matter of moments. Rather than a glorification in light and mystery, he humbled himself with a towel and some water. He washed their feet.

So striking was this gesture that nobody could say anything for awhile. And then of course it was Peter, always blurting out something, who manages a response. First Peter questions Jesus; and then Peter refuses him. The poor fisherman would never learn that less is sometimes more.

And now it is our turn to respond to the idea that the Lord of the Universe is prepared to wash our feet. Suddenly we feel Peter's dilemma, the sweaty palms, the confusion, even the denial. O Lord, don't do this. Don't humble yourself for the likes of me. But Jesus washes our feet anyway, because it is the only way we will know who we are called to be: precious children of a loving God. And once we see ourselves this way, we will recognize each other as well. And we will take up the towel and the basin, and start washing.

Questions for Reflection

- What are the lies and fictions of our culture which need to die so that truth might live?
- What does receiving the Eucharist, over and over again, teach you?
- Whose feet need washing in your community, to show them how precious they are in God's eyes?

Action Response

Practice serving with humility. Let others know by your service, not how good you are, but how loved they are.

It is Finished

FIRST READING: ISAIAH 52:13—53:12
Because of him kings shall stand speechless.

Human suffering is a terrible thing to witness, and innocent suffering is an outrage. How can God permit this? comes the cry from the depths of our hearts. Does God want it to be this way? If God does not want the innocent to suffer, why doesn't God do something?

God did something. God did an awesome thing. God saw innocent suffering and shared in it. God still shares in it. Though the rest of the world may flee from a tragedy, God stands with those who suffer, mourn, and die. The most hopeless and abandoned sufferer is in the company of angels, and God's Spirit testifies against a world which loses hope and deserts the victim.

God's people stand with those who are suffering and do what they can to strive against the unjust causes of the world's pain. Sometimes we may even be called upon to share the suffering of the innocent, as Jesus did. Sometimes we can bind some wounds, heal some hearts. But the one thing we cannot do is to look away and pretend it is none of our business. The reality of the cross insists: there are no innocent bystanders.

SECOND READING: HEBREWS 4:14–16, 5:7–9
Let us hold fast to our profession of faith.

Our profession of faith as it stands is an ancient document. It carries in its wake the combined genius and theology and response to heresy of many centuries of believers. It tells us what Christians believe. It also tells us, by default, what we cannot believe.

We believe, for example, in a God who purposefully created the world and everything in it. We cannot believe, therefore, that all of this is purposeless and pointless, spinning from chaos into oblivion. We believe that Jesus reveals the glory of God, and is "light from light." Therefore we cannot put our faith in the realm of darkness, cynicism, or despair.

The author of this letter narrows the focus of our faith to one image: Jesus, the true high priest. Unlike priests whose services come and go and must be performed again, Jesus the priest offered his great act of love once for all time. It is finished. His work is perfected. Of course this does not mean there is nothing for us to do. We must hold fast to our profession of faith and become what we profess. That is work enough for a lifetime.

GOSPEL: JOHN 18:1–19:42
When Jesus took the wine, he said, "Now it is finished."

The focal point of Christianity for all time is the image of Christ on the cross. Sometimes he is portrayed as gored and suffering, or hanging limply with closed eyes. Sometimes he stands almost detached from the cross in the robes of kingship. Sometimes he is draped in the stole of a priest. Christ in anguish and Christ victorious are two views of the cross, and both are true.

John's Gospel is more interested in telling the story of victory, and so Jesus marches to the cross in perfect control of the circumstances. Judas does not betray him with a kiss; Jesus steps forward and tells the mob, "I am the one you want." Jesus confounds Pilate by his own cross-examination on the source of authority. And in the end, Jesus announces his own death, "It is finished." He means his mission, of course, and not simply his life. No one takes his life, as he said. He laid it down.

Our mission as church is not finished. There is much yet to do. On this day of great and holy endings, we cannot forget that Easter and Pentecost are right around the corner. Death is not an end. Although something is finished, much more is begun.

Questions for Reflection

- Where do the innocent suffer in your community? How can you stand with them?
- Write a creed in your own words. What is it that you really believe?
- What images of the crucifixion are displayed in your parish? In your home? What do they tell you about Jesus?

Action Response

It is a good day for endings. Put an end to an old feud. Let a hurt go. Forgive yourself for being human. Resolve to start again, leaving past sin behind you at the cross.

Let There Be Light!

FIRST READING: GENESIS 1:1—2:2

God said, "Let there be light," and there was light.

On this night of nights, the light of Christ is revealed once more to our world. We see the light of the Easter fire burning at the entrance of our churches. We watch it advance through our assembly with the paschal candle. We hold our share of this light in our hands quite literally with smaller candles, knowing we are called to bring this light out of our assembly and into the lives of others. At the beginning of time, at the dawn of the first day, God called light to shine in the darkness, and that call continues to go out to those who have ears to hear.

SECOND READING: GENESIS 22:1–18

In your descendants all the nations of the earth shall find blessing.

Abraham was asked to choose between two dear allegiances: the spiritual love of God and the natural affection for his child. Tormented, he chose God, only to learn that to choose God does not exclude the natural affections at all. He made the right choice.

Many of us find ourselves divided in our hearts in a similar way. How can we turn from those we love to do the will of God? Unlike the idols of old who required human sacrifices, our God is the very essence of love, the perfection of the desire for whole relationship. The choice turns out to be no choice at all. If we choose God above all, God will perfect our relationships.

THIRD READING: EXODUS 14:15—15:1

Horse and chariot God has cast into the sea!

The struggle for freedom requires enormous courage. We have to be willing to leave our oppressors behind, something many of us are not willing to do, no matter how much we are suffering. We have to be prepared to leave the familiar and go off into the unknown. We can only take a small bit of our past with us, what we can carry. And we have to trust in God, with all our hearts. If we can do that much, we will live to see the enemy sprawled on the shore behind us, inert. If we refuse to do it, we will always serve an unworthy master.

FOURTH READING: ISAIAH 54:5–14

O afflicted one, storm-battled and unconsoled, I lay your pavements in jewels.

God knows what we need. There is no suffering in all the world that God does not see, no loss that God does not intend to restore one-hundredfold. Love will return, justice will come, peace is on its way in every hour. Though at times we feel abandoned in our pain, we are dearly met and attended. Angels guard our every step. There is no place we can go in this world where God is not.

FIFTH READING: ISAIAH 55:1–11

All you who are thirsty, come to the water!

The call to baptism goes out to east and west, north and south. Those of us who have answered this call renew our pledge, while those who await the living waters on this night tremble with anticipation. We stand together as baptized and unbaptized for the final hour. Soon our Elect members will be in full communion with us, wholly church, holy church.

SIXTH READING: BARUCH 3:9–15, 32—4:4

When God calls the stars, they answer, "Here we are!" shining with joy for their Maker.

We could learn a lesson from the stars. They are true to their course through the years, in correct alignment with the forces that created them. They do not try to be more or less than stars. They are obedient to the task of being what they are, and deliver their light faithfully. Baruch tells us poetically that it is the joy of the stars to serve their Maker. If we could know the simple joy of the stars, we would be the possessors of a wonderful secret.

SEVENTH READING: EZEKIEL 36:16–28

I will give you a new heart and place a new spirit within you.

The age of our hearts cannot always be determined by the number of our years. Often our hearts get worn out far in advance of our bodies, as our love is tried and disappointed time and again. But we have been offered what is hard to refuse: the chance to begin again with hearts not hardened by bitterness or betrayal. A new heart ready to love, a new spirit free of cynicism. All we have to do is say yes.

EPISTLE: ROMANS 6:3–11

You must consider yourselves dead to sin but alive for God in Christ Jesus.

We are dead to sin. We no longer have to pay the dues that sin demands: keeping up with the Joneses, conquering our competitors, looking out for number one. We are free from the bonds of sin and can put our talents and energies at the service of a new master. Instead of enemies, we see only friends. Instead of competition, community. And where we saw death, there is only life.

GOSPEL: MATTHEW 28:1–10 (YEAR A); MARK 16:1–8 (YEAR B); LUKE 24:1–12 (YEAR C)

"He has been raised up; he is not here."

Why look for the living among the dead? On this night we stay awake in the darkness, waiting for the light of the world to dawn once more in our hearts. We know that this night contains the utter brightness of God, the fulfillment of the promise, the joy of the world! We wait at the tomb, but we know we stand beside the tree of life. Death has been exposed as the great hoax it is. God means for us to share everlasting life, and nothing can stop the reign to come, not sin, not devils, not all the powers of hell. Christ is risen! Alleluia.

Questions for Reflection

- How will you bring the light of Christ to someone this day?
- Who is the real master of your life, you or God?
- What does your baptism mean to you today?

Action Response

Pray for the gift of a new heart and a new spirit. Use your resurrected heart to bring renewed love and hope to your family, friends, community, and church.

The Polished Arrow

FIRST READING: ISAIAH 49:1–6
God made me a polished arrow, in his quiver he hid me.

You are my servant, God said. You are Israel. "Who, me?" We can imagine the servant of the Lord being a little uneasy at this calling, flattering though it may be. "*I* am to represent your chosen people; *I* am to be light to the nations?" Whatever else it may mean, you can bet there are no paid vacations.

Yet the servant is ready to become the sharpened sword in God's hand, the sleek arrow at God's command. Though the hours will be long and the work seemingly in vain, the servant is going to trust that God's payroll is the best job security in the world.

How about you and me? Are we willing to labor long and hard, not making much of a dent in the world's poverty, its violence, lies, and injustice? Are we willing to accept an assignment on God's payroll, though the apparent benefits (in this world) are not exactly competitive? Will we allow ourselves to be sharpened for God's service, polished for the day and hour of God's choosing to use us?

SECOND READING: ACTS OF THE APOSTLES 13:22–26
"Look for the one who comes after me."

I wonder if there were moments, in those dark desert nights when John lay alone, if he thought about using his celebrity for his own ends. The moment comes to most preachers, teachers, and public servants who come to celebrity. They have to decide whether to lay down their fame for the sake of those whom they serve, or take it up and use its tremendous power for personal gain.

The papers report to us every day about those who take the latter course and falter along its dangerous slopes. Sex scandals, embezzlements, power plays, and people going off the deep end altogether are the usual casualties of human ego left unchecked. It is an intoxicating mix: plenty of ego and the power to feed it insatiably. Whatever John's midnight temptations, he wrestled them down by morning. And he continued to serve as the faithful signpost of "the one who was to come," who was the real story. He remained merely the storyteller.

GOSPEL: LUKE 1:57-66, 80

"Was not the hand of the Lord upon this child?"

Nobody ever expected more from a helpless baby than was expected of John, son of Zechariah and Elizabeth. Yet despite the fact that his father was a priest and had good connections, we hear nothing about John's fine education among the scribes in Jerusalem. Instead, we hear the peculiar news that he lived in the desert until his public ministry began.

What happened? Perhaps Zechariah and Elizabeth, quite old at the time of John's birth, simply died in his childhood and he was free to roam wild. Or perhaps Zechariah had connections with the religious desert sect at Qumran, the ancient keepers of what would one day be called the Dead Sea Scrolls. John may have been shipped off to a holy boarding school among the Essene monks there.

Whoever had a hand in his education, John emerged from the desert at the appointed hour, ready to be the voice crying in the wilderness that the world urgently needed. He came out breathing fire and preaching thunder. No man born of woman would be greater than John. And yet he had the humility to realize he was the least member of the kingdom he proclaimed.

Questions for Reflection

• Look at the images in the passage from Isaiah. Are you a sword, an arrow, a babe in the womb, or a light to the nations in your present circumstance?

• Are you the storyteller of God's divine story, or are you the only story your listeners hear about?

• John the Baptist was not diplomatic in denouncing corruption in his day, no matter how high or powerful it was. Which of our contemporary institutions might he rail against today?

Action Response

Take some of the power currently available to you—a seat on a committee, a surplus of money, a role of responsibility you exercise over someone—and put it at the service of God's reign, as John did. Be the signpost of the One who is to come.

A Remarkable Feast

FIRST READING: ACTS 12:1–11

"Now I know for certain that the Lord has sent his angel to rescue me."

In the Acts of the Apostles, we get the acts of Peter and the acts of Paul. But we never get the acts of Peter and Paul, because two more different men could not be found in the body of Christ. Peter was a self-taught fisherman, no stranger to error, who lived by instinct and followed Jesus from the gut. Paul was hyper-schooled, cultured, accustomed to perfection and the dictates of reason. If these two men had shared a table, Peter would have slurped his food and belched at the end. Paul would have used the right fork and noticed if the wine was good or poor. A friendship between them was not indicated, or likely to happen.

Both were fervent Jews who became fervent followers of Jesus. Both came to understand the salvation of Gentiles through dramatic revelations, though they disagreed on the method. Both gave their hearts and lives to Jesus, and died as martyrs in Rome.

Did it matter, in the end, that they were such different men?

SECOND READING: 2 TIMOTHY 4:6–8, 17–18

That is how I was saved from the lion's jaws.

Paul writes to his friend and protégé Timothy while imprisoned in Rome. The situation in Rome looks bad, and Paul is aware that he might not win his case. Timothy has been groomed to replace Paul, and he is content at the idea of relinquishing his work and his life.

Consider the two scenes as they are described for us. Peter in prison, in Acts, stumbling before the angel who offers him God's freedom. He does not believe in what is happening even while it happens. This is so Petrine, to be there and not get it! He needs the angel's explicit instructions every step of the way: get up; put on your shoes; get your cloak. Peter is slow on perception but quick with obedience.

Paul in prison is a different story. As a citizen of Rome, he has rights in these courts and places some hope in due process, which Peter, a mere Jew, could not hope for. Paul is reflective about his life and his chances, and knows the great work of his life is accomplished. Though no angel comes to the rescue, he counts on the Lord's rescue from the finality of death. This is the essence of the Pauline tradition.

GOSPEL: MATTHEW 16:13–19
"Blest are you, Simon son of John!"

So Peter gets the keys, and Paul gets the better part of the New Testament. It is ironic, really, that we Catholics base our authority on Peter, while Paul becomes the de facto pope of Protestants, who appeal to his authority as final.

It probably makes sense to the two men as well. Both understood the theology of reversals. Peter the underdog becomes the cornerstone of the future papacy, though reasonable people might have chosen Paul. Paul, the man of incomparable orthodoxy, becomes the champion of those who dissent from the center of orthodoxy. Only in the kingdom are such things natural.

The Feast of Peter and Paul in itself has something off-center about it. These men had one recorded encounter in Jerusalem and it was not exactly a meeting of the minds. Yet they are linked together eternally in this whimsical feast. Perhaps this is an ecumenical feast which offers hope for divided Christianity. Peter continues to speak to us from Rome, while Paul preaches to us in the heart of our Eucharist.

Questions for Reflection

- Have you ever found yourself, like Peter, rescued by forces you could not comprehend?
- If your "race" was finished now, would you feel your task on earth was completed?
- Answer the Gospel question for yourself: who do *you* say that Jesus is?

Action Response

Do something Peter-like: obey a prompting you do not understand. Do something Paul-like: reflect on your life and see God's hand in the events of your days.

TRANSFIGURATION

Lifting the Veil

FIRST READING: DANIEL 7:9–10, 13–14
I saw one like a son of man coming.

Truth wears many masks. We tend to dance around the truth with polite, correct phrases that will not offend, not recognizing that the truth in some circumstances cannot be prettied up or pretended away. When prophets speak, their words are blunt and unadorned, and they get put to death for that, generally speaking.

Revelatio is the root of revelation, and it means "lifting the veil" that conceals the truth from our eyes. Daniel, a prophet and truth-speaker, has a vision of the fiery seat of God and the ascension of a being like ourselves whose reign is established. The traditional understanding was that this vision referred to the favor that Israel enjoyed above all nations. Ezekiel mentions this curious character, "one like a son of man," in his writings, too. Jesus later adopts the metaphor to refer to himself. But he saw more than an ascendancy in the phrase. He saw all that led to it, struggle and passion together. When you lift the veil, there is no telling what you might see.

SECOND READING: 2 PETER 1:16–19
Keep your attention fixed on it.

Secondhand revelation is something to be taken with a grain of honest skepticism; but an eyewitness account leaves only one degree of separation between you and the event itself. The only thing better is to experience a revelation personally.

In the meantime, we are to keep the memory of Peter's experience alive within us as a lamp shining in a dark place. Sooner or later, the morning star will rise in my heart and yours, and the veil will be lifted for us as well.

GOSPEL: LUKE 9:28–36
How good it is for us to be here!

For the disciples, what starts out as another afternoon of napping while Jesus is praying turns into a terrifying visitation of the Divine. Just another reason not to close your eyes when Jesus is around! In this hour, Jesus is revealed as the fulfillment of both the law and prophecy (as represented by Moses and Elijah), not to mention the Chosen Son of God.

Peter's response is the understatement of the millennium: "How good it is for us to be here." He is spared embarrassment by the fact that he does not have a clue as to what he is saying, much less what is happening. Our response to revelation is often the same. Sometimes it takes a lifetime to figure out what happened back there, what God was doing while we were all but asleep.

Questions for Reflection

• Who are the prophets and truth-speakers in your life? What is their message?

• What events in your life have "lifted the veil" and helped you to know God or to believe more deeply?

• Jesus is "transfigured before our eyes" in every Eucharist. How is it "good for us to be here"?

Action Response

God reveals the divine presence and purpose in large and small ways. Be on the watch this week for the "burning bushes" alight in your path. Write a nightly reflection on where God showed up and what the face of God looked like.

ASSUMPTION

Blessed Among Women

FIRST READING: REVELATION 11:19; 12:1–6, 10
A woman stood clothed with the sun, with the moon under her feet.

A German artist has rendered a sculpture of Mary which I call "Mary on the Moon." She has a large arc of gold over her head and shoulders, inclusive of the boy she holds in her arms. She stands on a slice of silver, the moon of Revelation. The woman is very stylized, just a face and one hand and a sweep of cloak to suggest her. The focus of the piece is the boy, who balances cruciform on her hand.

"Mary on the Moon" is how I sometimes see the Mary of tradition. We do not know much about her. Popular culture has supplied more to us than Scripture. Yet still so often we see no more than a tender face, eyes cast downward, a sweep of cloak, and a boy.

Mary the woman has been replaced by Mary the symbol, and perhaps that is enough. Like John the Baptist, she was willing to serve and then to step aside. She prepared the way at the wedding feast of Cana, called Jesus forth into public life and then receded from view. She never asked for statues to be made of her, or holy days. She only asked, as she said to the steward at Cana, "Do whatever he tells you."

SECOND READING: 1 CORINTHIANS 15:20–26
Christ must reign until God has put all enemies under his feet.

Mary the symbol can be powerful and appealing, but Mary the dogma can be a lot more confusing. You have to wade through terms like *in perpetu* virginity (a virgin forever). Or try *Theotokos* on for size (she was the mother of God). Between the Latin and the Greek we have piled onto her, the real woman, even the symbolic woman, can be lost.

So when we say she was assumed bodily into heaven, what do we mean? Even in English, this is not very clear. Theologically it means she has special privileges afforded to her body since she carried the Son of God in her womb. But historically, the church has disputed whether or not this means Mary actually died. Some have preferred the term dormition, the idea that Mary just went to sleep and woke up Queen of Heaven. Others insist that she certainly died but just as surely did not suffer decay. How could the Ark of the Covenant, which carried God's holy word so immediately within her, know the spoil of sin in death?

Somewhere in the heart of history, a woman's body has been considered too holy to touch, too precious to lose. After twenty centuries, that is still news.

GOSPEL: LUKE 1:39–56
"Blessed are you among women and blessed is the fruit of your womb."

In a small town in a certain year, a young pregnant girl ran into the hills to find her elderly cousin and share some extraordinary news. The teenager was pregnant, and so was her old cousin! Neither of them should have been. Either this was from God—or the devil.

There will always be those who look at strange new life like this and name it evil. But these two women, one wise beyond her years and one very young in her heart, were able to accept astonishing conceptions and see the traces of holiness. There should have been fear, but neither of them gave evidence of it. Nor was there self-doubt, or blaming God, or protests that the timing is bad and the circumstances undesirable.

Both of these women embrace the life within them and call it good. They embrace each other and pronounce each other blessed. The collaboration and community these women found in each other changed the world forever. The greatest assumption of this day may be that these women assumed that God's words would be fulfilled in them.

Questions for Reflection

• What images of Mary have been significant or meaningful to you?

• Are women valued in your community? In your parish? How is this shown?

• How do you receive new life from God, with fear, doubt, protest, or something more?

Action Response

Find a way to celebrate life. Call your mother, hug your daughter, send goods to a home for pregnant teens, offer to babysit for a stressed-out relative. Be part of the chain of life.

Jesus Christ Is Lord

FIRST READING: NUMBERS 21:4–9

"Pray the Lord to take the serpents from us."

The people have lost patience with God, Moses, the manna, and the journey. The road is too long, and they have suffered too much. As if on cue, poisonous snakes emerge from the desert. Their fiery sting causes many to die. The people repent, and Moses prays for them. And then comes the peculiar part. God asks for the making of the bronze serpent. This is the same God who forbade the making of graven images at the start of the journey, so the fashioning of a bronze serpent is an odd proposal. But the serpent is not for worship. It is simply to be looked at.

The church wants us to think of this unlikely cure in the context of the feast once called the Triumph of the Cross. Why look at a cross? Every church has one, as do most Christian homes. We are reminded, at a glance, of the price of sin. We are also reminded, in this same glance, of how the world is healed of sin. The people in the desert had the same opportunity presented to them in the image of the bronze serpent, to know what sin does and what love does. Yet over time, the people forgot this message. By 2 Kings 18, the bronze serpent has become an object of worship in the Jerusalem Temple and has to be destroyed.

SECOND READING: PHILIPPIANS 2:6–11

He was known to be of human estate.

Solidarity is often the cry of the oppressed. We want leaders who can lead with some knowledge of our circumstance. We want a president who has paid taxes and struggled with the rent. We want priests who know what it is like to manage a prayer life in the midst of family and a full-time job. We want bosses who have worked in a cubicle like ours. Do not tell us how to live our lives unless you know what it is like.

So God took on flesh, and let go of the privileges of divinity. Jesus sweated under the hot sun and knew rejection and felt fear. And still he walked the way of obedience and love, and showed us it is possible, in a short life, to be holy as God is holy.

GOSPEL: JOHN 3:13–17
All who believe may have eternal life in the Son of Man.

Someone had to think up crucifixion: it is not a natural idea. Someone had to decide the way a body might be hung, and how to fix it there. Somebody had to consider how long and torturous a death it would bring. Death could result from many things: loss of blood, dehydration, asphyxiation, starvation. And all the while, a public death, naked, humiliated, while the crowds walk by along the road and hurl out insults about criminals deserving what they get. Someone invented crucifixion with diabolical creativity.

We celebrate the feast of a holy cross. This symbol of cruelty has been redeemed as a promise of life. We look upon the cross, not with a shudder, but with hope. We display it prominently in our churches, lovingly in our homes. We invent new meanings for the vertical bar (our reconciliation with God) and the cross bar (our reconciliation with one another.) When we see the arms stretched out on a crucifix, we do not think of the nails those hands received but of the love those arms extend. What the cross was meant to do is no longer as important as what Jesus meant it to do.

The condemnation of one man led to the salvation of all people. The original design of the cross is forever lost behind its new purpose.

Questions for Reflection

• Has a symbol of suffering ever become a source of healing for you? What would you create for your contemplation?

• How are you in solidarity with those who are less powerful than you?

• Has your contemplation of the cross changed over the years? If so, how?

Action Response

Find a response to the cross that helps you to value its meaning. Make the Way of the Cross, or contemplate the cross in your home parish or a favorite image of it in your home. Look for the shape in window-panes, trees, crossroads. Reflect on what you can learn from the cross.

ALL SAINTS
We Shall Be Like God

FIRST READING: REVELATIONS 7:2-4, 9-14

"Who do you think these are, all dressed in white?"

I like the scene of the four angels of destruction ready to go down to earth to tear apart the land and sea, halted by the angel of the east. Holding the seal of the living God, he means to put this seal on every servant of God before the destruction begins. If you have the seal, you are safe.

In its most fundamental understanding, baptism means you have the seal. Now, there are and have always been theological arguments about the innocent babies and good pagans who do not have the seal. It is the job of theologians to weave nets to catch those who fall through the letter of our laws. But don't worry about that too much: even when theology fails, God casts the bigger net. Baptism, properly understood, is not about exclusion but inclusion. It does not tell us who is out so much as who wants to be counted in. Baptism is the assumption of conscious membership in the church. Never mind most of us were half-asleep in our mother's arms when it happened. Even as tiny babies, we wore the white garment and were counted in. Baptism, we might say, is the easy part. Living out the vocation of being church is more challenging.

SECOND READING: 1 JOHN 3:1-3

We shall be like God, for we shall see God as he is.

I have asked children, from time to time, what God looks like. They show me amazing pictures: an old black man carrying a child on his shoulders; a fair young woman dressed in white like a bride; a basketball hero in sneakers; the Grand Canyon. When you ask to see the face of God, you never know what you might get.

Scripture is full of images: a smoking brazier, three mysterious strangers, a mother hen, One Ancient of Days on a jewel-like throne. "What color is God's skin?" we sang in children's choirs years ago. Does God even have skin? Is God more like the Grand Canyon, or Death Valley?

John's letter is very honest. We do not know what God is like, or what we will be like in the life beyond life. But how God is, is how we will be, if we incline ourselves in God's direction now. Because whatever else God is, God is love.

GOSPEL: MATTHEW 5:1–12
"Blest are the single-hearted, for they shall see God."

So here is the portrait of a saint: poor by worldly standards, yet rich in holiness, mercy, and peace. Humble, able to grieve without despairing, able to suffer insult or even injury without faltering. Single-hearted.

What does it mean to be single-hearted? Most of us have hearts like lilac blooms, with blossoms facing in every direction. We have many loves, many priorities, many, many longings, some of which we can scarcely put a name to. If we had to choose one above all the rest, we would raise our heads dizzily and not know how to respond.

The single-heartedness of the saint seems almost childish to us. When in doubt, choose God. And when dead certain, choose God. The saint among us does not choose God instead of people, but chooses God by choosing to serve others. The saint does not make time for God: all time belongs to God. The saint does not find special moments to pray: all of life is unceasing prayer. The saint does not "come into God's presence": the saint knows God is always present. Sainthood is billed as a heroic, impossible life-style. It is heroic, yet very possible, closer to us than we might dare to think.

Questions for Reflection

- Of what use is your membership in the church? How does it serve you, and how do you serve through this community?

- Page through a magazine until you see God. What does God look like?

- Is there a beatitude saint in your community? In the news? What makes this person wonderful, and what makes him or her like you?

Action Response

Find a saint that you can imitate. Their story might be told in *Butler's Lives of Saints*, or in the local newspaper. Find a saint who makes sense to you, and start down the path of sainthood this week.

Those Who Sleep Shall Awake

FIRST READING: DANIEL 12:1–3

Those who lead others to justice shall be like the stars forever.

Christians had a custom of remembering the dead from early on. Third-century writings speak of a need for purification before seeing God, and even among members of the Jewish community before Christ, some prayed for the dead (see 2 Maccabees 12:42). Though the Roman Church has spoken of a time for penance after death, the Eastern Church has seen it as a need for growth before entering God's presence.

On this day we remember all "who have gone before us marked with the sign of faith." A companion feast to All Saints, All Souls is an affirmation of our belief that the living and the dead are held together in one communion before God. In Christ, we share one body, and so our prayer for the dead and their prayer for us is "efficacious," in Augustine's word: it can effect change. In the turbulent time of Daniel's prophecy, as in our age, it is inspiring to hear that those who stand for justice on earth will share in the light of Christ for all time, radiant as the stars.

SECOND READING: ROMANS 6:3–9

One who is dead has been freed from sin.

Paul is a near-perfect example of the detachment Christians are invited to live. He understands that accepting discipleship in Christ is dying to worldly values and living only for the kingdom. Surrendering to the ways of the kingdom—love, joy, humility, forgiveness, among others—means being freed from the hooks that sin has in us, like jealousy, resentment, pride, stubbornness of heart. We cannot serve two masters, we know. If we serve the kingdom, we are dead to the empty claims of this world.

Death is always hard, because of the loss of the familiar. But being lost to the vain games of human culture liberates us for the sustaining joy of life in Christ. The problem with talking about this is that anyone who has not experienced this freedom thinks you are just talking about boring old religion. Real death with Christ leads to a life that is anything but boring.

"All that the Father gives me shall come to me."

In John's Gospel, Jesus repeats that he has come not to do his own will but his Father's. In light of this, I am embarrassed that so often I insist on my own will being done, particularly as I know God's will is infinitely wiser and better than mine.

When it comes to the last day, God has a plan that exceeds our hopes. All who have been given to Christ will be raised up on the last day. Narrowly viewed, that of course means all the baptized. But as Jesus himself says elsewhere (John 10:16), "I have other sheep you know nothing about."

The baptism of Spirit and fire was given to many so-called inappropriate people. Jesus' followers were upset when those not of their number cast out demons; the apostles were likewise astounded in Acts when the Gentiles started speaking in tongues. Those who are given to Christ might well surprise us in the end.

Questions for Reflection

• Whom have you known personally who stood for justice? How can you carry on that example?

• How much of your life is surrendered to the kingdom? How much is occupied with the things of this world? How do these two masters you serve come into conflict?

• Name three recent times that you have "looked upon the Son and believed." Remember, Christ is often met in the least of our sisters and brothers.

Action Response

Take time this week to pray for the dead. Pray for those you have loved. Pray for anyone who may have wronged you. Pray for those whom you have only read about in the papers.

DEDICATION OF THE
LATERAN BASILICA IN ROME
Building Up the Temple

FIRST READING: EZEKIEL 47:1–2, 8–9, 12

"Their fruit shall serve for food, and their leaves for medicine."

What is the Lateran Basilica, and why do we celebrate it? Built in the fourth century by order of Constantine, this church and surrounding dwelling was the official residence of popes for nearly a millennium. During its long history, it suffered two great earthquakes, barbarian invasions, a few major fires. It has been destroyed and rebuilt many times, and remains the highest-ranking Catholic church. Its proper name is the Church of the Savior.

Just as this building has a history of dying and being raised up, so too the church itself. Ezekiel's prophecy tells about the eternal spring flowing from the Temple in Jerusalem, and how paradise itself can be regained along the banks of this river. We who are the church know that in our long history, the church has been a source of life-giving water to all who seek salvation. Though the structures of the institution occasionally come down, the spirit of Christ's body remains the life force which sustains and compels us forward in history. It is, after all, a temple not made with human hands.

SECOND READING: 1 CORINTHIANS 3:9–13, 16–17

The temple of God is holy, and you are that temple.

The metaphor of building continues. Christ is the foundation of the church, and each of us builds our lives upon that according to our own materials. Gold, wood, or straw? Some things will last; others with fall away in time, now or at the hour of our death. We choose how strong the structure will be.

Recently I was with an elderly man who is very sick. Doctors have told him his body will not last another year. As he looks back over his life, a life that by most accounts has been highly lucrative and successful, he laments, "I amassed a fortune here, but I leave it all behind me. I go to God with empty hands!" The gold of this world has proved to be the straw of eternity, and he sees his life with the clarity of the dying.

Happily, it is not too late, for him or for us. Any moment of our lives can be the clarifying moment in which we see the work of our hands and resolve to start again. The Spirit of God dwells in us, and Jesus can raise up a new temple at the moment of our consent.

GOSPEL: JOHN 2:13–22
"Zeal for your house consumes me."

If Paul gives us a sense of what the Temple ought to look like, Jesus shows us forcefully what it can never be. Anything that means personal gain, or takes away from the pure pursuit of God's holiness and justice, is unacceptable. And more than unacceptable: it shall be destroyed.

What would you feel if someone from out of town came into your church and started tearing it to pieces? That is probably what those who watched Jesus were feeling. Some were frightened, waiting for God to strike him dead. Others were troubled and astonished, wondering what his motives were. Some cheered because of their own grudges against institutional religion, especially its more seamy and corrupt edges. All waited to see what would happen next.

Jesus identifies his own body with the Temple, which is why the church today speaks of being the Body of Christ. Anything that does not comply with that identity will always come down.

Questions for Reflection

• In what specific ways has the church been a source of life-giving water in your life?

• Draw, mold, or imagine the temple of God's Spirit you are called to be. Lay the foundation in Christ, and show what other materials you are currently building with.

• If Jesus were to come upon the temple of God that you are, what might he tear down in his zeal for God's holiness?

Action Response

Choose one of the weak aspects of your spiritual structure, (e.g., fidelity to prayer, charity, commitment to justice, sense of compassion, willingness to forgive) and resolve to build again with stronger materials. Spend the week fortifying your temple!

Scripture References